ETHICS:
THE CHALLENGES
OF MODERNITY

א ALEF
Series of works on universal logic and philosophy directed by
Michele Malatesta and Rocco Pezzimenti
A   **A**llgemeine **L**ogik Und Philosophie
L   Universel **L**ogik Og Filosofi
E   Logica Universale **E** Filosofia
F   Logica Universal Y **F**ilosofia

Volume 4: Rocco Pezzimenti, *Ethics: The Challenges of Modernity.*

ETHICS:
THE CHALLENGES
OF MODERNITY

Rocco Pezzimenti

GRACEWING

First published in England in 2013
by
Gracewing
2 Southern Avenue
Leominster
Herefordshire HR6 0QF
United Kingdom
www.gracewing.co.uk

No part of this publication may be reproduced, stored in a retrieval system, or transmitted in any form or by any means, electronic, mechanical, photocopying, recording or otherwise, without the written permission of the publisher.

The right of Rocco Pezzimenti to be identified as the author of this work has been asserted in accordance with the Copyright, Designs and Patents Act 1988.

© 2013 Rocco Pezzimenti

ISBN 978 0 85244 813 7

Contents

First Part

From Provisional Morality to the Provisional Nature of Morality

Ch. I. Moral and Juridical Formalism   11

Ch. II. The Ethics and Metaphysics of Non-sense
       Reserved for an Elite   53

    A) The Dilemmas of Will. Freedom and Responsibility:
       Arthur Schopenhauer   53
    B) The Ethics and Religion Split:
       Søren Kierkegaard   74
    C) Hyperactive Life without Reflection:
       Friedrich Nietzsche   82

Ch. III. Ethics Tied to the Moment   95

    A) The Norm, *still*, Relative: Hans Kelsen   95
    B) Morality Imprisoned by the Present:
       Martin Heidegger   104

Ch. IV. Atheism and Indifference: The Position of
       Dostoevsky and his Followers   107

    A) The Abandonment of Remorse: Charles Baudelaire   107
    B) Against the Drift towards Irreligiousness:
       Fëdor M. Dostoevsky   110
    C) Two Disciples   116
    D) Thomas Mann's Soul Searching   128

Second Part

The Problem of Social Moral Values

Ch. V. The Rules of the Comparison — 137

Ch. VI. The Person — 157

Ch. VII. Responsibility — 165

Ch. VIII. Pluralism, the Ethics of Conflict and the Right to the Truth — 177

Ch. IX. Tolerance — 181

Ch. X. The Sense of Limits and Faith in Society — 187

Ch. XI. Intelligence and its Development — 195

Ch. XII. Citizenship, Brotherhood, and their Corollaries: *liberty, dignity, equality, justice, solidarity* — 203

Ch. XIII. Security and Authority — 209

Ch. XIV. Work — 215

Third Part

Further Analyses

Ch. XV. Boudon and the Problem of Values: In order not to reduce Tocqueville to banality — 223

Ch. XVI. The Relationship between Command and Obedience and the Thought of Father Theodossios — 233

Ch. XVII. Brief Itinerary for an Historical Analysis   239

Works cited   245

Index of Names   259

FIRST PART

FROM PROVISIONAL MORALITY TO THE PROVISIONAL NATURE OF MORALITY

Ch. I. Moral and Juridical Formalism

1.1 *A necessary, preliminary word,* here at this point and not separately, so that it will not be ignored. I would indeed like to bring out two points. *First*: friends who have read this work in process have dwelt, on the first part above all, even in lively debates, not taking in account the second which seems to me the one which will be developed, and which has basically led to this study. I hope that those who read these pages will not make the same mistake. *Secondly* (and following from what precedes): I do not wish to seem anti-German. Goethe, Novalis, Schiller and many others up to Löwith, Mann are authors whom I greatly admire. For me these are the ones, who represent the true Germanic genius. My criticism in these pages is of a portion of German thought – and not only – which, I believe, does not follow in their wake and which is responsible for not a few of the contradictions in our recent history. I must say the same for the use, rare as it is, I make of the word Enlightenment, because I think that we should speak of enlightenments rather than the Enlightenment. I see, for example, many differences, enormous at times, between the French and English Enlightenments, but also in a few Italian and German Enlightenment figures. One need only think of the contrasts among thinkers such as Kant and others such as Beccaria or the Verri who were often at odds with one another. I shall return to this subject.

* * *

1.2 In a famous passage, Descartes honestly admits that during the difficult search for new paths, "he had to invent a provisional morality to enable him to live as well as he could during this time" (Descartes, 592). This thinker's honesty is beyond reproach in my opinion. What I would like to point out, however, is that since then, this provisional character has remained with us. Indeed, it has long been at the heart of philosophical enquiry or, at least, of a restricted fringe of intellectual circles, and has become more and more widespread in the last few decades to the point of becoming generally accepted. There are those who, appropriately in my opinion, have observed that Descartes' attitude is not all that different from that of his interlocutor Pascal, and Kant, too, despite his efforts to the contrary, fails fully to take his distance from a provisory morality (cf. Rigobello, 9 ff.). For Kant, indeed, morality separated from that God, which I can no longer show, remains, in any case, tied to a God that I must accept, even though I do not believe, as a hypothesis, if I wish to avoid the risk of causing the entire framework of practical reason to fall apart.

1.3 Kant knows quite well that he is facing a "difficulty" that offers no way out. He realizes that "this faith is based on the premise of moral feelings" and that these are not at all universal, so he comes to say "let us take one that might be totally independent of the laws of morality". In other words, he knows that the life he has embarked upon is not based "on a foundation, to which the most obstinate of forms of scepticism must surrender" (Kant, 1968A, 694). In the final analysis, he, too, is caught up in a provisional state. Faith is reduced to common sense. He himself says this quite candidly: "the most elevated of philosophies, cannot carry us further than the guidance it has offered to common sense, in relation to the essential goals of human nature"

(Kant, 1968A, 695). He likewise knows that the new moral approach, rather than being objective, runs the risk, despite intentions, of foundering in pure subjectivism. Suffice it to think that "I must never say: it is morally certain, that there is a God, etc., but: I am morally certain that, etc. That is to say, faith in a God (…) is so intertwined with my moral feeling" (Kant, 1968A, 693-694) that its certainty can never be communicated, as if to say that faith can only be communicated by rational means.

1.4 It would seem that existential morality was already lurking behind these considerations. The root is that moral feeling that has trouble offering objectivity even though it claims it almost instinctively. Instead of being the subjective, which moves freely in the area of recognized objectivity, it is a subjectivism, more and more unrestrained, which claims to lay the basis for its own objectivity. Sartre described it admirably and unequivocally. When he tells us that he was taught the Gospel and the catechism in a process we could call formal, without his being given the tools for believing, he adds that *"le résultat fut un désordre qui devint mon ordre particulier"* (Sartre, 1964, 209). He sought to observe the world with this.

1.5 "In Kant there is no opposition between choice and liberty, they are linked by the concept of duty. Duty is formally defined by law and is imperative, hence a source of obligation. The conflicts are purely accidental" (Rigobello, 47-48). If *law defines duty formally*, it follows that morality itself becomes formal and, with the changes in law, it could even lead to losing sight of the sense of morality itself. This already occurs in some of Kant's considerations. The idealists themselves realized this quite soon. Idealistic philosophy proposed a remedy: the "absoluteness of the conscience leads to the destruction of the objective world reduced to a phenomenon of the conscience itself" (Rigobello, 86). There is an aggravating circumstance: that of reaching the conviction that such a philosophical knowledge of the conscience claims to be totally exhaustive.

1.6 For Kant, as for Descartes, subjects are capable of deciding freely since they can act rationally, being, "by nature", endowed with the inclination to wish to obey moral law. However, the agreement between reason and will is not so consistent because the application of moral premises can be separated from impulses and inclinations. It follows that, in considering good and evil, Kant steers his course halfway between Socrates' position and that of Saint Augustine, preferring the former, obviously. In his opinion, there is no one who wants "evil for evil's sake, but a person can pursue evil goals driven by love of self. (…) For Kant, then, evil is above all a cognitive type of error and action is moral when it is properly performed from a logical point of view, only on behalf of duty, without the consequences, whether advantageous or not of the action being taken into consideration" (Crespi, 25). Kant steers his course halfway between Socrates' position and that of Saint Augustine because he conceives of love as the only egoistic factor capable of driving humans to the point of pure animality. It is against this, humans must constantly struggle if they are to escape the selfishness that dominates their instincts. It does not even occur to him that feelings in general, and love in particular, can bring to humanity this definitive improvement that reason by itself is not always capable of doing. It is still a feeling that determines the formal nature of reason: that of fear. Going against the rules of morality means distorting that formal order beyond which only anarchy remains.

1.7 There is more to be said, however. "Kant considered love for the very reason that it was divorced from will, as a feeling that was not free and, hence, morally irrelevant. He, too, saw, however, that he cannot give himself any will to will and so an attitude that precedes willing is necessary, a feeling, that is, to motivate will" (Spaemann, 228). The absence of this will to will, in reference to problems different from one another, can easily be understood if one thinks "that in Kant, even in reference to practical reason, morality, in the final analysis, places logical principles first when the experience takes place" (Crespi, 35). We seem to be dealing with theoretical ethics, the fruit of speculation rather than action. In other words it is a morality more studied than experienced, ethics in the Greek sense of the world more than morality achieved by embarking upon arduous path. From this comes the conviction, entirely of the Enlightenment, that a universal morality exists, written into rationality. It is practically a genetic code, capable of orienting choices. That does not, however, explain why certain cultures have established reference points, such as that of the person, which encounter difficulty being accepted even today.

1.8[1] The political analysis departs from these premises. Some have, appropriately enough, pointed out that in Kant "politics cannot be separated from reason" provided that "the powers and the limits" of reason are defined. At the same time, it must not be forgotten that reason "in so far as it is activity that produces awareness, is removed from the determinism of nature (...); it is therefore constitutively

---

[1] The points from 1.8 to 1.11, from 1.14 to 1.21 (1.20 presents some additions), 1.23, 1.26 and points 1.34-1.35 are again taken up in Chapter 17 of my work *The Open Society along the Arduous Path of Modernity, with letters from Isaiah Berlin and Hilary Putnam*, Leominster: Gracewing, 2011.

free". The ability to know represents the foundation of liberty, the idea of which constitutes "the transition point from pure to practical reason" (cf. D'Addio, SDP, II, 92-93). Among the duties of reason there is the pursuit of moral good which for Kant must not only be distinct from happiness, but must have unquestionable priority over it. Furthermore, morality is distinct from law: whereas the former refers to an interior determination, the latter only governs external action. For this very reason, law exists thanks to constraint. This is useless for morality because the will is free only if "it adapts entirely to the principle according to which it must be determined". Only will, in so far as it can perform an action or not, is free to choose (cf. D'Addio, SDP, II, 95). This conviction is a prelude to the dialectics of the objective spirit in Hegel.

1.9 Kant takes the basic features of his political thought from the letters of Montesquieu from whom he adopts the classical division of powers acknowledging that the sovereign power lies in the legislative branch. Only thus, as other contemporaries had also seen, can liberty, equality and the independence of individuals be ensured. Individuals have total freedom on the level of religion, as well. The State cannot intervene on matters of conscience and worship, it must only take care that nothing conflicts with the laws in effect (this is quite a delicate subject and it implies the appropriateness of taking exception. I shall return to this subject subsequently). The State which knows better than any other how to achieve the division of powers, having, at the same time the force and the authority necessary to pursue the desired goals and to coerce, is a republic whose constitution "is the only one which is perfectly adapted to the law of humans", even though some maintain (here there is a critical reference to Rousseau) that they would have to be angels (cf. Kant, 1968E, 233-234). A republican constitution is a better guarantee than any other of liberty, equality and the independence of individuals. He takes his distance from Montesquieu when he rejects the relationship between tradition and privileges since he does not grant the aristocracy any prerogative. This had happened in the United Kingdom, which recognized for all social classes, but the bourgeoisie in particular, equal opportunities to occupy positions or take office. Indeed, "no inequality can arise in legal status no submission to coercive laws, that are not those which the individual, as a subject of the single supreme legislative power, has in common with every other one (…) no innate privilege can exist for a member of the civil community" (Kant, 1968G, 148). This statement must be read, above all, with the eyes of those who have before them a feudal state structure which must be reformed. The State must reform landed property that is still tied to atavistic schemes and must have it at its disposition in order to accomplish public goals.

1.10 One of the basic perplexities to which Kant's thought gives rise, and which produces not a few corollaries, concerns the supreme postulate of law: "Only in the State does law become peremptory, and the conditions are found for it to be realized (…) The State is the idea of law implemented". It being understood that the State confers on law that force of coercion without which one would only remain on the level of good intentions, the limits of this force and the very basis of law leave us with more than a few perplexities. It can be a waste of energy to seek the empirical basis of law. The original contract is basically an idea originating in reason which is not necessarily formed on the basis of consent, but more likely on violence (it is truly curious that Kant, who uses an infinity of expressions taken from classical law, omits the expression *consensus iuris* itself, at least with the meaning that it took on from Cicero and thereafter. Cicero himself had taken it from tradition). The contract, finally, "is a necessary idea of reason" which lays the foundation for the legitimacy of the State with which each person identifies himself or herself (cf. Solari, 14), otherwise, there is the danger of actually losing liberty. Kant does not seem to have an optimistic conception of liberty at all, since he does not have faith "in enlightened selfishness governed by reason", as Locke maintains. Nor does he have faith in the "authority of reason against the excesses of selfishness", as Leibniz believed. He seems, in fact, to share the pessimism of Machiavelli and Hobbes to a greater degree than people may think (cf. Solari, 18). Those who do not think so should recall the considerations against the right to resist preconstituted power, a right which, in Kant's view cannot in any way be admitted. It gives rise to a dangerous state-worship in which the "State for Kant is not only the keeper and defender of law, but it personifies the needs of life associated, contemplated *sub specie aeterni*" (Solari, 19).

1.11 In actual fact, that of Kant is a veritable tyranny which imposes itself, despite life's necessities, claiming to enforce an *a priori* most often dictated by a sort of blind "reason of state", an obtuse divinity to whom one must, hence one can sacrifice everything. These are the moments when the universal nature of certain imperatives faces a crisis and it seems as if only some people had a particular revelation. For these, whether philosophers or politicians, it does not matter, for the others, what counts is obeying. How can one free oneself from this obligation if obeying the imperative is a deontological question? Obedience is obligatory as long as a law is what it is and has not been repealed and replaced by another. Is it then possible to speak of dissent? Absolutely not, because law has become the basis of morality of which it constitutes the precondition. It is the expression of a superior will which we must obey, even though we do not share it. Quite sincerely, to say that this is merely formalism seems to me to say very little. It is pure conformism, and the formulae of the categorical imperative say so, because our action must always be in conformity with existing law. Legislation thus becomes the basis of our morality, at least as long as it is in force. The universe of liberty does not find its basis in the conscience, but in conformity with the law that it must practice.

1.12 We all know that the Kantian imperative is categorical when it commands action for itself without there being any other purpose. Now we also know that "a principle exists *descriptive* of the will to be holy (God) whose will immediately conforms to it". If this constitutes moral law, and if "the will to be finitely rational does not immediately and necessarily conform to moral law" there is only one way out of this contradiction: that of conferring divinity on mankind and mankind's moral principles (cf. Fonnesu, 23). Hegel's *Gott mit uns* is already present in Kant and it is certainly no accident that religion, humanized, is reduced to morality or, to use Hegelian terms, ethicity. This is why the categorical imperative can command, whatever the consequences may be, if one remembers the case of falsehood. These consequences always find justification in what will be the universal legislation, a sort of *trick of reason* already foreseen by Hegel. However, what place can liberty have as a premise for moral action if the motivation of choice is impossible? Furthermore, doesn't thwarting liberty mean thwarting all Kantian ethics which become self-contradictory? It is in Hegel that we see the outcome:

despite the fact that he exalts the "free spirit", he always has the public dimension prevail over the private. "In the great dichotomy between public and private, the greatest risk, and the error of liberalism, is for Hegel that of the private prevailing, in other words private interest and subjective judgment are favoured". It suffices to say that the moral problem can be solved on the level of conscience, even though, in its implications, it is connected with the problem of evil. As has been appropriately observed, this "moral conscience" (whose German term *Gewissen* acquires its meaning throughout the subsequent philosophical tradition starting from Luther) is formed only within the sphere of ethicity and in its highest expression offered by the Ethical State (Fonnesu, 42-46).

1.13 "From this point of view, no doctrine of immanent duty is possible; certainly, here one can acquire a subject *from the outside*" (Hegel, 1986, § 135). This is tantamount to saying that all that an individual does must find its *raison d'être* in the totality. These are not free interpretations. One need only recall what Hegel says concerning freedom of the press. "Defining freedom of the press as the freedom to write what *one wants*, means passing liberty in general off as the freedom *to do anything one likes*. Such talk belongs to coarseness, superficiality, and being entirely devoid of culture" (Hegel, 1986, § 319). For Hegel this freedom finds its "guarantee in juridical laws and ordinances", but if these are oppressive, how can an individual possibly raise opposition since the person receives the mark of "ethicity" from the authority of the State? "Duty that obliges can seem to be a *limitation*, only in the presence of undetermined subjectivity or abstract liberty (…) but an individual finds his or her *liberation* in duty" (Hegel, 1986, § 149). This is formalism again, therefore. Rectitude, in fact, becomes pure conformism, adapted to that ethical vision with which one is associated and cannot in any way escape. The distance from this to that socially conditioned human conscience, of which Marx will speak is short. Marx, too, has his model of perfection to put into effect: it is that classless society where all disagreements and conflicts will wither away. If such were not the case? The followers of Hegel and Marx found the solution. Paraphrasing Spencer it might be said of those people of "that future", "if they are perfect enough to live, they live, and it is well that they live. If they are not perfect enough to live, they die, and it is better that they die" (from Fonnesu, 50).

1.14 Law, for Kant, must have universal value, but while it should be an aspect of legality, albeit fundamental, it becomes something exclusive for him. Solari rightly points out that "in practice law and the State are transcendental concepts for Kant, which draw upon intelligible reality and can only be constructed *a priori* outside of any experience. Only that which is *a priori* has objective, universal validity" (Solari, 23-24). Forgetting that law is also the prize of arduous achievements, it means to forget its deep relationship to morality and it means to take refuge in a conservatism which ignores legitimate aspirations upon which Latin and British juridical greatness are based. Not only that, when the objective validity of certain rights is called into question by the State, how can they be regained in a practical sense if not only resistance to established power is not allowed, but a body of law cannot be conceived unless it is capable of being constructed *a prior* outside of any experience? I do not believe that it is far-fetched to feel that Kant reaches these conclusions because he considers individuals the logical premise of the State, yet he considers them almost in conflict with society. The history of the best juridical experiences, however, tells us that individuals set up law, although they bring some *a priori* to bear, only if they create a society that guarantees the development of law; if anything, the problem is to see how to remain faithful to certain premises, keeping in mind, though, that society is the dynamic aspect of the coexistence of individuals.

1.15 Considering individuals the logical premise for the State does not mean for Kant that this is the expression simply of the sum total of the wills of individuals, but that it constitutes and represents a unified whole, a sort of general will of the type that Rousseau sought. Hence there is "the objective need for the State rationally to organize life in common". The wills of individuals must acknowledge a unifying will above them to which they must submit (cf. Solari, 28-29). This interpretation cannot be considered far-fetched. Kant's words leave no room for doubt: to achieve a "civil" consensus, "the will of all men *individually committed* to living in accordance with the principles of liberty in a legal constitution (that is that there be a unity distributive of the duty of *all*) is not enough. *Everyone together* must want this state (that is, that there be the *collective* unity of united wills" (Kant, 1968E, 230-231). The people are sovereign in so far as they are a collective entity and fatally (I would call it blindly) they must obey this rational need for unity. This is not an extemporaneous idea of Kant, but a conviction that runs throughout his thought. In *The Critique of Judgement*, speaking of the entire body of the State, he points out that every member "while contributing to the possibility of the whole, is in turn determined by the idea of the whole, in relation to his place and function" (Kant, 1968D, 323 note). It is now understandable why it has been said that if law expresses particular wills or even the sum total of the various wills it can be called unjust, "whereas even the harshest of laws is just when it comes out of the unified will" (Solari, 31), and because it is indeed an expression of this law, the State virtually becomes a moral person to whose development everyone not only can, but must contribute.

1.16 At this point it is quite understandable why Kant, departing from such a conception of the State, could not offer any possibility for the right to resist. As for Rousseau to some extent, disobeying the State is disobeying ourselves. Worse yet, the State aims at a Platonic sort of perfection which remains a constant point of reference, even though it can never be attained. A propos of the Platonic republic (never has a word been more inappropriate), in *The Critique of Pure Reason*, he expresses himself as follows: "although this latter case can never come to pass *(that is, achieving a perfect republic)*, nonetheless the idea that sets forth this *maximum* as an archetype is totally correct, so that in the legal constitution of men, observing it one may come closer and closer to the greatest possible perfection" (Kant, 1968A, 324, italics mine). This *"nonetheless the idea is totally correct"* cannot be ignored. Above all, who decides how correct the idea is? It can only be the State and obviously those who are qualified to do so on its behalf. Then, saying that no-one knows "the highest point, at which humanity must stop" does not solve the problem because, depending on the times, the various philosopher-kings of the moment, who interpret the various States, can design various models. This is so because, among other things, philosophers are masters at relating their ideas, political and moral, to the reality surrounding them. Thus, Kant hastens to say that "concerning nature herself Plato correctly sees manifest proof of its origin in ideas" (Kant, 1968A, 325-326). In Kant, this nature anticipates the deterministic model of Hegel, otherwise how could certain statements be interpreted?

"Nature still wants humanity to be obliged to implement on its own these like all the other goals to which it is destined (…) only by performing and completing that task can it achieve all its other goals concerning our species" (Kant, 1968F, 39). In other words, knowing the truth brings about the obligation, I would also say moral, to implement it. It is no accident that Kant calls this Platonic ideal a *respublic noumenon*, which is certainly not a senseless chimera, but a point of reference for an organized civil society, a *respublic phaenomenon*, which "can only be achieved laboriously through numerous wars and conflicts" (Kant, 1968H, 364).

1.17 Machiavelli's conception, based on the idea of political success, was mentioned above. It ultimately justifies any political event that prevails, thus Kant is in agreement with the Florentine secretary. While being opposed to any form of rebellion against the constituted power (even when not a few earlier theoreticians had suggested that various forms of resistance were lawful) and thus being opposed to any type of revolution that might lead to the conquest of power, however it was carried out and whatever the reason for it was, it must ultimately be justified. It follows that "the illegal nature of its origin and the way in which it has been established cannot free the subjects, as good citizens, from the obligation to adapt to the new order of things, nor can they refuse honestly to obey the authority which currently holds the power" (Kant, 1968B, 442). This means that it will be necessary honestly to obey Hitler or Stalin who, in the "new order of things", represent the "authority which presently holds the power". The justification is even more paradoxical because if anyone dared resistance, "this resistance would take place according to a maxim which, made universal, would destroy any civil constitution, so that the only state in which people can in general be in possession of their rights would be destroyed" (Kant, 1968G, 156). Even if the dissident were right, and it seems to me that history has shown this not a few times, resistance cannot be acceptable because, not being able to decide on which side the true right exists, in Kant's opinion, the would-be dissident would always end up "being the judge in his own suit. There would have to be a second sovereign above the sovereign, to decide between the latter and the people: which is a contradiction" (Kant, 1968G, 156). Such a figure does not exist and thus the right of necessity cannot be appealed to, only the obligation of submission exists, even if the sovereign were the worst of humans. The highly moral Kant is unaware of the moral obligation which so many of those who have fought in the name of liberty have felt, from Cicero to John of Salisbury and up to the present. The appropriateness of tyranicide does not cross his mind either because "the people have no right to coerce their own sovereign, since it is only through the sovereign that the people legally can apply constraint (…) a right (of resistance in words or in acts) to coerce the head of state can never belong to the people" (Kant, 1968G, 159-160). This is not merely a matter of principle as some people maintain. What has been said applies on a practical as well as a theoretical level. The head of state is also responsible for deciding what degree of well-being to attain and how to achieve it, setting forth which "provisions contribute to the prosperity of the State" (Kant, 1968G, 155).

1.18 Kant reaches these conclusions because of an erroneous approach to the moral problem. His deontology is perhaps based on a misinterpretation. He believes that "duty in itself is in fact nothing but the *limitation* of a will" (Kant, 1968G, 132-133). At best, that maxim is questionable. Sartre and most existentialists would say that duty, too, must be desired if it is to be performed, hence the performance of duty is the affirmation of the will itself rather than its limitation. Even considering duty the consequence of the principle of universal reason, its implementation always requires the free acceptance of the subject hence a full manifestation of the will. The problem is that Kant confers on reason requisites of absoluteness and truth which can only be denied *a posteriori*. "Reason cannot err (*Die Vernunft kann nicht irren*): every force has its path laid out. The condemnation that reason lays on itself does not take place when it is judged, but only afterwards, when one is in another position or when greater knowledge has been acquired" (Kant, 1968I, 774). Aside from the fact that here too, Hegelian rationality and "truth" can be perceived, not the slightest doubt arises for Kant when taking a decision that it can be erroneous or, at least, incomplete.

1.19 However that "duty in itself is none other than the *limitation* of the will" brings forth another holistic meaning in Kant which, taken to its most extreme consequences, is ultimately totalitarian. *I do not think that this conclusion* can be considered *too far-fetched*. Implicitly and even explicitly at times, Kant admits this. When he says that "each one in the state considers the body in common the maternal womb from which each obtained life" (Kant, 1968G, 146), in contradiction with the inalienability and universality of rights, he means that only the State is the source of right and no substantial right can be acknowledged for the person in himself or herself. So the State may apply the death penalty and even maternal infanticide. "The baby that has come into the world outside of marriage is outside the law (because marriage is the law), and it is thus not under the protection of the law. It has, so to speak, insinuated itself into civil society (like forbidden merchandise), so that it cannot fail to be aware of its existence and, as a result, its destruction, as well" (Kant, 1968B, 458). Statements of that sort must not astonish people if one thinks that it is "the maternal womb" of the State that is the sole source of right and not the human being. Here lies the clear difference between those who recognize the formality of law and those, on the contrary, who, not acknowledging that the state can be the sole and incontrovertible source of law, speak of the substantiality of law.

1.20 The concept of the person understood in that sense is obviously not exhaustive. Kant is clear in his definition. "The *Person* is that subject whose actions can be imputed" (Kant, 1968B, 329). The principle of responsibility is undoubtedly a fundamental characteristic of persons, but it is nonetheless restrictive, because, among other things, it is enough that "someone" not recognize them as responsible, or, they are not so for medical reasons. Any horror whatsoever may be perpetrated on a person. Someone, Kant himself for example, could speak of "the incompetence of the slave" setting history one dangerous step backwards, almost into prehistory more than into the ancient world, because many of his considerations on slavery had already been overcome by Roman law which itself is part of Kantian culture. What then is there to be said about the detached behaviour one must practice towards slavery? One must avoid allowing slaves even to adopt the simple "tone of familiarity" with us. No one must be allowed to influence our lives since, "in fact, no one can know my defects better than myself," (Kant, 1974, 452). Nor, can one think that often those who judge what others deem defects I can deem qualities from the pedestal of my presumed *a priori* morals. Does Kantian morality by chance want to bestow upon us the halo of sanctity, and only we, in the first person, can judge it?

Suffice it to reflect on the fact that at the end of his juridical work, perhaps his most important one, he states that "the best constitution is one in which power is not in people, but in the laws" (Kant, 1968B, 479), it is the latter that make us free. This was already Cicero's conviction when he maintained that in his republic the laws governed and not the kings as in Plato's, laws which protect our liberty because "legum servi sumus ut liberi esse possimus" (cf. Pezzimenti, 2011A, Ch. I and II).

1.21 As far as the death penalty is concerned it should be recalled that Kant accepts it in full. This cannot be justified by speaking of an era which had not yet reached maturity. It cannot because Kant participates in the debate of the most enlightened spirits of his time who were against the death penalty almost ridiculing it. The book *On Crimes and Punishments* was the centre of a European debate. Kant maintains, however, that "because of a pretentious humanitarian sentimentalism (*compassibilitas*) Marquis Beccaria maintains that every death sentence constitutes an *injustice*: This could indeed not be included in the original civil contract, because every individual among the people would have to consent to losing his or her life in case he or she had to kill another (among the people)" (Kant, 1968B, 457). For Kant this reasoning is a sophism and denatures law because *no-one can decide on his life* (!). In the original agreement or social contract "there is no promise to allow oneself to be punished thereby having the power to decide on one's own life. Indeed, if the right to punish were to be based on a *promise* of the guilty party to *allow himself* to be punished, he would also have to be allowed the faculty of himself declaring whether or not he deserves the punishment" (Kant, 1968B, 457-458). Rather than commenting on this statement, we should recall that the death penalty could also fall upon an innocent person who, not being allowed the right to resist or disobey an unjust verdict, must passively submit to the death penalty. Universal reason calls for this and the law of the State constitutes the source of law.

1.22 On this subject, it is useful to consider the example brought up by Kant several times and to which we shall return in connection with falsehood, the enemy who seizes me by the throat and asks me for my money. Here, too, there are useful reflections on the death penalty and the value of life. There could be those who desire something else before they desire money. As Kant warns, he could desire the woman who is with me. This person, "acts basely in every respect, indeed, as he conceived a desire for my girlfriend, he might conceive one for my wallet" (Kant, 1974, 451). Saying that such examples bring out Kantian misogyny certainly does not justify the absurdity of the comparison, which is still nothing if related to the umpteenth example, which, in his opinion, would be a justification for the death penalty. He reminds us "that in England, a woman who kills her husband by poisoning him is burnt at the stake, because if this practice were to catch on, no one would be sure of his own wife any longer" (Kant, 1974, 452).

1.23 On a juridical level, the individual is not the one who has the "right to the truth", an expression which for Kant is senseless, but all of humanity. Nonetheless the lack of truth, speaking on the juridical level obviously, directly harms whoever is primarily and tangibly the victim of a lie. "Lies therefore (...) always harm another, not a determined person, but rather humanity in general, since they contaminate the source of law itself" (Kant, 1968C, 638). We find ourselves face to face with the typical abstraction of formal law. It is certain that lies can harm all of humanity, but one who is directly affected is harmed in a different way. A lie which harms all of humanity calls into question the very foundation of law which is its certainty, but some of those directly involved immediately suffer an injustice and, not infrequently, a punishment as well.

1.24 Returning to the case where there is "an enemy who seizes me by the throat and asks me where I keep my money", it should be said that in his old age, Kant will deal with the problem in a substantially different way (Tagliapietra, 255 in nota). On the question of falsehood, he becomes rigorously intransigent. "It always harms another, however, not a particular person, but humanity in general" (Kant, 1968C, 638). To what Kant refers to as the sacredness of the commandment not to tell lies, a yet more sacred one cannot be sacrificed. Real characters such as *Salvo D'acquisto* or ones from literature such as *Jean Valjean* prove the opposite. Following the secularization of Christianity, to which he contributed not a little, Kant finds himself needing to make a principle absolute that no longer has anything absolute about it. A need for truth as an end in itself arises, which hides the need to inquire as to the very meaning of truth. It follows that more than being free thanks to the truth, *one becomes the slave of several concerns, which* no one "can elude, whether that harms him or herself or others" (Kant, 1968C, 640). A countless number of contradictions ultimately arise.

1.25 Kant quotes some statements of Constant for whom truth is a duty only towards those who have a right to truth. For Kant, however, the expression "*have a right to the truth* is meaningless" (Kant, 1968C, 637). Why should this be? Let us take the secret services as an example. If a secret agent reveals to the enemy what the latter is not supposed to know, he or she would cease to be a secret agent and would simply become a spy. An "Espion" (Big sneak) is, in fact, one who gives away a secret to another who must not know it (unless Kant wishes to consider spies, who act for money or for other sinister interests, an expression of moral life). Then, maintaining that "a man who, himself, does not believe what he says to another (…) has less value that of a simple thing" means reiterating a belief in a formal right more than a substantial one. The dignity of human beings and their rights cannot depend exclusively on their behaviour. This could cause the total loss of their rights, ignoring the fact that some are inalienable.

1.26 One of the innovations in Kant's juridical and political thought is erroneously thought to be the division between public and private law. Not that this division is not important, but it is certainly nothing new in western tradition. Kant himself cannot help but recall that "this division can easily be made according to Ulpian" whom he credits with having created formulas that "make it possible to develop and introduce" modern innovations. When these basic points are dealt with several contradictions arise which are not of a secondary nature. When speaking of the division of law, Kant rightly maintains that equality must be considered innate because it rests on the original independence so that one cannot "be constrained by others to anything more than we can constrain them mutually". However, since this principle may, at times, be called into question, why should human beings be prevented from defending this principle by having recourse to the various forms of resistance? This is still Kantian formalism which universally sets forth a principle that can then, in practice, also be disregarded. This formalism also comes out when Kant speaks of the social and civil states. Regarding these the juridical terms used must be clarified otherwise great confusion will result.

Maintaining that "there can certainly be a society in the state of nature, but not a civil society" merits a not inconsiderable explanation if one has used Ulpian as a starting point, and has also referred to Cicero. For classical law, referring to civil society is a useless tautology because, etymologically speaking, society is either civil or it is not. Departing from the concept that *ubi societas ibi ius*, the Kantian distinction is not only useless, but also dangerous. It is no accident that the Hegel and Marx's concept of civil society will be based on that distinction with all the consequences that we are familiar with. In other words law is either the basis of society or it becomes *uniquely* its superstructure.

1.27 Going back to the norm, which, over time, is codified in law, and sets forth the appropriate forms of coercion in case of failure to obey the law itself, it must be said that this encounters very precise limits that also become limits in the codification. *Without these limits, inalienable rights for persons would not exist.* If they exist, it is because a single individual finds in all others with whom he or she comes to interact, some forms of recognition that no one can call into question or fail to acknowledge. This means that each person is obliged, "in all conscience", to accept in every person his or her "personal" rights independently of the existing formal law. *Law* thus is required, and I would call the obligation absolute, to *abstain from legislating* on those subjects which concern the "most intimate" sphere of the person.

1.28 We shall return to the problem of limits. Here, it is useful to emphasize Kantian formalism, which, in his desire to divorce himself from any experience and base his conclusions only on an *a priori* reason, the universality of which has been anything but verified, ends up being purely utopian. Kant himself points this out to us, criticizing the efforts of those who attempt to refer to experiences of institutions of the past and exalting the Platonic Republic seen as a model of perfection to which one must aspire. "Indeed, nothing can be found that is more harmful and less worthy of a philosopher than that trivial appeal to an alleged experience (...) nor is the idea entirely accurate, that sets forth this *maximum* (that is, the perfect order) as an archetype, in order that the legal constitution of people comes closer and closer to the greatest possible perfection by following its form" (Kant, 1968A, 324). Unwilling to pit his strength against tradition or reality, *Kant proposes perfect models*, at times impossible to bring about, and representing the narrow and risky Platonic theme of those who can devise, interpret or propose to (impose on) others such models. In other words *like Plato, he feels he is a philosopher king*.

1.29 Kant, feels, basically, that he is conveying "a theory which determines practice and not vice versa (...) he concedes nothing to the foundation of the state which must be oriented by the law of reason (...) Kantian thought comes to a halt on the idea that it is impossible for anything to be valid just in theory, but not in practice" (Brandt, 4-5 and Falcioni, 21). Not only is he unaware of Latin juridical tradition, but even the elementary political virtues, on which political practice has been inscribed in the most eloquent way, and then exalted by great political thinkers. In this case, the claim to go back to models which are considered perfect, thwarts all the moral efforts, or, in any case, all that the gradual attempts and various historical experiences have produced in order to improve the human condition. It is true that Kant, in his old age, considerably softened this position, acknowledging the importance of the existing "juridical and political orders", but these are always seen as transitory. As has been rightly said "the position of an unappealable *no*, gives way to a *not yet*, as if pure (!) practical reason was becoming prepared for contamination" (Brandt, 11) with what is experienced, which, often, on the moral and also juridical level knows more than abstractions.

1.30 As has been appropriately observed, the chance of a Kantian *pax* rests on a very precise claim: "peace must be perpetual (...) and not simply lasting. In the German language, the distinction between perpetual and eternal is not offered; the term *ewig* must be used in any case". This is not an insignificant explanation, but a position that rejects any other solution that offers chances for a lasting peace. "It is not a question of unacceptable proposals because they are devoid of that unconditional character, which, on the contrary, is essential to the Kantian *pax*, which aims at a peace without conditions" (Falcioni, 17 and 18). This peace design, in other words, is presented as a categorical imperative and was such *not only for Kant, but* also *for those who*, consciously or otherwise, *were influenced by him*. One need only think of the Marxist classless society, which abolishes all the motives for conflict and sets in motion no less than the regeneration of humanity. This, too is a *categorical imperative* which one cannot escape but which "must induce" us to fight those who, by means of a misleading economic vision, wish to impede this other form of perpetual peace.

1.31 Even though it may not seem so, not a few Kantian statements carry us towards the prospects just referred to. Saying that "the concept of good and evil must not be determined before moral law (of which this apparently must be posited as the basis)" means corroborating that principle which advises: "operate in such away as to be able to want your maxim to become a universal law". Obviously, a position of the sort is rife with consequences. A just action will come about "from conformity of the will with the claim made by that principle, that is, one which is in compliance with legislation (…) which ensures the compatibility of external actions with universal law" (Falcioni, 29). Falcioni concludes that, in Kant, the only legitimate source of law seems to be reason, which, as we shall see, almost ends up being "raison d'état".

1.32 Statements of that sort may, upon first sight, seem to be too peremptory, but such is not the case. "The work of the future, the realization of a peremptory body of law, guides the action of the present, where a provisional law is in effect – according to the expressions that were to be introduced in the *Rechtslehre*" (Falcioni, 41). I would say that a tactic is involved that can utilize various tools as long as it accomplishes the goal which is that of *peremptory law*. Here, too, a way has been opened, which will go far. On can give thought to the fourth part of the *Manifest*, where the relationship between Communists and other political forces are discussed. As all of history has brought out, think for a moment of the Chinese experience, while the *peremptory goal* remains an assumption, in this case the revolution, the interlocutory phase, may justify any *temporary* alliance. "Every policy must bow before the law and only that way hope that it will arrive, however slowly, at a level at which it can shine with lasting splendour" (Kant, 1968E, 244). Until this is achieved, those actions, which operate towards its accomplishment can be justified. This would also explain that sort of love and hate which relate Kant, in various portions of his writing, to Plato.

1.33 At times, however, Kant seems to lose himself as if immersed in an unsettling realism. "As the government becomes larger, the laws lose their force, and a soulless despotism, which has uprooted the seeds of good, ends up degenerating into anarchy" (Kant, 1968E, 225). What, then has happened to the moral law based on *a priori* principles if so little is needed to sweep it away? Here, nature comes to the rescue, with the two famous equal and contrary laws of *sociable-unsociability*, regulates and takes best advantage of the antagonism present in society.

1.34 Keeping in mind the classic concept of society, Kantian unsociable sociability, which the classics had examined departing from different premises, becomes more understandable. Saying that man seeks harmony because nature, almost as if thanks to an arcane mystery, calls for discord, and can be dangerous because the mystery of uncontrollable forces among people is included. Kant, almost recalling Spinoza, is the one who uses these nebulous words: "*Nature* the great craftsman, from whose mechanical course, the goal of drawing people away from discord, harmony as well, even against their will, becomes evident." It is as if this goal were "called *destiny*" (cf. Kant, 1968E, 217). For classical jurists there is no destiny, nature, understood to be the Great Craftsman, has no better knowledge of what is good. Individuals know that together they can pursue their own tangible interests but they also know that they must control their selfishness, which is capable of various abominations. They therefore agree, while realizing that they do not have pure hearts. This is why Lucanus reminds us that his contemporaries were already speaking of *Concordia discors* (cf. Pezzimenti, 2011A, II.24).

1.35 Society, understood as a group of members who, abiding by a set of rules, pursue their objectives is the environment in which a certain *modus vivendi* is to be established, one which guarantees security and stability or, perhaps, the salvation and prosperity of those associated. I spoke of salvation because the word from the classical authors which Kant uses is *salus* taken from the *De legibus* of Cicero. However, the quotation is not accurate. Kant takes the maxim *salus publica suprema civitas lex est* which he acknowledges to have "unchanged validity and authority" forgetting that in Cicero and the classical authors, a different work is used. The second word is not *publica* but *populi*. It is not an oversight typical of those who quote from memory nor is it a misunderstood term. Kant wishes to express another thing. For him "the public safety, which is to be taken into consideration *first and foremost*, is precisely that legal constitution that guarantees each person liberty through law" (Kant, 1968G, 154-155). Certainly the word *populi* implies all that, but makes a concrete reference which removes law from its formalism. I do not think that this specification is a hair-splitting one, otherwise it would not be possible to explain why, in ancient times, the evil-doer, who, however, enjoyed the right of citizenship, that is, belonged to the people, was to receive forms of punishment that could not go beyond a certain limit, for example crucifixion unworthy of the *civis*, because he belonged to the *populus*. For Kant, such is no longer the case and he wonders if "the respect due to humanity in the person of the ill-doer" must still be taken into consideration. One cannot wonder at the fact that he goes so far as to state: "I consider that as far as the form is concerned, the *ius talionis*, is the only idea that can determine the principle of criminal law *a priori*" (Kant, 1968B, 487). What about where the law of retaliation is not possible, for example, in cases of rape and pederasty? Kant does not hesitate to maintain, in the subsequent sentence, that guilt of that sort must be punished with castration and exile "*ad perpetuum* from civil society". It is a bit like Rousseau when he returned to the idea of excommunication, so greatly vilified.

1.36 Still on the subject of *concordia discors*, a difference between Kant and Marx should be considered. For the former, harmony cannot be accomplished being stimulated by competition, indeed, without this, human beings would return to the precariousness of the primitive condition. *Paradoxically, it is the criterion of utility*, so berated in moral theory *that again unifies* mankind and directs it along paths that lead to perpetual peace. From this comes the idea of a "great federation of peoples", albeit with all of its contradictions so that, as Falcioni has shown quite excellently, which is set above the idea of confederation. The core of this federative union should be carried forth by a "powerful and enlightened people" such as the French, who gave rise to those ideas, which, since the end of the eighteenth century, have been contaminating all of Europe (cf. Kant, 1968E, 231 ff.). This people, I dare say, which, for Hegel, will, in future, be the Germans, for Marx it will be the proletariat and some might say, today, the American people capable of exporting not only democracy but the idea of a federal union anywhere. Why the French people? Above and beyond the historical and revolutionary motivations there is an element, which is not of secondary importance: the creation of the Republican State is considered by Kant a determining element for the accomplishment of perpetual peace. Is the French Republic, however, appropriate to accomplishing this purpose? For Kant it matters little if it is *ex novo*. For him, the institutions seem to be given *a priori*, coming from a reason, in this case: revolutionary.

1.37 It can easily be imagined that Kant ends up falling back into the emptiest of abstractionism not only concerning institutions, but also individual laws. His statements do not leave the slightest doubt. "If, however, it is only possible for a people to agree to a law, they have the duty to consider it just, even though the people found themselves in such a situation and in such a state of mind that, if they were consulted on it, it is highly likely they would deny their consent" (Kant, 1968G, 153-154). This all means that one cannot speak of inalienable laws. It is possible to speak of a "republic of reason" according to the dictates of the French Enlightenment. This model is not easy to attain, however and, at times, it seems to serve only as a goal, so that it is the concept itself of that institution, which splits up "into a *respublica nuomenon* and *respublica phaenomenon*". A terminology comes out of all that, which "turns out, in some cases, to be misleading or at least uncritical" (Falcioni, 83, note 19) and it, quite often, reveals the temptation already expressed by Rousseau, to believe that the republic is a system only for divine beings.

1.38 Departing from the assumption, subsequently exacerbated by Hegel, with the theory of the State, that surrendering private considerations takes place after the awareness of the superior ethicalness of public, left up to the monopoly of the force of the State, Kant maintains that even the devils, that is the divine beings, would agree on such a statement. Indeed, the devils would be willing to give up their freedom in a calculated surrender, that is, in anticipation of peace. This supposition leaves one perplexed to say the least: were the devils, in our tradition, not the princes of falsehood, so abhorred by Kant, those who brought war and discord more than peace? Is this not why they disobeyed God and should accept obeying human beings and their precepts? Now, solely to make those who should tempt and condemn to live in pace, do they suddenly discover themselves to be "republican spirits"? These are not catechistic-like and unrealistic questions because it is the premise around which much Kantian thought operates.

As can be read in the *Anthropologie in pragmatischer Einsicht*, for Kant there are people who, however rational they my be, are nonetheless in truth evil, even if they are endowed with inventiveness and an inclination to be moral. As their cultural sensitiveness grows, they feel with greater force the evil that is committed out of selfishness. A change and the rectification of some of their forms of behaviour should come out of this, but can an evil reason really feel certain necessities? For Kant, yes. It is as for peace: it will be reason that convinces human beings over time that a war is not advantageous for anyone. That same war that "has driven people to populate even the most deserted of regions; through the same means, it has forced them to unite in more or less legal relationships" (Kant, 1968E, 319-320). Couldn't a reason, always pressed diabolically by irrationality (a danger which Kant seems at times to be unaware of) show some advantages, which in actual fact are non-existent, and drive people to consider actions plausible, which "the after us" show themselves to be exactly incompatible with reason itself? There is no need to return to prehistory. The century, which has just concluded offers us a wide sample of similar absurdities.

1.39 This path, as has been well brought out (cf. Falcioni, 112), seem almost to put a blind force into play "which has no regard for the will of individuals". It is a Natural course of events and nature "does it whether we like it or not" (Kant, 1968E, 323). That concept of necessity, more than that of liberty, appears here. It is cherished by Hegel, who is capable of justifying everything that happens with the notorious "trick of reason", that, to give an idea, which justifies everything as long as the desired goal is achieved, one capable "of obtaining harmony from the discord among human beings, even against their will". That is all "irresistibly" (*unwiderstehlich*) willed by nature (Kant, 1968E, 217 and 225). To be sure, one can speak of identity between *nature and reason*, but the fact remains that Kant considers that the fundamental premise of law. An *a priori* law, of universal dimensions, and one, which is acceptable in the light of the French Revolution (today, one might "say" exportable) at any time and anywhere.

1.40 If the French Revolution intends to cancel out all that has been, Kant takes a further step: "behind the pantomime of the struggle against privileges of the nobility, the true plan provides for no less than the revocation of original sin, cancellation of Adam's guilt (…) In other words, the rigid, transcendental morality of the Kantian philosopher allows mankind to be prohibition and sin, apple and serpent, guilt and redemption" (Tagliapietra, 16 and 19). This is all by virtue of a morality based and dependent upon reason. Morality must always relate to this reason, the source of law, which politics must obey. This is Kantian reason, obviously, and not an historical one, which cannot be based on *a priori*-s. Hence, it is clear that universality of morality depends on an equally universal reason which founds and maintains a right, which can be applicable everywhere. Now, the meaning of Kantian formalism becomes clear: "Human beings, for Kant, are always confronted with the law, but this being confronted with the law means the inexhaustible paradox of formality, which never tells us the essence of the command, but simply *how* to carry it out. As a result, the famous categorical imperative, too, which seems to reveal to us the essence of the law, actually ends up relieving it of comprehensibility" (Tagliapietra, 26). The absence of this intelligibility, which I believe is a lack of objectivity, is such that the dimension of evil and sin is subjectively resolved in the secret dialogue each person carries on with his or her reason, convinced that it is possible to offer universally valid solutions. In actual fact, once again the Protestant side of Kant comes out: "the drama of sin is played out *in interiore homine*" and, more or less consciously, leads to self-deception (cf. Tagliapietra, 27). It can be and has been said by many, that there is no longer a need for the divinity to justify the problem of evil, but one could conclude that there is no longer any need to save oneself from and be redeemed by the divinity. The foundations of human reason are sufficient.

1.41 Kant thinks that "starting from the principles of reason" he can found new moral criteria which would acquire authority based not on tradition but on rationality: this is the root of his formalism. These new principles, however, must, in any case, be authoritative as were the preceding ones. This is the source of their rigorousness, of which someone must be a guarantor in the exteriority of moral life. This someone can only be the State in the guise of supreme legislator according to reason. Once again, Hegel can be perceived here, and it is certainly no accident that against this supreme form of authority "there can be no legitimate resistance", only submission. Upon closer examination, it cannot be otherwise. That explains the peremptory Kantian statement: "Law must never be regulated on the basis of politics, but politics on law" (Kant, 1968C, 642). As has been appropriately written "the entire development of Kantian philosophy turns on the metaphor of the court, in which reason and the arbitration of force agree to meet" (Tagliapietra, 33). To be sure, if human beings were different, the problem would not arise, but then one could ask oneself: are these principles of reason universal or not? Kant's observations on this subject are totally clear: "If all human beings were good, they could show themselves openly, but for now, this is not possible" (Kant, 1974, 445). That *for now* is truly interesting. It is as if to support the possible movement towards a universality of morality that is not yet such, that is, a regenerated humanity that becomes the source of a new, moral life. On whom does that regeneration depend? On a few exceptional individuals endowed with new principles? Impossible, Kant replies, "since these exceptions negate universality, and so they are called principles" (Kant, 1968C, 643). Then, however, we find ourselves in a vicious circle from which it is impossible to escape.

1.42 The opposite of what Kant set forth for himself and, in actual fact, wanted to avoid seems to occur. A law of which the State becomes the supreme guarantor must guarantee what were to be inalienable premises, to be defended at all costs. However absurd the Kantian imperatives may seem, they fail to "guarantee Kantian precepts more than a provisional reality. To make those rules effective, a public juridical order is necessary, one which is capable of instituting peremptory law" (Falcioni, 2001, 108). Here, too, Hegel with his ethical State can be perceived, a State, which personifies only the force of law.

A Brief Digression on the Problem of Falsehood.

1.43 In the meantime, how are those, who believe in this universality, supposed to behave? The answer is simple: as if such universal principles did not exist. There is Kant's own example, concerning the possibility of concealing thoughts by making poor use of the truth. Returning to the case referred to above, we think of "an enemy who seizes me by the throat and asks me where I keep my money". In this case "he does not have the right to expect the truth from me" (Kant, 1974, 447). Then, is the principle of truth valid abstractly and when there is money involved, it is no longer valid! Let us clarify, *I do not mean* that we must allow him to cut our throats as long as we do not lie, I mean that Kant does not at all think so for more serious cases. Although I did well because I saved a life, Kant believes that I "am a liar anyway, because I acted against the rights of humanity". False information not only harms one person in particular (here I would have not a few objections) but all humanity. The fact remains, however, and Kant says this, that if we wished to abide faithfully "by the truth, we would quite often expose ourselves to the malice of those who wish to make ill use of our truth" (Kant, 1974, 448). It seems to me once again, that every one of us is subjectively inclined to justify his or her behaviour, even knowing that objective *a priori* principles exist. Kant himself says this, too: "An evaluation of the case of necessity is entrusted to each person" (Kant, 1974, 448). Is all of that not pure Machiavellianism!

1.44 To answer that question, we must again return to the opposition between falsehood and truth. Derrida provides us with an explanation as to why the great critics of Christianity attacked Saint Paul on no uncertain terms, as did Nietzsche, for example. The reason is that an authentically Christian spirit, this is the case of Augustine's, "constantly continues a dialogue" with him (cf. Derrida, 9-10) and at the end, questions itself on the problem of the truth. Yet, rather than being a manifestation of the truth, history seems dotted with continual falsehoods, which are there for everyone to see, so that it would be more logical to speak of the history of falsehood. However, wonders the French philosopher, "who would dare to relate the history of falsehood?" (Derrida, 15). I believe that we should ask a question, more fundamental than this one: is it possible to speak of falsehood without reference to the truth? Is any one, who relates a history of falsehood not obliged at least to be true to himself or herself, insofar as this is possible? How can we trust one who relates this history of falsehood and fails to start from the need to tell the truth about that history? To relate the history of falsehood, too, there must be the *intention* to tell a story in accordance with truth.

1.45 Saint Augustine said that the intention was to some extent the desire, the explicit will to tell or not to tell the truth. If there is this *intention not to tell the truth*, there is falsehood. There is another complication, however: "a distinction must be made, too, between the history of the *concept* of falsehood and an history of *falsehood in itself*" (Derrida, 31). This problem arises from another subtlety insofar as there can be some truths (cultural) related to those who experience a critical detail from history and who can claim, quite tranquilly and with all the best intentions, a particular statement to be true, which only subsequently turns out to be false (think of those who considered the earth flat, or who maintained that travelling around the globe, they would reach the Far East, unaware, as they were of the existence of the new continent). For the very reason that what characterizes falsehood is intention, in those cases errors of unawareness will be referred to, until one finds oneself faced to face with evidence that one would like to deny. What counts is that in order to speak of falsehood, there must be a reference to the truth, otherwise, falsehood would not be such. One might even speak of a reference to the sacredness "or the holiness of truth, outside of which it is impossible to condemn, or even identify a falsehood" (Derrida, 34). Basically, liars are such not because they tell a lie, but because they know the truth and do not tell it.

In other words, just about everyone knows that the false presupposes the true.

1.46 What should be emphasized is that this truth cannot *either* be totally detached from a situation *or* totally dependent on it. In the *first case* there would be a merely formal truth, In the *second,* only a contingent and utilitarian one. The first case concerns Kant and his morality which, like his understanding of law, ends up being rigorously formal and inapplicable, unless absurdly so. In order not to succumb to the danger of excluding any reference to historical events, as Kant indeed does, Saint Augustine presents a highly intricate set of cases. For Kant, in falsehood, too, there is an *a priori* "bad" which lead him to conclusions that are questionable to say the least. Indeed, even before killers who asked if your friend, whom they are pursuing, has taken refuge in your house, it would be a crime to lie. On this subject, the Augustinian position, for the very reason that it is not rigidly formal, turns out to be far richer, even though it departs from the assumption that lying is an evil.

1.47 Saint Augustine departs from a very precise conviction: "language was created certainly not because people deceive one another, but because each makes the other aware of his or her own thoughts. So, using language to tell falsehoods against one's original goal, is a sin" (Ench. 7, 22). He shows considerable ductility and, for this reason, even without ever contradicting the truth, he presents a complex and rich set of case histories. In some cases, he went so far as to speak of *honest mendacity* while not approving of it, arousing the perplexity of Saint Jerome, who preferred to speak of *honesta dispensatio* (cf. Augustini, 1969, 75 and 82). Speaking of falsity, the Bishop of Hippo, notes "any falsehood that unjustly harms another person is immediately to be excluded" (Augustini, 2001A, 11.18). This is to be condemned "without any hesitation whatsoever", if then it causes harm to no one the question still remains as to "whether one who offends the truth to take advantage of another does not cause harm to himself or herself" (Augustini, 2001A, 12.19), an aspect which is often neglected.

1.48 Given these premises, let us again take up the paradox of Kant that even face to face with killers who asked if your friend, whom they were pursuing, has taken refuge in your house, lying would be a crime. Augustine presents a fairly similar case, which reveals his noteworthy sensitivity and the great value he places upon existence. "One does not sin when fleeing from capital punishment but when the sin for which that punishment is deserved is committed. In Christian doctrine, furthermore, it is taught that one should not despair of mending one's ways and not to cut anyone off from access to penitence" (Augustini, 2001A, 13.22). Is it possible to respond to the Kantian paradox by saving truth and not yielding to falsehood? Relating a similar case, Augustine says 'yes'. A bishop from Tagaste had hidden a man who had taken refuge with him to escape the death penalty. The guards who went to the bishop's to arrest the man were told that he knew where he was hiding but had no intention "either of lying or of revealing the hiding place of the fugitive". He was tortured for this and eventually brought before the emperor who, admiring his courage, gave grace to the convict and modified the penalty (cf. Augustini, 2001A, 13.23). In other words, Augustine would have replied to Kant that *firmness cannot be mistaken for stupidity*, like truth for pure formalism. For this reason, "it must be recalled that it is not the same to hide the truth and proffer falsehood. Although everyone who tells falsehoods wants to hide the truth, not all who want to hide the truth tell falsehoods. There are numerous cases where falsehoods are not told in order to hide the truth, but one is simply silent" (Augustini, 2001B, 10.23).

1.49 Returning to a truth totally outside of time has perverse effects. One of the effects of the attempt to do this is totalitarianism. Put in these terms, this statement might seem paradoxical, but, upon closer examination, as Todorov reminds us, totalitarianism can be considered "*un mal extrême*" because it has claimed to be the sole truth, even with the intention of making people forget all that could contradict it (cf. Todorov, 11). The most radical of untruths lies in the fact that where totalitarianism aims at nullifying mankind, it makes "*une promesse de plénitude, de vie harmonieuse et de bonheur*". For this, it claims to possess "*absolu et définitif* knowledge" (cf. Todorov, 28 and 34). The destiny of individuals shows itself to be "*sans importance*" for this monstrous Leviathan which "*nie radicalement l'altérité*" (cf. Todorov, 38 and 44). Degradation of human beings and all their personal relations becomes total, even the independence of love becomes a hazard. Hence, totalitarian power is hostile to traditional religions (cf. Todorov, 25). To reinstate the truth it is necessary to reaffirm the primacy of the person.

1.50 At this point, I should once again like to return to a point in Kantian formalism. From what has been said up to now comes a dramatic conclusion, brought out by some, but seldom considered: "For Kant an act is moral when its maxim is a maxim that can be universalized, raised to a rule that universally commands the behaviour of every human being. It is this universality of the maxim of the act that constitutes the moral goodness of the act itself" (Maritain, 745). Moral good, therefore, does not serve as another foundation. It is clear that a purely formal ethic is involved because its deductive regulatory framework is distinct from any situation in human life and refers to those principles of reason that should be universal only because it is reason itself that dictates them. While this reason concerns the practical sphere, as Kant himself said, it was necessary to refer to principles of pure-practical reason, because it is considered "only from the point of view of the exigencies of logical universality". That explains why, in Kant's view, one such as Massimiliano Kolbe was exclusively a liar and senseless person. The reasons of charity cannot be put in opposition to those of pure rigorism. In the final analysis it is the pure aprioristic exigencies of reason that dictate the regulatory character of any moral act. Outside of these, inalienable rights of persons do not exist because they must be normalized by reason in order to exist. Referring to moral principles to moral principles far from aprioristic exigencies is senseless and can be considered the result of an emotional conception. This is the typical position that will lead to logical positivism and already finds in Ayer a convinced advocate, since he is of the opinion that the principle of an ethical symbol in a sentence adds nothing to its content as the phrasing of an act (cf. Ayer, 158).

1.51 Then, there is another problem worthy of consideration: as time goes on, some forms of behaviour judged morally correct in the past, can seem to us, if not improper, at least unseemly. What at first seemed good or bad, perhaps seems to us more or less good or bad. This means that our "moral consciousness" can improve and gradually become more and more demanding. It is said that our manner of judging becomes more high-minded and we should ask ourselves with respect to what. The fact remains, however, that our *intelligence* becomes more *penetrating* in the etymological sense of the terms. Here, too, the question again arises: in relation to what? The moral considerations refer then to a goal on which the dynamism of moral life depends. If not our happiness, at least our satisfaction depends on this aim. Kant may say that happiness cannot condition our moral life, pursuing the quest of an ethic based on "absolute autonomy whether, let us say, upwards (religion), or downwards (the doctrine of prudence or doctrine of happiness)". This, in any case, means, "the leeway for moral action is not determined from the outside, divine laws or perceptible conditioning are involved" (Fonnesu, 17). A being so created, however, is a robot and its intelligence is artificial. There is no cause that can justify, or rather, be considered the motive for a moral action. Furthermore, for human beings, the robot dimension, brings up a question, which is not secondary: from what does the morality of an act come about? Does it depend, as Maritain would say, on it conformity with reason, or on the liberty from which it comes and which it expresses? ...or else, I am taking the liberty to suggest, from both positions, which, to some degree, seek to overcome the gap between theory and practice.

1.52 It should be kept in mind that Kant wants to uncouple moral action from any reference because he believes that the latter can constitute an egocentric conditioning of moral action, which would end up no longer being such. If, for example, we considered happiness the foundation of moral life, we would run a great risk "since the principle of happiness is structurally egocentric and corresponds to the principle of self-love" (Fonnesu, 19). Speaking thus, however, we want to ignore an infinite number of acts, great or minor, which, as Saint Augustine would say, have nothing to do with self-love (*amor sui*), but which, on the contrary are profoundly altruistic, gratuitous, and which seek to emphasize the *amor Dei*. Not only is Kant unaware of Augustinian dualism, but even of examples like those of Salvo D'Acquisto or Massimiliano Kolbe, who express the maximum forgetting of self. Figures such as these are troublesome in a rationalistic ethic, as Kierkegaard noted quite well, then ended up not considering them ethical at all, all of this without losing sight of the fact that if we also considered self-love only (*amor sui*), that those who choose one moral action rather than another still want it with a goal in mind. It is impossible to desire without the *specifics* of desire, even if these specifics were the essence of duty in itself, that is: finding satisfaction in desire, duty for duty's sake. This act placates my moral consciousness, anyway.

1.53 Without accounting for the fact that, if a moral action separated from any reference were possible, should we ask ourselves why such a moral command exists in our consciences? What is this *prius ontologico* based on? Without it, it is impossible to speak of morality, since it is certainly not exaustive simply to speak of *a priori*? There can only be one answer: "The genuine principle of morality universally and necessarily valid, cannot be material, but will have to be, on the contrary, *formal*" (Fonnesu, 20). Furthermore, if this formalism, with all its ascetic being, becomes so objective, what happens to liberty devoid of any sort of reference, which may guarantee the possibility of choice?

Ch. II. The Ethics and Metaphysics of Non-sense Reserved for an Elite

A) The dilemmas of will. Liberty and Responsibility: Arthur Schopenhauer.

2.1 In Vattimo's opinion, Schopenhauer caused a crisis for various aspects of "systematic" knowledge. In so doing, he emphasized several points, expressions of a sort of "common sense", to which not a few thinkers of our era refer. This conviction also applies to "ethics, in which tender compassion for a living person seems practically the only point on which our culture (…) seems to agree when good or evil, the just and unjust are spoken of" (Vattimo, 1989, XI). It is appropriate to point out immediately that that sense of compassion, of *pietas* which Nietzsche himself would fight (but then benefit from as I shall point out later), is not something new, but constitutes one of the salient traits of our religious tradition. Apart from tradition, for many years, in the throes of the greatest dialectic delirium, from Hegel and his followers, historicism in rigorously Machiavellian terms had been evident. Whoever wins is always right and "never feels shame": this conviction had contributed to blurring that tradition. When the dialectical daze had given up its narcotic fumes, it became apparent that such a deep feeling would come back into fashion. One only had to be patient.

2.2 Setting aside Adorno's analyses, of *Negative Dialectics* or *Aesthetic Theory* which revealed a pessimistic Schopenhauer, the expression of a bourgeois world in crisis, and a line of thought which had perceived the limits of Hegelian reason came back into fashion. Along with this was the attempt to rationalize everything within a technical and scientific method. Wittgenstein expressed this failure quite well in the twentieth century. In his opinion: "Whereof one cannot speak, thereof one must be silent" (Wittgenstein, 1985, prop. 7). This is tantamount to saying that the destiny of total rationalization failed miserably. If any possibility of using reason or rather, as seems more opportune to me, the need to set limits to it, is another problem with which Schopenhauer cannot help us, it seems to me. To be sure, Schopenhauer definitively relieved us of the illusion of knowing the thing in itself, but he did not tell us, as some present-day sceptics would have us believe, that we were forbidden to think of it, to suppose its existence as a guide to our actions. The very fact that the will, the spring of actions, does not have its origin in the phenomenon, but "pours out from within our intimate selves, from the immediate consciousness, in which each person recognizes the essence of the individual self", should make us reflect on not a few consequences.

2.3 Saying that the metaphysical need "arises not so much from the wonder of which Aristotle spoke, but from the experience of death, grief, the relentless passing of everything and from the unhappiness that accompanies this" (Vattimo, 1989, XXIV), certainly does not help us to understand how such a need is satisfied. Nor can we be consoled by the fact that philosophy does not offer a remedy for suffering, because, otherwise, what would the use of thinking be? To be sure, thought can induce us to admit that philosophy cannot give us definitive solutions. This is already a contribution, and it can encourage us to find them elsewhere. Some can say, furthermore, that "the redemption, authenticity, and happiness of human beings consist in the recognition of the true structure of being and in accepting this as a norm of behaviour" (Vattimo, 1989, XXIV), but that *acceptance*, to be sincere, seems like *resignation* and an admission of *failure* for a reason that claimed something quite different. One thereby arrives at irrationality, which conceals pessimism, in the manner of a Machiavelli as to the impossibility of the moral betterment of humanity. The aesthetic solution, reduced to being a palliative, cannot be considered exhaustive either because, among other things, it presents itself as being elitist, hence, unsatisfying. Schopenhauer honestly admits this himself: in order to find redemption, happiness or salvation, he was obliged to find a way free of will, even the will to live, which the original guilt in the being born gathers up, and which is so reminiscent of nature, the cruel stepmother, evoked by Leopardi. This *flight from the will*, even if a difficult operation and certainly not within everyone's reach, *already evokes* that idea of the superman that Nietzsche will propose as a new "existential", hence moral, solution. It is *obviously moral* not in the classical sense, since it involves going *beyond good and evil* in the traditional sense of the words.

2.4 Speaking of morality, it must be said that despite the fact that Schopenhauer criticizes the vision of Hegel and the other "sophists" of his time, who are under the illusion that they are pursuing a systematic vision of philosophy, is convinced that philosophy cannot escape a systematic approach properly understood. "A system of thoughts – he clearly writes – must always be arranged in an architectural form"; and slightly earlier: the "thought I feel I must communicate, manifests itself in the form of what has been called metaphysics, ethics and aesthetics, while it should, in actual fact, be all of those things taken together" (Schopenhauer, 1986A, 7). It is the totality that often makes it difficult to discern the value, as well as the destiny of each individual branch. Indeed, the "value which is usually the destiny of good in every form, will be recognized late (...) since I always saw falsehood and, finally, the absurd and the meaningless, as the object of honour and admiration" (Schopenhauer, 1986A, 14). In other words, the just and the true need time if they are to be understood.

2.5 Departing from these premises, Schopenhauer puts us on our guard against one of the recurring ills of philosophy and which, more than any other, bring out his crisis: the use of philosophy as a political tool, but also as fashion. Being basically anti-philosophical, all that decrees its demise. Worse yet, it turns philosophy into an instrument of gain and career, in other words, in sophistry. Making such use of it, one pursues vacuous things and charlatanism, more than absolute thought (cf. Schopenhauer, 1986A, 16). It all leads to the degradation of philosophy and constriction, truly ignoble, to go about, as did Petrarch, *poor and naked*. This is an ongoing danger. "*The feverishness inherent in vile gain*" is the expression of a world taken up by the dimension of money than it is of thought. In order "*not to abandon your magnanimous undertaking*" you must be strong and intrepid in solitude because "*you will have few companions if you take the other path*" (Petrarch, 35).

2.6 To liberate philosophy one must free it of the fable, thought up by some "philosophers", "and which has become indispensable to them, of a reason which immediately and absolutely knows, intuits and perceives" (Schopenhauer, 1986A, 24). In other words, the limits of reason must be recaptured to define its areas and confines, but also to establish that, above and beyond those boundaries, there is an entire universe, often existential, towards which reason, as Kant already perceived, seems naturally driven. Criticism, just, towards a reason which knows in an absolute way, is replaced by what Schopenhauer calls "support of the world", that is, the subject. "What knows all, without being known by anyone" (Schopenhauer, 1986A, 33). The risk of arriving at a dangerous subjectivism is overcome by the fact that "the subject ends where the object begins". These two goals are always indispensible for thought as well. Subjectivism, however, is overcome by use of the pure intellect's way of knowing, recalling Kant.

2.7 Schopenhauer arrives at a vision of life similar to that of Descartes, when he was subject to "temptations", no longer being able to distinguish between dream and reality. It is indeed true that "using that criterion to find out whether something was a dream or reality, is a highly difficult and often impossible undertaking (...) Life and dreams are pages of the same book" (Schopenhauer, 1986A, 48-50). Isolating a page can be senseless, given the close connection that brings dream and reality together. Prudence comes to our aid. "Rigorously speaking, [it] means the intellect placed in the service of the will" (Schopenhauer, 1986A, 55). Not everyone is capable of acquiring prudence, however. "A stupid person does not come to comprehend the connection between the phenomena of nature" and, in this respect, is worse than the animals, because his or her intellect is "below the animal level" (Schopenhauer, 1986A, 56). The fool cannot grasp the connections between the various representations. The wise person, indeed, has only this advantage, by using the intellect. It cannot be forgotten, in fact, that "science cannot capture the ultimate essence of the world, it cannot go beyond the representation: science, in the final analysis, only offers us relationships between representations" (Schopenhauer, 1986A, 63-64). This actually means perceiving only the outer appearance of reality.

2.8 "Every science consists of a system of truths, laws and rules, universal because they are abstract, relative to any category of object whatsoever" (Schopenhauer, 1986A, 85). This is now a dated conception of science. Scientific laws and rules, too, eventually go out of date or they are valid, as Kuhn teaches us, within certain paradigms. This is not all. "The greatest strength of knowing, or abstract knowledge consists in communicability and in the possibility of being preserved in a set form" (Schopenhauer, 1986A, 100). In the light of these conclusions, one can, in part agree, "that reason is not the source of virtues" (Schopenhauer, 1986A, 104) as is true for artistic genius. I say in part, because moral like aesthetic life cannot be fulfilled on the level of often too rigid knowledge, but it cannot be completely do without it, either. To be sure, that leads to the crisis of Kantian morality because the "moral value of an action, its being produced in terms of abstract, purely rational maxims" cannot be considered (Schopenhauer, 1986A, 107). Moral life is surely something more. In this point and more than any other, Kant is affect by the French Revolution and the height of the Enlightenment, believing that moral maxims can be universal, like the rights proclaimed by the revolutionaries.

2.9 "The cause of error is certainly to be sought in hastiness or in imperfect knowledge (...) Error is thus perfectly analogous to illusion" (Schopenhauer, 1986A, 131). This means that in order to avoid making mistakes and deceiving oneself, perfect knowledge must be acquired. This all seems to me a camouflaged form of Hegelianism, unless one is willing to admit that some of the unknowable must always remain on our gnoseological horizon. In other words, a thing "absolutely obscure: science must then leave the intimate essence unexplained". Elsewhere it is said that that intimate essence, "must remain an eternal unknown"

(Schopenhauer, 1986A, 133 and 155) This means marking off the territory of the comprehensible and giving up Hegel's assertion according to which: all that is real is rational and vice versa. Now it can be understood why "for philosophy all is equally unknown to an equal degree, all is a problem" (Schopenhauer, 1986A, 134). For the German philosopher modern thought "does not ask itself about the problem of the origin and end purpose of the world (...) the why is subordinated to the what". In other words, teleology, or rather escatology can be considered old-fashioned. Why, then, have a series of surrogates come in existence ? This is a question that sagacious spirits should ask themselves. This is all the more so because we, "in virtue of knowledge *in abstracto*", are capable of going beyond the present, embrace the entire past and the future" (Schopenhauer, 1986A, 137). This all has a moral value as well. We can indeed evaluate planning and, above all, we can experience a series of feeling such remorse, for example. Hence, morality cannot be reduced, as Kant wished, to "an absolute duty, which is tantamount to saying that it has fallen from heaven" (Schopenhauer, 1986A, 137).

2.10 It is well know that the solution to every enima lies in the will. This also shows itself as the act of the will and action of the body that constitute "one and the same thing which is given to us in two, basically different ways" (Schopenhauer, 1986A, 158). This statement may sound strange but it is clearly repeated in a sort of "refrain". So "this will is something I know (...) only in its single acts, hence in time which is the form of the phenomenon of my body" (Schopenhauer, 1986A, 159-160). Where does this will come from, however? It is impossible to know since it is impossible to penetrate into its essence. Yet, there must be some reason if this will induces one to act one way and not in another? Otherwise, we would be obliged to admit that, all that brings it about, in some way, "belongs to it by chance (...) that the act itself is, in general and in its essence, only the phenomenon of a will inexplicable in itself" (Schopenhauer, 1986A, 166-167). By chance (even if the reflections made on life and light seem to exclude it) and inexplicable, are two different and contradictory conditions. As far as I am concerned, they are unsatisfactory. It can be misleading to say that the intimate essence of every phenomenon always remains inexplicit, if phenomena produced by the will are involved. For one who undergoes (or even participates in) an action of another the intimate essence of the will can be inexplicable, but can we say the same for the author of the action? Even Schopenhauer seems to be obliged to entertain some doubts. Indeed, he cannot deny that it is the will "that comes forth from our intimacy, from the immediate consciousness, in which each person recognizes the essence of his or her own individual" (Schopenhauer, 1986A, 172-173).

2.11 Despite that, however, the will remains without a basis. This is what makes it free, otherwise, even whoever rejects the dialectic process, would be forced to admit its necessary and necessitating logic: it becomes immediately clear, however, that this is an illusion. "Only *a posteriori*, after the experience, does a person, to his or her great surprise, become aware of not being free, but subject to necessity" (Schopenhauer, 1986A, 175). Can we be happy and secure? In the principle of necessity, reduced to that of sufficient reason, love, the will, liberty, etc., should be involved, but are we really sure that all that can happen? Without a basis or points of reference, the will "while becoming more and more distinctly objectified as it moves up from one degree to the next, nonetheless, it does not operate unconsciously and by blind force" (Schopenhauer, 1986A,

222). Hence, the logic of *homo homini lupus* is accepted, which brings out the existence of the identical logic of imposition in all the various levels of nature. This is a sort of "determined and invariable direction" the result of a will, which "takes on character". A propos of character, it is surprising that, almost anticipating Nietzsche, it is possible to maintain that in "some people, knowledge reaches the point of freeing itself from this servitude" (Schopenhauer, 1986A, 225). This is as if to say that only some supermen can overcome the principle of necessity.

2,12 "Will is always the will for something, hence it has an object, a goal". It is not a trivial matter to ask oneself why, otherwise it would be ridiculous "for a long time to continue the game of the perpetual passage from desire for satisfaction and from satisfaction to the next desire" (Schopenhauer, 1986A, 238 and 241). It is only that the German philosopher ends up giving an exclusively Platonic explanation for all that. Indeed, when he speaks of "objectification of the will", he maintains that "then what is known is no longer the particular thing as such, but the idea, the eternal form, the immediate objectivity of the will at that given level" (Schopenhauer, 1986A, 257). It is a sort of thing in itself, which Plato and Kant have in common. Art, poetry and music in particular arrive at this form of "pure contemplation". "Its unique origin is the awareness of ideas, its unique end the communication of that awareness" (Schopenhauer, 1986A, 265) is, obviously, as Croce would say, that it as an awareness having a different nature. The fact should be emphasized, however, that here too, all of that is reserved to whoever, as Nietzsche will later point out, can rise to such "pure contemplation". It is reserved, that is, to a rare portion of humanity, whose "genius therefore consists in the attitude of keeping oneself in pure intuition" (Schopenhauer, 1986A, 266). This is not a gift granted to the common person, since this person "is all filled with and satisfied by the ordinary present". This is an elevation to a *caste mystique*, which, *differently from the traditional one*, certainly has no bearing on simple and uneducated people. The "populace herd does not see", notes Schopenhauer.

2.13 With a sense of superiority that evokes said premonitions, he draws a sketch of ordinary people. These, "goods from nature's factory, which produces thousands of them a day, is, as we have said, incapable, at least with any degree of continuity, of that apperception, permanent and disinterested in every way that is true contemplation" (Schopenhauer, 1986A, 268). Complete lack of sensitivity to beauty and to the sublime is to be observed in this example of the common herd. Those people are under the yoke of the will; its basis of slaves who celebrate "the Sabbath after a week of forced labour (…) Under this conditions, there is no difference between contemplating the sunset from a gaol or from a palace" (Schopenhauer, 1986A, 280-281). Yet, at times, such is not the case. The pure simplicity of willing, and loving, is capable of bringing light even where light is not to be found, as so many simple and heroic accounts have done, even behind prison bars, watching the sun in patches or not looking at it at all. Not understanding this leads to an incorrigible pessimism about human nature, typical of the "lamentations of the great" of all times. These lamentations "seem to come from today, and this is the case because the human race is always the same" (Schopenhauer, 1986A, 332). This anthropological view is typically Machiavellian since humanity is "in its intimate essence, in its idea, always the same in all of its manifestations" (Schopenhauer, 1986A, 345).

2.14 Nonetheless, our awareness of this immutability is always temporary and incomplete. "Our philosophy will remain in the area of immanence (…). The real and knowable world will remain the constant object and limit of research (...) so rich that the farthest-reaching investigations of human genius are incapable of totally grasping it" (Schopenhauer, 1986A, 377). Here there is a just critique of philosophies of history. which claim to account for all the real in the rational, but, like them, the philosophy of Schopenhauer explains all the *raison d'être* of events in terms of immanence and, finds in it his justification. "From this point of view, the individual, who has sprung forth out of nothing (...) plunges back into nothing" (Schopenhauer, 1986A, 380). Here, one might speculate that a beginning of nihilism is involved, but the position is more complex. Individuals are being spoken of, who have lost their *raison d'être* and found it once again, as Feuerbach would say, in the dimension of humanity. "Nature is not aimed at the individual, but at the species, at the conservation of which she operates in all seriousness and prodigality". However, *take care* because, from this point of view, "nature is always ready to sacrifice the individual" (Schopenhauer, 1986A, 382). Here is a different form of the "ruse of reason" whose effects we have felt dramatically! Moreover, it could not be otherwise if death is a sleep in which individuality is forgotten and, hence, can be forgotten without any trouble.

2.15 It matters little whether it is superman or super-humanity: the positions appear already to be defined. "A being which loves life as it is, who asserts it with all its power, can, without scruples, consider it as infinite". That of having to die is considered an "abstract persuasion" which, however, "only human beings bear (Schopenhauer, 1986A, 387 and 388). Can an individual, however, who "perishes as a phenomenon", still deem the criterion of responsibility to be valid or does this, too, not come under the *mare magnum* of the species?

2.16 "The philosophies of Bruno and Spinoza, purified, to be sure, of their "imperfections" would also lead to the same result". This all corroborates the fact that, in addition to imminence, that philosophy brings "liberty [back] to its relationship with necessity" (Schopenhauer, 1986A, 392-394). To what degree then can the will call itself free, and thus responsible? It is possible to "demonstrate the necessity of every phenomenon and all that nature contains. Liberty is reduced to being blind in the uninterrupted chain of causes and effects, set as binding, necessary, and immutable. Why, then, appeal to Seneca's statement *Velle non discitur*? If will is not something one learns, it does not seem to be such a necessary phenomenon. If one is to be consistent with what the German philosopher has said, the statement: "my repentance will not, then, be able to fall on what I willed, but only on what I did" can certainly not be accepted (Schopenhauer, 1986A, 407). If will and consequences are so separated, how can one speak of necessity? Furthermore, if, out of fidelity to a certain immanentism, will is reduced to a sort of *anima mundi*, why should that will experience a hard struggle between opposing desires only on a few occasions?

2.17 Let us depart, then, from another assumption of the German philosopher: "every act of living is by its very essence suffering (…) the activity of our spirit, too, is only a constant effort to chase away boredom". How, then is it possible that we have "affection, in any case, for life and make every effort to prolong it as long as we can"? Pain indeed seems essential to life and "its level is set by the nature of the subject" (Schopenhauer, 1986A, 426-427 and 435-436), as with joy; then, any excess is to be deemed an error or an illusion. Who can measure feelings of the sort? Who can thwart the illusions considered healthy by some and harmful by others? Or rather, according to what criterion can such a judgement be formulated? Then, what can it mean that "happiness is never innate nor does it come to us spontaneously, but is always due to the satisfaction of a desire" (Schopenhauer, 1986A, 438)? If the desire for happiness were so, sooner or later, it should be placated or find peace. But that does not happen! Not even the greatest of pleasures bring to an end the need for another form of happiness. Does the fact that this can never totally take place not perhaps suggest that its deeper need comes, indeed, from a "primitive situation"?

2.18 If these questions are senseless, we must resign ourselves to having a life without sense. The German philosopher himself is the first to admit this, and seems to bring it out on more than one occasion. "Humans are like clocks that are wound up and run without knowing why" (Schopenhauer, 1986A, 441). If they do not know, why should they have the awareness, however, of having a will, which "flings itself into the infinite"? Is in not, perhaps, from this infinite that the need to live beyond the present comes, which no temporal happiness satisfies?

2.19 The principle of responsibility that is explained in terms of immanence claims to "carry out" complete justice within history. "Responsibility for the existence and organization of the world falls on the world itself: who else could take it on? (...) Thus we can say that the court of the world is the world itself" (Schopenhauer, 1986A, 480-481). At this point, we unwittingly slide into that dramatic trick of reason, invented by Hegel, which has justified the most ferocious acts committed in the twentieth century. A sort of delirium, which no longer knows where and how to justify it penetrates all of this thought. Thus, he goes so far as to maintain that "the distinction between one who inflicts pain and grief and one who bears them is a simple matter of appearance (…) the torturer and the victim are one and the same, and both deceive themselves (…) They fail to realize that the tormented and the tormentor are in themselves a single being". All "are only aware of the good of the moment" (Schopenhauer, 1986A, 484 and 488). Again, the meaning of the species, it is this that cancels out the singularity of the person and that person's sense of responsibility. With Hegel, Machiavelli and Hobbes return and continue to make their ways. They had been sharply criticized, yet they were ever present in the search for that success that characterizes part of modernity.

2.20 We remain with the fact that personal responsibility for existence is excluded. The "affect" of the conscience should be immunized, by having recourse to a strange prayer: "The prayer *lead me not into temptation*, means *let me not see who I am*" (Schopenhauer, 1986A, 500). It is obvious to anyone that this is a total misrepresentation of Christianity, but what is more serious is the fact that *here, one prays in order to become irresponsible*: a person who does not want to see who he or she is, hence, who her or she has been is just that.

2.21 Yet, this "irresponsibility", always seems to drive us toward the objective that Schopenhauer seeks: The "rejection" of will. "Will, then is cut off from life, and feels the horror of all the pleasures, which result from it. Mankind arrives at a state of voluntary renunciation, of resignation, of perfect peace, and the complete suppression of willing" (Schopenhauer, 1986A, 515). Isn't a further act of will, however, necessary in order to arrive at that point? Is the "mortification of the will" not always in need of an act of will, which might discover another purpose in willing? Resignation itself is an act of will. Denying the will is somewhat like denying liberty, even its rejection requires a free act. Here it is appropriate to bring out another observation on the so-called rational premises of Kantian morality, which, if accepted, would end up exposing merit or guilt to ridicule. This error was already criticized, as Schopenhauer reminds us, as he quotes an amusing epigram of Schiller: I do good on behalf of my friends, but unfortunately I am inclined to do so, and thus I am often tormented by not being virtuous (cf. Schopenhauer, 1986A, 107).

2.22 It is truly curious, moreover, that only at the end does one come to the point of "seeing in perfect holiness the negation and sacrifice of the will" (Schopenhauer, 1986A, 554). Is a philosophical journey necessary to reach this form of perfection? If such is the case, how, according to the German philosopher, can the fact be justified that the highest form of ascesis, indeed its "true personification", was attained by Saint Francis, who seems to me the saint of the will and, for this very reason, of renunciation? Furthermore, what need is there for the various philosophical doctrines if, among these, only Christianity "not only recommends supreme charity, but also renunciation" (Schopenhauer, 1986A, 522 and 525)?

2.23 When "the omniscience of the preceding dogmatism and the despair of Kantian criticism" are overcome, the only thing that remains to be done is to return to religion, since the mystery of life cannot be explained. "In fact, something quite different lies behind our existence, something, however, that we cannot attain, unless we shake off the yoke of earthly life" (Schopenhauer, 1986A, 578 and 549). It is understandable, behind this act of surrender, why one speaks of the despair in Kantian criticism. This criticism uses faculties such as intuition only in mathematics and neglects it in the other forms of consciousness.

2.24 Before moving on to the specifics of ethics, it is useful to recall that Schopenhauer, criticizing Kant, does not come to a liberal, Enlightenment sort of vision, but to an "inflexible, tragic conception of a natural and social world dominated mainly by the instinct for cruelty and selfishness" (Vasoli, 9). This conception, therefore, is typical of Machiavelli and Hobbes. Saying, indeed, that human will is the cornerstone of every action does not help us understand "what each reasonable (…) being may wish or not wish". Basically, the answer lies in selfishness, since each person ultimate "wants only what is best for him or her". Is it not because true goodness is an exception, which the State invented to combat the prevalence of injustice and violence? This is the proof that the universal morality desired by Kant is objectively denied by reality (cf. Vasoli, 27-29). Furthermore, the stimulation to perform good acts is so weak that, often, bestial instincts seem to predominate in human life. They are, we seem still to be hearing the voice of Machiavelli, selfish, bitter and "malevolent". Would they ever reach an agreement if it were not for that yearning for well being which always and everywhere characterizes them? Here lies the main cause of actions (cf. Vasoli, 39-41).

2.25 This cause of actions seems to be the immutable essence of mankind and it is curious that Schopenhauer finds himself criticizing Kant while relying on a premise that we could call "metaphysical". A Machiavellian vision once again returns: "The individual, rigorously determined in all his or her manifestations given an immutable and innate character" (Schopenhauer, 1986C, 705) seems not to know any law but that of personal advantage. In short, "in the moral sphere the decisive element is an innate one", why this should be so, then, is not explained. It is to this being, certainly not to actions, that faults and merits are to be attributed, that is to "the primitive, interior mechanism" that determines what we are and what we do (cf. Vasoli, 55-57). Here, as already pointed out, there is an anthropological view still typical of Machiavelli, which reaches even beyond personal relationships to those among various peoples and States. Among these, too, a more or less concealed utilitarianism predominates. One need only think "the customary jargon of justice among peoples is, as is well know, only a bureaucratic style of diplomacy". Everything is obviously based on a human nature inclined towards evil, to such an extent that when we find an honest person, we are forced to exclaim with Hamlet: "*To be honest, as this world goes, is to be one man pick'd of ten thousand*" (Schopenhauer, 1986C, 688 and 722).

2.26 Schopenhauer departs from the assumption that religions base morality on a precise dogmatic apparatus, a conception in which Kant himself was decidedly trapped, and yet, which he had firmly criticized. The result was that, in spite of himself, he used unquestionably theological roots. What, indeed, can be said of the categorical imperative itself which can only have value on a hypothetical level? In conformity with what has been said about human nature, it seems to have a purely metaphysical value in that it refers to rare life experiences anchored to transcendence. The same must apply to moral "law" since it either makes use of the explicit Biblical text of the Decalogue, and so has religious and teological validity, or it falls in the category of civil laws and is the result of an historical necessity. It follows, furthermore, that the sense of duty itself has value only in face of a threat of coercion. Schopenhauer's words leave no doubt on the subject. He is convinced that religion "prescribing morality does not postpone it, but gives it dogmatism for support" and it is curious that Kant himself, having to cover himself, is *forced to admit* that "metaphysics must come first and without it cannot be said that there is morality" (Schopenhauer, 1986C, 634).

2.27 To be more explicit, that metaphysical premise is to be found throughout Kant because, in spite of everything, one must speak of the metaphysics of nature, metaphysics of customs, and the metaphysics of the beautiful. Those approaches "presuppose one another and only in their entirety do they carry out the explanation of the nature of things and of existence" (Schopenhauer, 1986C, 635). Kantian morality is thus an artificial construction and difficult to accept. Human actions are determined as if it did not exist at all. On the contrary, human action follows the path of legality, and not always out of conviction. That shows that "what in human actions is legal, worthy of praise and approval, will appear inspired by purely moral feelings but only a small portion of those actions" (Schopenhauer, 1986C, 636). Indeed, Kant was well aware that it is not possible to "find a more efficient motivation for morality than a teleological one". Who could oppose the will of the Almighty, if the Almighty were recognized as such? Kant demolished this conviction, believing that principles deduced from reason could be equally authoritative. To support that conviction, naturally, he had to make use of an idea of universal "reason". Otherwise the risk would be that his attempt would fail.

2.28 There is more, and it is more serious, however. Kant purged ethics of any eudemonism taking away that approach which had characterized the ethics of the classical authors, which had been incorporated into Christianity, and, not a small matter presented the doctrine of salvation. *From this came a morality without any sense*, which *gave rise to the modern monstrosities of ethical States, veritable "teological" structures.* Plato had already foreseen all of this: "his ethics are not eudemonistic, but become mystical" (Schopenhauer, 1986C, 643), indeed, State mysticism. Upon closer examination, however, the Kantian operation is all a matter of appearances. Eudemonism remains and becomes an essential element. This is what saves a tiny portion of Kantian ethics. What little there is of *a priori* laws Schopenhauer would have called laws of nature, without intending any metaphor. Hence, recalling the revealed origin of Moses' Decalogue, it is possible to understand why in Christianity, "philosophical ethics unconsciously took on the form of teological ethics", thus they could be "basically imperative" and they drew this strength from an eschatological promise recognized over the centuries and which not even Locke had called into question (cf. Schopenhauer, 1986C, 646-648). The eschatological promise, which should constitute the premise for moral action, for Kant becomes the result. At the conclusion of this reasoning even he fails to realize that changing the order of the factors, the result does not change, and it is that of re-presenting the old teological morality, twisted, but based on Enlightenment - hence abstract reason, which *considers universal that which is not universal. To stimulate it, he must have recourse to postulates.* Schopenhauer could not reach different conclusions once he had admitted that, what he calls pure duty, offers, in actual fact, *very few examples*. On the contrary, quoting Kant himself, he says: "it is absolutely impossible to establish with certainty through experience a single case in which a proper action was based only on the idea of duty" (Schopenhauer, 1986C, 661). If such were the case, moral action would risk falling into a dangerous mechanism because this *decisive* sense of duty would also require a precise knowledge of the character of a person and his or her motivations, so that "these actions could be calculated with the precision of a lunar eclipse" (Schopenhauer, 1986C, 671).

2.29 From this, the need arises to "create a moral utopia named *the Kingdom of Ends*" (Schopenhauer, 1986C, 694) to sustain a will without cause which holds up the framework of an abstract morality. *For this reason, post-Kantians have felt the need for new metaphysics*, a new theology that would be fully developed in Hegel and in his various followers (cf. Pezzimenti, 2008). Yet, in order not to fall prey to such a danger, Kant wants to eliminate any human inclination in moral action, maintaining that this must come about only out of duty. He thus foresees, as has already been said, that meaningless morality, which has not only brought about the monstrosities of modernity, but would also characterize several aspects of post-modernity as well. This point merits close attention: on the pretext of eliminating particular goals of moral action, *Kant* not only attacked the crudest form of individualism, but *came close to exalting the lack of love in moral action, reducing the ethical view to the most absurd formalism*, to a sort of absolute necessity which would successfully combat human selfishness.

2.30 The above conclusion is a contradiction in terms and Schopenhauer himself could not avoid pointing this out. It is indeed absurd that "mankind conceives of an idea to investigate a law, to which his will should adapt and submit". Thus, even Kant, when speaking of morality, is forced to use "only Latin juridical expressions" as if to identify" in the intimacy of our soul a complete court with a trial, judge, prosecutor, defendant, and verdict". This is a trial of thought whose founder, guarantor and judge are individuals themselves who, as experience has shown, ultimately orient their actions towards what is most advantageous to them. To avoid such a drawback "we must think of the internal judge as different from ourselves" (Schopenhauer, 1986C, 700-702). This is surely an unavoidable necessity since, excluding "a small portion of purely moral content", human actions "are due to motives whose efficacy goes back to selfishness (…) the main and basic stimulus in mankind as well as in animals" (Schopenhauer, 1986C, 636 and 727).

In order not to behave this way, human beings must be saints. What a discovery! Are Saints, however, not people who orient their actions towards a prospect of which they do not consider themselves originators and to which they *con-vert* their wills?

2.31 What happens as a result of all this? The "divinization" of reason, instead of the simple, but noble, effort to us it in terms of its real possibilities. According to Schopenhauer, there is another contradiction in Kant. The latter indeed *criticized* "rational psychology", *but*, in actual fact, *he failed to free himself of it*. Realizing the contradiction, he began to exalt "human dignity", an expression that was "received most favourably", but which, in fact, is a mask for the destruction of a basis of morality itself. Kant realizes this perfectly well to the point that he rediscovers the so-called "interior judge" as one "different from us", in order to arrive at a moral judgment which keeps a minimum of objectivity (cf. Vasoli, 26 and 30-32). *Without objectivity, morality is reduced to an expression of the will of an individual, in any case, the strongest one.* When ethics are spoken of from the social point of view, the strongest becomes the class, the race, or worse yet, the *State which can also be an expression of one or the other*, thereby claiming to satisfy the "metaphysical need" of its citizens.

2.32 To overcome all of this, "compassion" must be brought to bear (this word should be kept in mind for a discussion of Nietzsche), that is the disinterested participation with others in need. All that refers to compassion almost seems the fruit of a "mystery", "a mystery of ethics, its primordial phenomenon" (Schopenhauer, 1986C, 741). It cannot be seen in any other way, since the evangelical and insuperable love of one who gives his or her life for others is reflected. It may be selfish and malicious, but there is also this impulse towards compassion in people that Schopenhauer fails to explain to himself but which stimulates the will. Compassion seems to be part of the very nature of mankind. As if it were a sort of "natural right", "it manifests itself in all countries and in all eras". The fact remains, however, that it "arises in noble souls" (Schopenhauer, 1986C, 745-746). In the others and in the multitudes? Here the anthropological pessimism re-emerges of one who sees only a few beings as capable of experiencing certain feelings. The disconcerting statement on education shows it as well, namely that education "can modify the choice of means, but not that of ends" (Schopenhauer, 1986C, 793).

2.33 Schopenhauer, a systematic philosopher, seeks to find a logical basis for ethics. Ultimately, he seems to find it in metaphysics, but what metaphysics are involved? The continual appeal to mystery, which accompanies the foundation of pity and compassion itself, justifies this question. Mystery, furthermore, underlies all of Schopenhauer's thought. To say that the world is basically will, of which individuals are phenomena, cannot hide the central problem of this will, the manifestation of which is without a goal, "a meaning or an objective end" (Fonnesu, 87-89). In other words, ethics without sense, and as they are without sense, they end up being pain itself, even though they have unquestionable dignity. The very solution of denying the will, ultimately negates what is represented as the reasons itself for the world.

B) The Ethics and Religion Split: Søren Kierkegaard.

2.34 As far as ethics are concerned, the position of Kierkegaard is no less problematic. His merits as a critique of Hegelian dialectics, his effort to bring back the religious significance of mankind and his pressing need for the infinite are beyond any doubt. Another great merit of Kierkegaard is likewise unquestionable, that of identifying in the *aesthetic moment the real condition of modern human beings*. Now, people live "with no more valid references to good and to the truth". The reality of aesthetics has become, in other words, "the modern pseudo-religion and pseudo-salvation, the ultimate form of treachery and the decomposition of Christianity" (cf. Quinzio, XXIII). This is none other than a new attempt, the latest, to manufacture a new myth: while "wanting to uproot all myths, he himself produces new ones" (Kierkegaard, 1963B, 140).

2.35 The fact remains, however, that Kierkegaard, by relegating ethics to a middle way between aesthetics and religion, has, in the end, deprived them of any relationship to faith, relegating them to the area of pure and simple bourgeois coexistence. "The area of what belongs to ethics can thus seem – as in fact it already seems in Luther – the area of the demonic itself" (Quinzio, XV). So a veritable split *between ethics and religion* comes about, between what is human and which transcends the human, between the dimension of sin and the absoluteness of the divine (cf. Fonnesu, 86) to such a degree that it is even impossible to formulate rules of conduct in order to experience the religious dimension.

2.36 How can one experience faith? Can simply abandoning oneself to the force of the divine be sufficient? Does not human will find, in pursuing the divine, an itinerary which involves an adaptation of faith to teachings, better yet, to a Person, who orients our lives in one way rather than in another? Living within the religious dimension means a choice for Kierkegaard. Even if this choice involves a sort of leap, immediately thereafter, it involves a series of choices, which imply a considerable sense of responsibility.

Is it possible, then, to elude the moral sense of the choice in favour of religion? Answering yes is tantamount to considering ethics a baggage of conventions, which is not only foreign to religion, but actually places obstacles in its path. Finally, if experiencing the aesthetic moment "means living in necessity and dependency (...) in the immediate, in change and in dispersion" (Fonnesu, 84), living in terms of the ethical moment means living in the blandest of conformity. We are quite far from that abstract sense of duty proposed by Kant which was to have universal value insofar as it was based on reason, but we are also far from a morality which, simple common sense, is to be understood, in any case, as a qualitative leap forward in the sense of an ability not to resign oneself to doing everything that everyone else is doing.

2.37 Another hazard, no less important, can be discerned in the choice of religion: that of misrepresenting relationships with fellow creatures. One can thing of the strange relationship with the Queen-fiancée. She is put aside because this could compromise the longing for the *infinite*. The priority to be given to God implies the impossibility of allowing oneself another relationship which consumes itself in the narrow *finite-finite* perspective, which would sacrifice the other *finite-infinite* one (cf. Fabbro, XLVII). There can be no objections about the exclusiveness of certain choices. The fact is, however, that Kierkegaard is not even affected by the idea that that infinite can be present in the other, which calls upon us to observe a particular moral conduct. The other is, I would say almost always, an obstacle as is improperly understood ethical life.

2.38 The protagonist of ethical existence, Wilhelm the Councillor, clearly personifies bourgeois ethics as he adapts to a situation which seeks a static order and wants only to keep away from scandal, this, too, understood in a bourgeois sense of the word. One wonders how Kierkegaard actually opposes Hegel, at least on the ethical level. The ethical moment, personified by the State, calls upon individuals only to bring their views of things to coincide with a uniform, general view. From this perspective, ethics indeed becomes Hegelian ethicity. There is no doubt but what this ethical dimension throws the Danish thinker into a state of uneasiness and disorientation. "My conception of life is completely without meaning" to such a degree that he can no longer interpret reality. To justify himself he re-evokes the evil genius of which the early Descartes was so fond. This "evil spirit has put a pair of glasses on his nose. One lens magnifies things out of proportion while the other shrinks them, likewise, out of proportion" (Kierkegaard, 1962, 28). If my life drags on without meaning, the only approach seems to be that of nihilism: "The outcome of my life is fading into nothingness" (Kierkegaard, 1962, 31). The very link between cause and effect, to which Schopenhauer had been so attached, now turns out to be meaningless. "At times enormous causes bring about a tiny effect without any importance, at times even nothing at all; at times a small cause brings about a colossal effect" (Kierkegaard, 1962, 28). Can it then be true that all that is real is rational or all that is not, at least, meaningless? Yet, for the great majority of individuals, this is a question that has no sense. Therefore "in our times no one stops at faith any longer (…) Would it not be better to stop at faith and is it not revolting that everyone wants to go further?" (Kierkegaard, 1963A, 10 and 36).

2.39 For Kierkegaard the greatness of each person is in proportion to "the greatness against which he or she struggles". Like Abraham, a person is certainly greater when "quitting his or her terrestrial intelligence and taking faith unto himself or herself" (Kierkegaard, 1963A, 18). Faith asks reason to step aside. This is the conviction of the Danish philosopher who sees no possible collaboration between faith and reason. In his eyes, Hegel does nothing but re-present the reason of the Greeks that Christianity had contained and reappraised. After classical speculation "there is no need for any other category other than that of Greek philosophy or those that coherent thought can derive from it. This Hegel should not have hidden, since he was well versed in Greek studies" (Kierkegaard, 1963A, 52). The fact that faith is a passion, which gives meaning to human life, did not appear in his thought. It is not only the fact that faith has reasons which common reason cannot grasp, as Pascal believed. Here, further steps are taken. "Faith is a marvel, yet no person is excluded from it" (Kierkegaard, 1963A, 62).

2.40 At times, and despite the fact that it can seem paradoxical, given the strength of his convictions, Kierkegaard seems quite disoriented. His famous three moments, the aesthetic, the ethical and the religious seem impossible to define: "the melancholy possesses above all the sense of the comic, the sensual often has that of the idyllac, the debauched a moral sense and the skeptic a religious sense" (Kierkegaard, 1962, 24). The world around him seems not to help him. With great genius and foreseeing the way of thinking which today we call post-modern, Kierkegaard sees a decline in seriousness in the conduct of daily life. The need of the era seems to be that of emphasizing a certain frivolity that ridicules the tragic sense of the great heroes. This is why "our whole era deals most of all with the comic". Resembling Schopenhauer, he ultimately says that our era has lost a sense of compassion, thus "it is losing itself and is becoming comical" (Kierkegaard, 1962, 131 and 134). Ethics have been lost with that seriousness. For that reason, it is no wonder that, "everyone wants to dominate, but no one wants to take on responsibility" (Kierkegaard,

1962, 131). This admission does not, however, lead to a re-evaluation of ethics, not even when he speaks of Abraham, he underscores the degree to which this personage is so far from us today, because, among other things, people today seek to be admired. What is of interest today is ostentation, which, however, seems devoid of any precise itinerary, and anchored in a certain extemporaneousness.

2.41 The gap opened between ethics and faith cannot be bridged, to be sure, because ethics is understood as that conceived of, albeit differently, in exclusively rational terms by Kant and Hegel. Kierkegaard's doubt in part reflects his Lutheran spirit. The religious quest comes to be laden with scruples. Using the word *Anfaegtelse* (Ger. *Anfechtung*) it must be kept in mind that the term, as Fabbro perceptively notes, was placed in circulation by Lutheran theology, and it indicates a complex state of mind, a mixture of doubt, uncertainty, temptation, slackening of faith and liberty (cf. Fabbro, 207 note 21). It is from here, from the "paradox of existence", that faith arises. It is from a sense of vertigo, which one seeks to come out of after having had a glimpse of faith. Abraham "nullified all of ethics by his act" (Kierkegaard, 1963A, 55), but it would be worth while pointing out that he simply nullified the drab bourgeois selfishness, laden with conformist formalism more endowed with an ethical view. Christian ethics are something different. They are what fights sin. The problem is that something else is meant by ethics, because "ethics which are unaware of sin, are a science which is perfectly useless" (Kierkegaard, 1963A, 90). This statement seems for a moment to be in contrast with the uninspired dimension of the ethical state.

2.42 Such a contradiction or, if one will, a simple doubt often accompanies Kierkegaard in his later years. Christian morality seems to be necessary to create a genuinely Christian spirit. "The relationship of the Christian situation with life (in contrast to the distance from life that is inherent in science), or the ethical site of Christianity, constitutes precisely the uplifting moment" (Kierkegaard, 1963C, 67). Kierkegaard regrets the loss of the moral sense, which led to the lack of a sense of sin in modern humanity. He goes so far as to say, in no uncertain terms: "an ironic-ethical correction is what our times need most of all. It is perhaps the sole remedy for a person in need". Sin is no longer comprehensible "since the ethical moment has been abolished to the point that a word with a sound ethical meaning is hardly ever heard" (Kierkegaard, 1963C, 145 and 165). Here it is evident that when Kierkegaard speaks of this healthy ethical sense, it is far from those bourgeois ethics, which characterize the second level of his existential dialectics, that of the bourgeois "bienpensant" who spontaneously adapts to the reality that surrounds us. "In Christianity he is a Christian (in perfectly the same sense as in a pagan world, in which he would have been pagan, or, a Dutchman in Holland), one of the cultivated Christians" (Kierkegaard, 1963C, 112).

2.43 The ethics that are presumably needed are those which suggest a continual effort to adapt to an ideal which seems too high for us and which gives rise to a sort of interior disease of which it is difficult to be cured. "In the area of the spirit, or when humans consider themselves as spirits, health is as critical as disease; the immediate health of the spirit is not given" (Kierkegaard, 1963C, 84). This confirms the need that a moral effort must always accompany a Christian to the very end, as a person who can never consider himself or herself definitively saved under any circumstance. Even when one is close to despair, there is a need for a change, a veritable moral effort in order to seek the longed-for infinity.

The commitment is not felt by "many who live their lives in an approximate way, cheated out of the most blessed thought". Schopenhauer would have said that these are individuals who do not have the will to understand the real meaning of living. What people are those! "A person who does not have a trace of will is not a self; the greater his will is, the greater is the awareness he has of himself" (Kierkegaard, 1963C, 85-86 and 87). Here the moral question comes back since the will is always the premise for acting.

2.44 A serious morality also makes it impossible to exaggerate or even to distort the religious moment. "The relationship with God is rendering oneself infinite; but a person rendering himself or herself infinite can be drawn into dreams to the point that nothing but a sort of intoxication is the result" (Kierkegaard, 1963C, 90). To avoid running these risks, not to become alienated, in other words, a great need exists for a strong sense of responsibility in day-by-day actions. This is why bearing witness daunts people. A morality experienced that is a cause for reflection on the part of whoever thinks of the religious dimension is needed. This person ultimately sells the best part of himself or herself to the world. This person is all caught up in business, and cannot even breathe in liberty. He or she cannot understand the meaning of sin. "A divine revelation is needed to teach a person thus fallen what sin is" (Kierkegaard, 1963C, 149). Even if it is acknowledged that this can happen, what happens then? What happens to this self? "If one desperately wants to be oneself, there must be awareness of an infinite self. This infinite self, however, is only the most abstract form, the most abstract possibility of the self (…) With this infinite form, the self desperately wants to be its own master or create itself, make of itself that self that humans want to be (…) through its infinite form, it wants to construct it itself" (Kierkegaard, 1963C, 122-

123). However, this remains a good intention. This striving to realize one's own self is not upheld by an adequate moral itinerary, as will be observed, for example in the ethical conception of Rosmini.

C) A Life without Reflection and Hyperactive: Friedrich Nietzsche.

2.45 For Nietzsche religions, Catholicism in particular, have led to the annihilation of existence, modifying the will to live. Religion has fused and confused possession of the truth with the manifestation of domination: "the very things that are the opposite of what we venerate today have, for a long time, had the conscience on their side and God as their custodian" (Nietzsche, 1980B, 357). That has practically brought about violence against us, which has found expression in a sort of crushing of the soul to pursue the insane idea of "becoming day after day" more worthy of living. Only the collapse of this absurd Christian morality will bring about the collapse of its dogmas and, as a result, of its teachings: "thus must Christianity, too, *as morality*, collapse – we are on the threshold of *this* event". Here too is a subtle criticism of Schopenhauer and his noluntas. It all leads to a total rebellion against what has been, "against the fundamentalist premises of life. However it is and remains a *will*! ... and, to repeat by way of conclusion which I have already said at the beginning: humans still prefer to desire nothingness, rather than not to desire ..." (Nietzsche, 1980B, 410 and 412).

2.46 From what has been said, a clear-cut criticism of German philosophy from Kant to Hegel can be inferred. Nietzsche identifies an essential evil in the philosophical perspective that preceded him. It is necessary to free himself from it: the taste for the absolute. Towards this, one must have a "lighthearted diffidence, the pleasure of mocking something". These "are signs of good health: everything that is absolute belongs to the pathological" (Nietzsche, 1980A, 100). Not even this sarcasm, however, has been able to keep him away from the danger of himself absolutizing his own positions, ultimately putting another absolute in place of the one he had fought against: that of the superman. In the final analysis, it can be said that Nietzsche is a "Manichean" (Bergson, 237). He is a Manichean because what is set in opposition to his view of the new man, what will have to be the superman, falls in with that philosophical view that must be rejected. This is the origin of the contempt, not only for philosophical morality, whether Kantian or Hegelian, but also for Christian morality. Reduced to a slaves' morality, Nietzsche sees in it the premise for an order against which one must react because it condemns inferior and ignoble individuals to find peace and aspire to transcendence. All of this is to the advantage of a few "priestly aristocracies" which, from time to time, preaches a coming Kingdom of God (cf. Nietzsche, 1980B, 264-265). It is considered inopportune to rebel, because only the aristocracies as mentioned are aware of the time and modalities of the goal. Rebelling is to be avoided; nonetheless, there are those who are beginning to do so. "All of that is of unbounded interest, but also the blackest, murkiest, most exhausting of miseries; we must keep ourselves from peering for too long in these abysses" (Nietzsche, 1980B, 333). A dangerous "tyranny of the diseased over the healthy" (Crespi, 32) is created, to give birth to that meek animal that the human being is. The consequence of all that is also felt in interpersonal relationships. "In Nietzsche we can observe that negation of the relationship with reality coincides with the dissolution of the person and the negation of his or her unity. If I am not someone who can be conceived of as such, then I am no one at all, but just something. (...) If I am not a you, I cannot even be an I, but am a conglomerate of states, which are not states" (Spaemann, 88).

2.47 Nietzsche's destiny is truly curious. If it had not been for this morality of compassion characteristic of "meek" spirits such as his mother and sister, much of his work would have been nullified, because of having been dispersed. The danger of aspiring to an absolute, underscored several times by him, is, however, characteristic of a philosophy which, wanting to make the absolute imminent, needs to impose it and certainly not to suggest it. When the reference parameters were confused, a war broke out against every moral conception as well as any reference that could somehow provide its basis. Criticism, of all the foundations is also a criticism of any concept of truth or falsehood, because everything is reduced to the extemporaneous. Thus, every position becomes undefendable, yet every action becomes, in any case, equally justifiable (is this not the position of Vattimo, Rorty and many other post-modern thinkers?). From this comes vitalism, an expression of the will for power. This is capable of encouraging any form of exaltation whatsoever. From this point of view, everything finds justification and legitimate research.

2.48 Criticism of Christianity is part of the broader criticism by Nietzsche of all of western philosophy. It is pointed out that "Christianity is Platonism for the people – in Europe it created a splendid tension of the spirit as had never existed on earth heretofore" (Nietzsche, 1980A, 12-13). He set forth the problem of the truth placing it within reach of every person, even those whom Nietzsche deemed "ill". How will those people cope without that truth which the "healthy", the supermen, have disproven? Criticizing this truth, opposing it "involves a risk and perhaps there exists no greater risk" (Nietzsche, 1980A, 15). The "healthy" are a new order of philosophers, coming ever closer, "philosophers of the dangerous *perhaps* in every sense". They are the ones who will proclaim the end of the truth as believed in up to now, and thus will be viewed with suspicion. "To admit non-truth as a condition of life: undoubtedly means to set us in dangerous opposition to the usual feelings of value: and a philosophy that dares to do this sets itself, for that reason alone, above and beyond good and evil" (Nietzsche, 1980A, 17-18).

2.49 What seems to interest Nietzsche is just the instinctive reason for the moral judgment heretofore made by the philosophers who preceded him. "Every instinct, indeed, desires to dominate: and as *such* seeks to philosophize (…) there is nothing at all impersonal in a philosopher, and his or her moral in particular offers resolute and decisive evidence of what he or she is" (Nietzsche, 1980A, 20). In other words, not only is philosophy a means for emphasizing supremacy, but also a sort of self confession justified by that supremacy. Nietzsche totally fails to see that what he calls self-confession can be made with the most diverse of intents and not just in a spirit of supremacy. Who can say that the *Confessions* of Saint Augustine or Rousseau were motivated by the same intents and set forth for themselves the same objectives? Furthermore, if philosophizing means wishing to express a certain supremacy, if living is expressing a certain morality, how can anyone put every philosophical reflection on the same level and then wonder: "Is living not perhaps assessing, preferring, being unjust, being limited, wanting to be different?" (Nietzsche, 1980A, 22). What difference can we speak of if all morality and philosophy expressed up to now are considered equal because of a single intent: that of dominating?

2.50 When Nietzsche speaks of philosophy, he refers to a very precise one. "It always creates the world in its own image. It cannot do otherwise; philosophy is this same tyrannical instinct, the most spiritual desire for power, for *the creation of the world*, for a *prime cause*" (Nietzsche, 1980A, 22). Hegel's shadow can easily be perceived behind these lines. Those philosophies must be believed, considered true, and faith in those who sustain them is necessary. In Hegel's case, a faith in absolute reason is involved in his panlogism, which ends up being what discriminates between good and evil. To be sure Nietzsche is far-sighted here: what seems to be a claim of philosophy is now becoming one of science, as well, for example, of physics, as should be the case, however, "only an interpretation of the world and an order imposed on it (…) and *not* an explanation of the world" (Nietzsche, 1980A, 28). It should also not be forgotten that mankind does not know what to do with it, only being interested in the explanations about its ego and that which concerns what is outside of this ego. Ego means not only singularity, but also that humanity which can be understood in relation one's peers.

2.51 This is the consequence of selecting one will over others, a relationship that gives rise to a certain moral problem. "In every will commanding and obeying are absolutely involved, on the basis, as has been said, of a social organization of many *individuals*; (…) that is, a morality understood as a doctrine of the relationships of supremacy from which the phenomenon *life*" draws its origins (Nietzsche, 1980A, 33-34). This is not, however, morality *tout court*, but Hegelian morality, that of the master-servant relationship, which, with its highly disparate implications, will interest much of contemporary thought. It even seems that Nietzsche contemplates it in its dialectical relationship which never ends and which experiences the alternation of positions in domination relationships: "basically, the subjected race has come to prevail here (...) and this guarantees modern democracy for us (...) but does this not signify an enormous repercussion"? (Nietzsche, 1980B, 263-264). Nietzsche's sarcasm about democracy is to be found entirely in that weariness of humanity, a thought characteristic of him. Democracy means peace arbitration in place of war, the return of religion as compassion, equality in the rights of women, in other words, "declining life". Expressions of this are also those thinkers who have wanted to base democratic life on the idea of a contract. Anything that smacks of a pact is decadent. Those who are capable of commanding (who "are naturally rulers") will have a despotic spirit rather than a democratic attitude (cf. Nietzsche, 1980B, 403 and 324).

2.52 Returning to the master-servant "dialectics", I wish to emphasize that I do not at all intend to reduce it to banality as something useless or misleading. I believe, however, that it cannot be all inclusive in the perspective set forth by Hegel or his followers, otherwise Nietzsche would be right in maintaining that the moral question goes back solely to the "problem of two, radically opposed sides, even if always in a profoundly personal guise" (Nietzsche, 1980A, 36). If this is the morality to which Nietzsche appeals, there is, however, no question but what the outcomes are different. He certainly does not think like Hegel, who saw the eternal alternation between servants and masters, nor does he think like Marx who visualizes the definitive victory of the subordinate class in a paradisiacal outcome of history. Nietzsche reproaches the servants and their alleged morality. He does not wish for their deliverance at all. Indeed, he is downright contemptuous of them: "the odour of simple people always remains with them. Where the people drink and eat, even where they pay homage and direct their veneration, there is only a stench". Giving up this view of life and morality, is what Nietzsche aims at, and he proposes the recovery of the historical phase that preceded philosophical, hence moral reflection. "We call this period the *premoral* period of humanity: the imperative *know thyself!* was totally unknown at that time" (Nietzsche, 1980A, 49 and 50).

2.53 This *premoral* phase of humanity means not only a criticism of Christian or, more generally, religious morality, but also a criticism of morality in general, even Greek morality, which had the clear intention of achieving happiness. "No one will so easily consider a doctrine true, for the simple fact that it makes people happy or virtuous" (Nietzsche, 1980A, 56). One must understand that a new era is before us which could be qualified "as extra moral", that term meaning that these new "immoralists" are motivated by a *non-intentional* component: that is, that action is not based on decisive values. Moreover, it is almost impossible for Nietzsche to deny that "morality, with the meaning held up to now, hence as the morality of intentions, was a prejudice". The consciences of today propose "going beyond morality, in a certain sense, the self-going beyond morality". Morality, any morality whatsoever, speaks of ridiculous profundities and "all that is profound loves a mask" (Nietzsche, 1980A, 51 and 57), but all this gives rise to falsities, superficiality, and estrangement from real life.

2.54 It is in this real life that it must be shown "that one is destined to independence and to command", but who is to be commanded? Nietzsche makes no secret of the fact that this new view does not place people on an equal level, but that it gives rise to a new command-obedience relationship. Our heart, our intentions must not be linked to a ridiculous "sense of compassion". The facts will turn out differently: "great matters are reserved for the great, abysses for the profound, forms of finesse and thrills for the subtle, and to sum things up in a single word, rare things for rare people" (Nietzsche, 1980A, 58-59 and 60). *Above and beyond good and evil* is, in other words, a formula that cannot concern all people but rather a way in which "superior spirits" succeed in protecting themselves from "being mistaken for the others" (Nietzsche, 1980A, 62). It is a veritable distinction, then, for the many who are still living, and, in many respects, we could say that they will always live, a morality of slaves.

2.55 Nietzsche does not hide from facing the difficulty of such an enterprise; I would also say the tragic aspect as he describes it quite clearly in the famous passage of The *Gay Science* in which he speaks of the death of God. From time to time, he seems to feel almost nostalgia for the true, albeit few, men *of religion* as Pascal had been, for example. Nostalgia, or interest – whichever it is – it is suddenly mollified by rejection of the idea itself of sacrifice which goes with every religious and, above all, Christian, choice: "the sacrifice of every liberty, of every bit of pride". These aspects only encourage submission. He does not know and cannot see anything else. "How is a negation of the will possible? How is a saint possible?" (Nietzsche, 1980A, 66 and 68). *Is it not this "absurd" idea of holiness that has sought to negate contemporary philosophy?* Nietzsche is lucid in his reply to this question. *The attack on holiness is an attack on Christianity*, but modern philosophy has not succeeded in eliminating the need for religiosity, but has created dangerous surrogates for it. It has focused human needs and aspiration on this. "As a consequence, does modern industry, noisy, making good use of its time, proud of itself, stupidly proud of itself, educate people in incredulity more than any other thing?" (Nietzsche, 1980A, 76). Yes, modern life, against reflection but *hyperactive*, only creates continued and wearying restlessness, incapable in any case of asking questions that go beyond every-day activity.

2.56 To react, it is necessary to reject that religion, Christianity in particular, which, up to now, has manifested only a "ruinous presumption of itself". Nietzsche overcomes this love of mankind for the love of God, a principle often overcome. "What is done for love, is always above and beyond good and evil" (Nietzsche, 1980A, 99), thereby giving a forced interpretation of Augustine's motto "love and do as you like". It would seem that it is sufficient to be aware of what is being done. Nietzsche seems unintentionally here to go back to Socratic ethics since, when a wicked one acts badly, it must be supposed that "he would not do so if he knew that evil was evil" (Nietzsche, 1980A, 111). The ethics of Socrates seem not to be disposed of, nor do those of Kant. This does not take into account the impossible of knowing what is evil once the reference to good and evil is lost and without failing to know of the inability to reach truth, since, "basically, we have been used to falsehood from time immemorial" (Nietzsche, 1980A, 114). We must keep in mind, however, that Nietzsche well knows that "disinterested" judgments cannot be formulated that do not take into account specific feelings or objectives. On that subject, it would perhaps be appropriate to recall criticism of Kant on the question of the beautiful that cannot be "what is pleasing *in a disinterested guise*" (cf. Nietzsche, 1980B, 347).

2.57 That, however, is not enough. One must also reflect on the mediocrity of the majority as opposed to the energy of the new and few noble minds. Here too, the Judaic and Christian tradition is guilty for the slave morality. The Jews are a people "born for slavery" – Nietzsche goes so far as to quote Tacitus – and the Christians are their heirs. They made the word poor a synonym of holy and friendly. That revolt of the slaves in the morality that we still have before our eyes began with the Jews. All of that gave many people a sense of disgust. "I have yet to meet any German who has any benevolent feelings towards the Jews" (cf. Nietzsche, 1980A, 116-117 and 193). Furthermore, the seeds of that claim to love desired by Christianity are to be found in that history (cf. Nietzsche, 1980B, 268). The "evil plant" of modernity likewise germinated at that point: here we are back with the idea of democracy and its intrinsic mediocrity! There is no doubt that "the democratic movement is the legacy of the Christian one". Democracy offers no objective foundation or criterion: The "objective" human being is an absurd postulate. In all life's events, as in grief, human beings "strive to reflect on their afflictions, but in vain" (Nietzsche, 1980A, 125 and 135). Needless to say, this pointlessness comes from the lack of objectivity.

2.58 This objectivity could be dangerous because, in Nietzsche's opinion, it could be reduced to being a mere convenience. From this came a tailor-made life, conditioned by a sort of well being "which immediately makes humans ridiculous and contemptible". This all takes them away from those doubts that should make them great and capable of freeing themselves from the petty concerns of normal and predictable life. "*Measure* is foreign to us, let us recognize the fact: our concern is indeed that of the infinite, of the boundless". Are these not the painful quests of philosophy that have always existed? No! Here they are not seen as the conditions of an itinerary. Rather than conditions for growth, they are seen as goals of a perennially anxious existence. This is the new nature of humanity finally renewed! We, the new supermen are that way "we are in *our* bliss only when *we are* also in greater *peril*" (Nietzsche, 1980A, 160). We come out of our greyness with a concern that does not seek solutions, but continues to be an end in itself.

2.59 To be sure, this state of concern can appear to be madness to most people. Nietzsche seems to be concerned about this: "But every form of greatness was, in the beginning, nothing other than madness!" This will give rise to a new aristocracy, which, like all aristocracies, is a barbarian caste at the beginning. In the beginning as in every beginning, "humans were more complete (which, at every level, also means the same as more *complete* beasts)" (Nietzsche, 1980A, 182 and 206). Bestiality and madness, on these the renewal, indeed the regeneration, of humanity is based. Bestiality and madness will give life to a morality of the noble to distinguish them from that of the slaves. The latter are incapable of freeing themselves from the morality of convenience and well-being that Nietzsche continues to call "utilitarian morality", and which might better be called hypocrisy. They will do so only if forced to by the bestial madness of the newly elected. It matters little if that renewal takes place by force, above and beyond good and evil, merit does not count are there is no room for penalties or rewards. Matters of religion, as with mercy and compassion, are destined to disappear, as is the idea of holiness itself. "The compassion of the saint is compassion for the foulness of the human, overly human (…) but what importance has mercy for those who suffer! The *absence of virility* (…) is the first thing, in my opinion, that leaps before my eyes" (Nietzsche, 1980A, 226-227 and 236). Now, one most go further, into the realm of the superhuman.

2.60 This sense of compassion is perhaps generated by the fact that one feels oneself indebted to a transcendent being, which is as illusory as it is ridiculous. "The sense of indebtedness towards the divinity has not ceased to increase for many millennia". It has made us lose the true sense of original innocence, an innocence that can be regained by removing the debt to the *First cause*. For this, atheism must be energetically promoted. "Atheism and a sort of *second innocence* are intrinsically connected" (Nietzsche, 1980B, 329 and 330). The superman will be capable of overcoming this metamorphosis. He will have to usurp the place of God if he does not want others to take his place. He will have to become God himself. "For a sanctuary to be built, *a sanctuary must be smashed to pieces*; this is the law (...) This antichrist and anti-nihilist, this victor over God and nothingness – *must come one day*" (Nietzsche, 1980B, 355 and 336). Thus, atheism constitutes the new, the authentic way to liberation, life that extinguishes even the idea of indebtedness and makes the superman indebted only to himself. However, one must be aware that this "debt" is certainly not created by chance. Only thus shall we know what has up to now prevented this new possibility for coming to know and establishing a different life. This hindrance comes from New Testament teachings. To the *Old Man* "goes all my respect! I find in it great men, an heroic landscape and something extremely rare on earth". In *that which is new* there is something totally different!.. "God himself who makes the supreme sacrifice due to mankind (...) the creditor who sacrifices himself for his debtor, out of *love* (must we then believe this?), out of love for his debtor" (Nietzsche, 1980B, 393 and 331).

2.61 Must we believe this? Nietzsche's secret lies in this question. There is a misunderstanding of Christian values. Good cannot be necessarily associated with actions that are not selfish ones. Love, the Augustinian *amor sui,* the source of every form of selfishness is again called upon and praised at the expense of every form of love which, with the excuse of being altruistic, actually conceals plebeian mediocrity. Responsibility is thereby rendered banal and it is cut off from the concept of liberty. "This is indeed the long history of the origin of responsibility, this task of raising an animal which can make promises" (Nietzsche, 1980B, 293). In other places Nietzsche has emphasized the difficulty of the task and he himself often feels a sense of vertigo and disorientation. He almost does not know where he is: "but what should I say, my friends? About whom am I talking to you? Have I forgotten myself to the point of not even recalling his name?" What does it matter? All this has long been known! "Oh, how *happy* we are, we people of awareness, since we are able to keep quiet for quite a long time" (Nietzsche, 1980A, 237 and 1980B, 250). This silence is worrying. In human relations, the word is indispensable, but humans are what Nietzsche intends to do without. All that is human is permeated with a sense of nausea and fatigue. "The sight of humans is tiring now – what else is nihilism, is it is not *this*? ... We are tired *of mankind*" (Nietzsche, 1980B, 278). So much for Nietzschean anthropology!

Ch. III. Ethics Tied to the Moment

A) The norm, *always*, relative: Hans Kelsen.

3.1 Elsewhere I have already said (cf. Pezzimenti, 2011B, CH. XVII) that Kant's juridical conceptions do not seem at all innovative to me, especially when they are compared to others formulated in his era. Here I think it is appropriate to emphasize that when he formulates his thought concerning public and private law he opens the way towards a trend in contemporary cultures, which has still not entirely disappeared, even though it began to be criticized almost immediately in Germany. Basically, Kant maintains, and Kelsen will state it later, that only the creation of a *power monopoly* can ensure the distinction between my and your outer selves and ensure that that distinction is abided by. This point is undeniable except that the *power monopoly* must somehow be subject to limitations and made responsible. Here is where the first source of perplexity arises. Above all, everything implies that, for Kant, public law ends up being compared to a private law, which was already on the way to being established first. Here I do not wish to repeat that wondering which form of law arose first, public or private, is a bit like wondering which came first, the chicken or the egg (cf. Pezzimenti, 2004), I wish only to cite a valuable conclusion with which I am in full agreement. "Fully to achieve the *neminem laede!* it is necessary to abandon the State of Nature and enter a Civil State where everyone can be assured of what belongs to him or her, following the formula of *suum cuique*" (Falcioni, 136). This is tantamount to saying that, without a superstructure, the social structure itself with its *negotia* cannot itself be developed. Who would operate economically if he or she did not feel there were safeguards when running the risk of losing everything?

3.2 It may seem rash to say that a body of thought such as Kelsen's must be seen in the wake of Kant's, but if one goes back to what was said on juridical formalism, the parallel would not be so strange. If Kant sought to found a morality free of any metaphysical and religious reference, Kelsen not only did the same concerning law, but also for the very conception of the person, which is the very first point of reference of law. He not only eliminates naturalistic and psychological references from this concept, but also every metaphysical premise. This is all with the intention, and this comes from Kant, too, to bestow on the science of law those prerogatives of objectivity, which other references could compromise. Already in the *Preface* of his most famous work, he says that in speaking of the knowledge of law, he has sought to "bring his results as close as possible to the ideal of science: objectivity and correctness". From this comes the need to appeal to "objective requirements" keeping a due distance from all those other needs which have a "subjective character" (Kelsen, 1994, IX-XI) and which, as should be recalled, would, in a short while, have burst with the crisis of the basics and scientific certainties.

3.3 The opening itself of the work is indicative. Kelsen says that he wishes to answer a question: "what and how is law, but not the question as to how it must be or must be constituted". In other words, jurisprudence has to be "purified". From time immemorial, it has been confused with psychology and biology, ethics and theology" (Kelsen, 1994, 1). Rather than enrich it, these had compromised its efficacy and objectivity. Certainly Kelsen was not unaware that law, being a social phenomenon, had "an object completely different from Nature", but because of its being a social phenomenon, in its quest for objectivity, it was subject to all the limitations of human sciences and of all those interconnections with other disciplines that enriched rather than limited it. The very existence of the case should confirm the impossibility of totally purifying law of other disciplines: and it is proper that it be thus. Since law must regulate life in its great variety of cases and events, it certainly cannot be surrounded by a series of other human disciplines, which enrich and complete it rather than hinder its objectivity.

3.4 Saying that "the pure doctrine of law neither refers to spiritual processes or other physical events when he attempts to discover the norms and understand anything whatsoever in a juridical sense" (Kelsen, 1994, 6), is not only questionable, but does not exclude the possibility that those processes and events actually exist. Making law pure or "neutral" could otherwise lead to veritable aberrations. We will have juridical knowledge, hence the possibility of formulating judgements, only when this knowledge connects that event established with the law. We shall devote no attention to wilfulness or matters of conscience, even though these have their importance in every event and crime. Above all, we will reach the point of saying that law "includes any event only in so far as it involves juridical norms, that is in so far as it is established by juridical norms" (Kelsen, 1994, 11). Aside from the fact that such considerations give rise to nothing other than relativism, one can ask if they do not reduce law to pure formalism, since only one who goes against a law issued by a legitimate State ends up being sentenced. Not only does this compromise the so-called inalienable rights, but all the efforts of international courts to judge are also in vain, when it comes to judging people who have gone against criteria which might still be called meta-juridical within their own State and applying the laws thereof. Kelsen's intention is clear in any case. "That the law be valid always means that what refers to events that can happen in any place and time is valid for a determined space and for a determined time" (Kelsen, 1994, 8).

3.5 Then, saying that "the norms of a universal morality doubtless refer to all human beings (...) whereas juridical norms bind and authorize only determined categories of people" (Kelsen, 1994, 9), should give rise to the suspicion that that contrast could lead, at least some people, to consider the former superior to the latter. The history of dissent has amply demonstrated this. With acute intuition, Cicero maintained that dissent could only be dealt with in a climate of consensus. This is indeed further proof that law must contemplate something more than mere facts, even when it wants to be scientific. Kelsen seems convinced of that when he states: "As a moral category law means nothing other than justice. This is simply the expression of the just social order, an order which attains its purpose in so far as it satisfies everyone" (Kelsen, 1994, 13). Is it possible to find such a paradisiacal condition that it satisfies everyone? This seems pure utopia as well as pure formalism, and certainly no less dangerous. Yet that is not all: "The trend towards justice considered psychologically is the eternal tendency of humans to attain happiness, which they cannot find as individuals and so seek in society. Social happiness is called justice" (Kelsen, 1994, 13). This statement is as questionable as it is downright paradoxical. Is it really true that humans cannot find happiness as individuals? At times, such is not the case. Furthermore does the quest for happiness in society always lead to the desired effects? Does social happiness depend only on justice? The various attempts, made in the twentieth century, as well, to create "Perfect Cities" as realms of social happiness have led to veritable hells. To be sure, we must pursue what Kelsen seeks for the just and justice: "the judgement of justice expresses only the value pertaining to conformity with the law. Justice here is only a different word for legal" (Kelsen, 1994, 13). In that case, why not use the term "legal" and leave it at that, without using another that is so pregnant with meanings and facets that are not solely juridical like the word justice"?

3.6 Maintaining that it is impossible to understand what justice consists of, Kelsen thinks that it is worthwhile to reduce it solely to a juridical dimension. "Justice is an irrational ideal (…) humans are only give positive law or, more precisely, that as an object of research" (Kelsen, 1994, 15-16). This is a simplification that suffocates justice itself and, never more than in this circumstance, can the saying *summum ius summa iniura* apply. Without forgetting the fact, furthermore, that justice is for many disciplines the "object of research", it is also such for law itself, unless one wants to tie oneself down with some preliminary considerations that actually end up being prejudices.

3.7 There is a reason why Kelsen feels that he must free law from the criteria of metaphysical justice: nowadays "law is no longer assumed to be an eternal and absolute category" (Kelsen, 1994, 19). In actual fact, however, to ward off a hazard, one ends up face to face with a more serious one and, to avoid law understood in terms of immutability, law becomes understood as formalism. In so doing, it can be forgotten that something in between can exist, typical of Latin jurisprudence. Obviously, the latter recognized the bodies of positive law typical of historical contingencies and specific traditions, but, at the same time, considered some bodies of law that we now consider inalienable, that cannot merely be a function of conventions. Cicero, for example, is extremely clear in recognizing that not all the concerns the laws can be based on decrees of the people or the deliberations of those governing. If such were the case, who could prevent a majority from approving the right to steal, falsify, etc. There exist, in other words, laws that no legislation can cancel so that then as now, a *referendum* cannot be allowed. If that were not the case, it would be a very serious error. "Among the most absurd things is that of considering all principles sanctioned in institutions and in the laws of peoples as just" (Cicero, DL, I, 15; cf. Pezzimenti, 2011A, points I.46 ff.).

3.8 Let us return to the need to "purify" law however. "The pure doctrine of law attempts (...) totally to distinguish the concept of juridical norm from that of the moral norm from which it arose and ensure the independence of law from morality, as well" (Kelsen, 1994, 21). If, however, a juridical norm is always the expression of a widespread feeling, otherwise it would be an illogical imposition it follows, as Kelsen himself acknowledges, that it is always derived from a moral norm. How can anyone claim to be able to distinguish it completely from the latter? It would be like cutting out its roots and preventing it from living and being observed. Kelsen provides a typically Kantian solution. It could not be otherwise, given the fact that, in the final analysis, both find themselves dealing with pure formalism. His words leave no doubt: "This comes about by acting in such a way that the juridical norm, contrary to traditional doctrine, is understood not as an imperative on a par with moral law, but as a hypothetical judgment which explains the specific relationship between a conditioning fact and a conditioned consequence" (Kelsen, 1994, 21-22). Only thus should the norm free itself from what Kelsen calls the "magic and metaphysical character". Only a norm of this sort can be accepted by everyone without being contested. Aside from the questionable nature of that conclusion, there is no doubt that such a juridical category comes from a typical Kantian approach and, once again, Kelsen brings it out clearly: "In the sense of Kantian philosophy, it is gnoseologically transcendental, not metaphysically transcendental" (Kelsen, 1994, 24).

3.9 The concept of the illicit, which is one of the keys to Kelsen's thought, must be interpreted in this light. What does it mean, however, that the illicit must be conceived of solely as law? It means that it "it gives up its extra-systematic nature in which only a naïve pre-scientific jurisprudence can keep it and takes on an intra-systematic position" (Kelsen, 1994, 27). With statements of this sort I perceive a clear Hegelian background. Saying that something takes on an intra-system position, means totally historicizing the concept of the illicit which, a bit like the concept of truth or morality, is valid only at the moment it is posed. This is the essence of Hegel. This *may be correct* for a scientific truth, but I doubt that it can apply on a juridical or moral level. If such were the case, we would find ourselves in a position of always considering licit that which imposes history with its logic and its force, and it could be that of a majority, of a class, a party, a State, etc. These are the perspectives that have led to considering, in a Machiavellian perspective, "licit" all that guarantees political success, even to the point of ignoring the inalienable. From this comes the point that "the end justifies the means" and Kelsen certainly does not help us take up a position against this gloomy thesis. Otherwise, he would not tell us that law must be seen "as a specific means (...) law is a coercive mechanism, which in and for itself does not correspond to any political or ethical value, a coercive mechanism whose value depends more on the purpose which transcends it in so far as it is a means" (Kelsen, 1994, 32).

3.10 Kelsen seems to realize all that, and so he states that a pure doctrine of law cannot "do without adequate penetration and a systematic working out of the spiritual structures which, above all, give meaning to law" (Kelsen, 1994, 36-37). Upon closer look, however, this, too, is seen in Hegelian terms. It involves giving rationality to something real that imposes itself by the force of coercion as long as it finds an adequate justification. This is so because "law does not embrace human beings in their totality with all their spiritual and corporeal functions, but qualifies only clearly determined human acts as obligations or authorizations" (Kelsen, 1994, 52). Clearly the very concept of the person takes on a profound new dimension in this view. The person, in fact, is only "the unity of a plurality of obligations and authorizations, that is, the unit of a plurality of norms that establish obligations and authorizations" (Kelsen, 1994, 53). What room is then left for the person, beyond this formalism? The question is not only legitimate, but also extremely appropriate.

3.11 There is a crucial point in Kelsen's thought, which merits being recalled because it brings out an essential, knotty problem in contemporary political and juridical thought. "If the traditional doctrine of law and the State puts law in opposition to the state as a being different from it and yet conceives of it as a juridical being, it does so because it considers the state as a subject of juridical obligations and authorizations" (Kelsen, 1994, 115). These juridical obligations and authorizations should set several limits, which safeguard the personal rights of each person. These are considered the *legal status of the individual* in private-law theory. Once, it was "supposed that this preceded objective law logically and in time, that is, the juridical order" (Kelsen, 1994, 115). It was this precedence *that constituted the real limit to the excessive power of the State*, since, in the absence of this limitation, it remains the sole source of law. Now this "traditional" dualism had to be abandoned to the sole advantage of the State. "Here it is not so much a matter of understanding the essence of the State, as it is to reinforce its authority" (Kelsen, 1994, 117). All that means aiming at perfect identity between law and the State. Our times have dramatically shown how risky such statements are.

3.12 *Dualism,* judged to be out-of-date and contradictory, *must be replaced by a rigorous monism* capable of ensuring juridical and political effectiveness both. "Considered from a gnoseological point of view, the dualism between the status of the State and the legal order is parallel to the dualism, analogically contradictory, between God and the world" (Kelsen, 1994, 126). In other words it is an unsustainable dualism. What must remain hereafter is only and solely the State, without entities that could limit it. From this perspective, the State needs no one to control it. It should not be forgotten that for a believer, it is inconceivable that God can sin. It is equally unacceptable that the State can commit a crime. Kelsen will return to this conviction in *Gott und Staat.* Another dangerous statement comes out of what has been said: one, which leads to criticism of every principle of legitimacy. Overcoming dualism constitutes the total negation of what Kelsen calls the "very widespread ideology of legitimization". In his opinion, this is inadmissible and the identity between State and law ultimately confers on the former an absolute and unlimited ability to express juridical norms.

3.13 Habermas has offered an interesting reflection on this subject, one that, however, leads to more than just some perplexity. This has been appropriately observed after a reading of *Facts and Norms. Contributions to a Discursive Theory of Law and Democracy*, one wonders whether or not "a moral justification is given to the legal order (…) If this is morally justified, then respecting the juridical norms becomes something that is not only legally obligatory, but also a moral duty" (Petrucciani, 51). The importance of this problem is hardly negligible. Another one comes out of it: Is it possible to ignore, when human beings "prepare to seek valid norms, an impartial attitude, that is, such as to take into considerations the interests of others on an equal basis with one's own interests?" (Petrucciani, 52). This is tantamount to saying: Is it possible to formulate a body of law without a moral feeling in common? In my view, absolutely not! Even though there must be agreement on that *moral feeling in common.*

3.14 For Habermas the democratic principle is placed on a different plane from the moral one, and he maintains that the former, the democratic one, must absolutely not be subordinated to the latter, the moral one, as Kant would have it (cf. Habermas, 111-112). That is all done in consideration of the problem of to what degree that subordination, in Kantian morality, is actually essential or exclusively formal, given the undeniable contractions that arise from it. Habermas himself seems to get caught in this position when he attempts to justify the legitimacy of the norms (cf. Habermas, 193-194). The fact that laws are formulated in democratic debates only after confrontation between the majority and the opposition shows that differing interests to be sure, but values, hence different moral conceptions behind the laws, are brought out. A law is never the neutral product of a legislator. It is not sufficient to say, either, in apparent self-contradiction that "positive law always contains an indelible reference to morality" (Habermas, 137) to recognize, even unwillingly, subordination to moral laws. It is not enough, because the problem remains of explaining the *ubi consistam* of those norms to escape vagueness, which could become too dangerous. The foundations and, above all, the limits of a morality that continues to be understood in a Kantian sense are yet to be explained.

B) Morality imprisoned by the present: Martin Heidegger.

3.15 Heidegger's reflection is to be found at the end of this itinerary in which, as many critics have pointed out, the ontological and existential constitution of the Being there is based on time and, perhaps, it would be useful to add that it finishes in time as well. It is certainly a conclusion that must somehow be dated, even though no one fail to be aware of the consequences it led to. It was when some thinkers felt the need to react to that crisis in fundamentals, which mathematics as well as other sciences had encountered (Heidegger, 9). Hence, the need was felt to clarify the "meaning of being". This ultimate finds its basis in temporality again. This is all with an interpretation, at times forced, because what cannot be temporal is ultimately circumscribed in time: "The *non-temporal* and the *ultra temporal* are *temporal* in being" (Heidegger, 18).

3.16 The reference to being works itself out in everyday life. In fact, only this represents, "the being that extends *between* birth and death" (Heidegger, 233). Being is fully determined only in existence, and only as long as existence lasts can the being say that it exists. This is not an interpretation, because the author of *Sein und Zeit* clearly maintains the point: "If existence determines the being of Being and if its essence consists of a may-be, it follows that the condition of being, as long as it exists, still has something of being" (Heidegger, 233). It follows that *the moral problem*, of the behaviour of Being, *concerns only the present* and *has no implications* for the hereafter. So, as long as there is being, something may always be lacking: this process comes to an end with death.

3.17 "But death *is* adapted to Being only in an existentive being-for-death" (Heidegger, 234). Temporality becomes the dimension of Being there and of its end. Time and the "calculation of time" become the element constituting being. "The design of a sense of being in general can only be put into effect in the horizon of time" (Heidegger, 235), as if it were easy and universally acceptable to explain the meaning of time!

3.18 This placing oneself in the temporal dimension implies that being means having the courage to consider the possibility of our non-being. In other words, the fact of having to die implies acceptation of our finiteness. The fact that that gives rise to "other emotional tones, is clear if phenomena such as tedium, sadness, melancholy and despair are examined" (Heidegger, 345), not to mention fear and anxiety even though the first always refers to something in the sense that one always fears something, the second is not as well defined because it is difficult to circumscribe the sense of anxiety. Suffice it to think of the anxiety of death, or rather, of dying, in which we feel the presence of nothingness in its manifestation of total nullification. Death is the possibility that all that we are immersed in may become impossible from one moment to the next. It is the possibility of the sooner or later, as a temporal fact, because, as a fact in itself, no one can escape death, so that one can say that the authenticity of existence is to be found in its being-for-death. "The authentic being-for-death, that is, the finiteness of temporality, is the hidden basis of the historicity of the Being-there" (Heidegger, 387).

3.19 This "being for" even gives meaning to history and its meaning comes from the fact that the totality of the entity "changes in time" (cf. Heidegger, 379). Now, this changing is determined and determines a change in all that concerns the being there in time, obviously including morality, which is seen as product of the time. Despite the subtle reasoning, it remains to be understood why the *Dasein*, "effectively thrown away, can *take* time and lose it" (Heidegger, 410) in a dimension that surrounds it so that it cannot place itself above it.

Ch. IV. Atheism and Indifference: The Position of Dostoevsky and his Followers

A) The abandonment of remorse: Charles Baudelaire.

4.1 Baudelaire is the poetic expression of that view of life that breaks away from the sacred with a mixture of irreverence and nostalgia. He senses, as do few others, the persistence of a certain inclination towards evil, in which there is no longer a sense of remorse. In his forward *Au Lecteur* he says that evil draws us into a spiral for which there is no exit:

> *Sins are stubborn, remorse is vague*
> *... ... ...*
> *Revolting*
> *objects seem attractive to us*
> *and each day we are a step further along on the way to Hell*

4.2 This condition gives rise to *"that delicate monster"* that is ennui *"plunged into wildernesses"* (Baudelaire, 1975A, CIX), like the albatross, he ridicules those who seek to free themselves from its inane clumsiness. As in Nietzsche, however, the solution is to be found in a sense of pagan nostalgia:

> *I love the memory of the naked centuries*
> *when Foebus brought gold to the statue.*
> *Agile, without feigning or suffering,*
> *man and woman savoured joy,*
> *whole and high instruments of themselves*
> *caressed by a benign torpor* (Baudelaire, 1975A, V).

4.3 Just as in Nietzsche, at the end of this quest, the solution is to be found in regaining instinct and unawareness. In this way of understanding life, all is sacrificed in a state of almost religious exaltation. One feels like "*a monk without a cowl*", without the forms of consolation of monks of the past:

> *Once on convent walls was painted*
> *the 'holy image of Truth*
> *to make gentler, by warming the hearts*
> *of the faithful, cold austerity* (Baudelaire, 1975A, IX).

4.4 A feeling of "*hurt pride*" can be sensed, but everything is done to suppress it. It was not so in the fabulous times when theology flourished. As it faded away everything changed for human beings. "*Its reason for being vanished*", with the meaning of life itself and "*all the chaos tumbled over heads ... from that day which, like a stray animal ... wandered about in the fields, oblivious to summer and winter, hideous, useless and dirty like an unserviceable object*" (Baudelaire, 1975A, XVI). A sense of aristocratic presumption leads the poet to a perspective typical of the superman and he says, in the *Journaux intimes*, "*only the aristocratic government is reasonable and safe*" (Baudelaire, 1975B, 684). Here, too, Nietzsche is anticipated as he thinks of an actor in whom "*crime and charity act together, when necessary, confused*" (Baudelaire, 1975A, XXI). It is clear that in that sense "*living is evil. It is a secret that no one ignores*" (Baudelaire, 1975A, XL). Everything is thus thrust, as Baudelaire says several times, into the terrible oblivion that camps on the shore of the dead. Nothing can save us since one tries even to suppress remorse, considered an implacable and ancient enemy, but "*in what philtre, what wine, what potion*" (Baudelaire, 1975A, LIV) will we have to drown it? Is drowning possible or does one always wait in vain? The result of this attempt is dramatic as it is described in the sonnet *Le mort joyeux*

(Baudelaire, 1975A, LXXII). From its carcass there emerge "*worms ... sons of putrefaction, libertines full of wisdom, go, go without remorse, go through my decay*".

4.5 Meaningless life shows itself to be atonal and dissonant, a cracked bell (Baudelaire, 1975A, LXXIV) that, albeit old, tends to "*hurl out its cry of faith*". An injured soul does not come in tune with faith, but moans like a dying and forgotten soldier forgetting that he is making an effort to die, but in a society which has been able to "*make gold for me has not been able to extirpate the corruption from my body*" (Baudelaire, 1975A, LXXVII). In other words, *the technical does not save*. This is the dramatic cry of a soul in despair, which, as if trapped in an avalanche, feels driven towards ruin. A soul: "*trapped, a crystal prison, and which seeks to discover by what fatal compulsion it has ended up there ... a torch of satanic graces*" (Baudelaire, 1975A, LXXXIV, I-II).

4.6 What Baudelaire calls "*the divine Chance*" involves a life lived extemporaneously and without any goal, since "*only chance moves eternally*" (Baudelaire, 1975A, CXXVI, I). "*My mind sought in vain, to once again to take over the helm ... an old barge at the mercy of a monstrous and endless sea!*" (Baudelaire, 1975A, XC). It is impossible to reason otherwise, despite the fact that there are those who are under the illusion of finding causes beyond our restricted earthly space: "*what will they seek, all those blind people, in Heaven?*" (Baudelaire, 1975A, XCII). The solution can only be tragic. This blindness certain does not help to cheer one up. On the contrary, it makes them frantic, malicious and "*the impatient person turns into a beast*" (Baudelaire, 1975A, XCIV). That awareness that makes him human suggests another prayer: "*Oh God, give me the courage, the strength to look at my flesh and my heart without feeling disgust*" (Baudelaire, 1975A, CXVI). What is the result of all that? Dostoevsky was to make the basis of his thought what Baudelaire anticipates in an extraordinary line: "*What do we care about justice or injustice?*" (Baudelaire, 1975A, II). From this perspective, as comes out in the sonnet *Le gouffre*, there remains only to envy "*For Nothingness nothing*" and, as he would write in his *Journaux intimes*, "*those who do not believe in the immortality of their being take justice into their own hands*" (Baudelaire, 1975B, 696). What can result from this is there for everyone to see.

B) Against the irreligious tendency: Fëdor M. Dostoevsky.

4.7 In Dostoevsky's view of universal history there is the firm conviction that Russia does not live exclusively for itself, but also for Europe, and the Russians can even claim to have two countries (cf. Dostoevsky, 446). The conflict between Slavophilism and Occidentalism, which comes up again and again in his writings, must be seen in the light of this. The conflict was to become sharper since the West seemed to be giving up the authenticity of the evangelic message in order to embrace new, universal ideas, such as utopian socialism, which held out the dream of attaining heaven on earth. Russia would offer Europe another contribution, which the old continent did not imagine that it needed. It was the struggle against that nihilism which was present in Russia, too, and was contaminating the minds of youth (cf. Lo Gatto, XXI ff.). Fortunately, the Russian people would be able to resist this, due to their profound spirituality, as long as attempts were not made to corrupt them. There was a "polite dispute" between Dostoevsky and Tolstoy, which was "taking away from the Russian people all that was most precious, the principal meaning of its life". Dostoevsky's works can be read in this perspective. Starting from the invaluable source of his *Diary*, they can be seen as a "spiritual necessity", since, for him, true liberty and true equality are only possible in Christ (cf. Lo Gatto, XLIV and L).

4.8 Dostoevsky interprets a state of uneasiness, to which he certainly does not want to submit, typical of contemporary mankind. The ability to think and to understand has been lost with the crisis of spirituality. "Reflection, too, is impossible in our times: it is very costly. It is true that lovely, ready-made ideas can be bought. These are for sale everywhere, and also free of charge". These are fashions, intellectual for the most part, typical of those who want to cut themselves off from reality, disdaining simple people and the people themselves. Where are these intellectuals headed, in fact? "Cutting themselves off from the people. They have naturally lost God as well. Among them, the worried become atheists, the half-hearted and the calm, indifferent" (Dostoevsky, 5 and 8). *Atheism and indifference*: these are the contemporary evils that Dostoevsky sought to combat with all his strength. Both of these evils have a single goal, in fact, that of wiping out religion with the intention of giving life to a scientific savouring that can really save mankind. They have forgotten, however, "that reason, science and realism can create an anthill on their own, but not a social harmony where human beings can find their places". Without religion, the moral bases of society are denied and this conviction, "denying the moral responsibility of individuals, ultimately meant the denial of liberty" (Dostoevsky, 10-11). Responsibility and liberty have a sort of reciprocal recognition.

4.9 The effect of this new culture has, on the contrary, been to relieve individuals of responsibility to give responsibility to the surrounding world. Thus, "the conclusion has gradually been reached that crimes do not exist at all, and the surrounding world is guilty for all this". Dostoevsky believes the opposite: "If we become better, we will add to the environment as well and will make it better", otherwise we will arrive at "even considering crimes a duty (...) Since society is badly organized, one cannot assert oneself in it, except with a knife in hand" (Dostoevsky, 19). From this point of view, what sense have humans perfecting themselves and their efforts to improve? Improving oneself is returning to the truth. That is no easy task. Untruth is always lying in ambush and fascinates even those would not capitulate to such a point that "if just one person tells a lie and comes out of it well, he develops a great taste for it", but this is not yet the most serious point, which appears when "untruth taken for truth always takes on a more and more dangerous appearance" (Dostoevsky, 180 and 192). There is an interior propensity towards evil on which one must work in order to improve. Inner life is the real realm of morality. This is what Christianity proclaims, and this is why it is so opposed by the representatives of European culture most in view. They go so far as to say clearly: "When Christ is repudiated, the human intellect can accomplish stupefying results" (Dostoevsky, 201), whereas the Russian writer is of the opposite opinion.

4.10 The outcome of this antireligious is catastrophic. From whatever point of view one wants to see it, it leads to vice and half-heartedness. There are two expressions of materialism and scepticism. That is how "people began to worship getting rich without working, enjoying without fatigue; every deception, every crime is cold-blooded; people are killed only so that someone can take a rouble from their pockets" (Dostoevsky, 249). Whose fault is this? If it is the fault of the surroundings, it is that of everyone and no one. Of course Dostoevsky does not wish to deny the problems, often insurmountable, with which some people are obliged to live. He does not, however, want to give in to a purely sociological view of evil. The problem of poverty must also be confronted from a social point of view, *but it certainly cannot be restricted to it*. However, this reasoning appears absurd to the Europeans of today. Many of them seek salvation in the new social visions. People should, however, have the courage to see beyond this error caused by a precise design of many intellectuals, who "having repudiated God, worship humanity". Fortunately, the people in Russia have been holding out because they do not feel that these people are on their wavelength. Europeans should thus be eternally grateful to the Russians, and for their history up to now. "For a thousand years (the Russians) had to fight ferocious enemies, who, without them, would have spread throughout Europe" (Dostoevsky, 371). This happened because the Russian People, throughout their history, felt their religion more and more, and it became their soul and their culture.

4.11 Having given up its religious spirit, Europe plods along in a state of constant dissatisfaction. It has lost the sense of life and of words themselves, and no longer knows how to regain an orientation. Commenting on a current event, Dostoevsky reminds us that regaining meanings is not so difficult after all: "I most timidly take the liberty of observing that evil had to be called evil, despite any humanitarianism and not be elevated to the status of an heroic act" (Dostoevsky, 424). Confusion about the basic problems of existence leads to no improvement. Crime itself is no longer recognized as such, but as "just an illness which comes from the abnormal condition of society" and this only in order to "depersonalize people, depriving them entirely of independence and life, equating them with a grand of sand swept away by the first gust of wind" (Dostoevsky, 595), "nullified" people, in other words, cogs in a machine that can sacrifice them when it wants because it cannot take responsibility.

4.12 The paradox of all this becomes truly dramatic. It leads to a "logical suicide". It could not be otherwise since humanity, by setting aside the "necessity and inevitability of believing in the immortality of the human soul (...) arrives at the inevitable conviction of the absolute meaninglessness of human existence on earth" (Dostoevsky, 693). The Russian intellectual "class", contaminated by some "European" philosophers, has become a champion of this atheism. As a result, the "indifferentism in our era is almost a Russian characteristic". Indifference is the result of a lack of loftier ideas to which our actions can be related, and "there is only *one* loftier idea on this earth and that is the immortality of the soul". All evils come from the loss of this idea. In other words, evil has a metaphysical basis, as well. Indeed: "evil lies exclusively in the loss of faith in immortality" (Dostoevsky, 693-694). When this point is reached, suicide becomes inevitable and logical. It doesn't need to take on the tragic tones that everyone can imagine, but manifests itself in the rejection of life and in an existence that rises only "slightly" above that of animals. Without faith in immortality, any vital tie fades away.

4.13 We could almost say that suicides "are due to a single spiritual illness". Dostoevsky believes that such an illness has even struck childhood and youth. It is easy to see that even the younger generation "suffers and languishes because of the lack of higher goals in life". Education and the school are also to blame. "They have become too indifferent because of other, more practical tasks and ones more of interest to modernity" (Dostoevsky, 698-699).

4.14 These aspects "more of interest to modernity" should be given some thought. It is not that they are not important. Dostoevsky points with pride at Russian science and scientists, but he does not want to run the risk of turning science into an absolute, and assign tasks to it that do not belong to it. Indeed, not a few maintain the opposite and "openly claim that no brotherhood is needed, that Christianity is a form of delirium, and that future humanity will be organized on scientific bases" (Dostoevsky, 797). This is also an underhanded attempt to take mankind back to the level of the animals. Science is not enough to build a better society. "Ants know the formula of their anthills, bees that of their beehives (...) but human beings do not know their own formula". Science is important but not all embracing. The "moral perfecting of individuals" is also needed. Without this there is no true improvement (cf. Dostoevsky, 1305).

4.15 Behind this presumption another conviction is also advancing. It is that "science attempts to explain what life is, itself seeks to know about it, in order to teach others how to live" (Dostoevsky, 879). But how many people, even illiterate ones, know what life is and live better than a great many haughty, educated individuals? Dostoevsky's characters can all be summed up in this. Not only that, but those who decide to follow consolidated moral criteria are often seen as idiots, as a novel of that name shows. Those who ridicule this character do precisely what presumptuous people of science do. They reduce all evil to a "physical" question whereas its roots are metaphysical. These presumptuous people do not accept a simple postulate: "Evil existed before they did". Not admitting it, they dream of earthly paradises in which evil will disappear by magic without the personal effort of everyone to be better. "Perhaps all these utopias will be possible only when we grow wings and all people turn into angels" (Dostoevsky, 1013 and 1125). That is not an ironic quip, but a conclusion that comes out of a simple observation: "The spiritually richer a nation is, the richer it is materially" (Dostoevsky, 1088).

C) Two Disciples.

4.16 For Soloviëv, Dostoevsky was one of those rare writers that still conserve the image of – and resemblance to – God. This is why he could be considered a creative spirit, because only people of faith really know how to create and how to create life. Both, convinced, as they were, that the Church was destined to reign over the entire earth, they possess a sort of philosophy of history, which, however, Soloviëv develops more precisely, in a less literary but more philosophical fashion. In his opinion, the outcome of this itinerary is unavoidable and will take concrete form in the mutual, peaceful and necessary union between East and West. The destiny of Russia will thus be fulfilled, that of saving Europe from the crisis of spirituality towards which it is heading (cf. dal Santo, 8-9). Both, in any case, were convinced that they were writing above all for the future, maintaining that the authentic philosophy and that comes from it, could only by that of Christianity. This is why Soloviëv, inspired by a love for the people and disgusted with the impositions that they might be subjected to, never accepted the atheistic position of a certain socialism, which could end up usurping the religious consciousness of human beings. Hence, the union of the "two" traditions of Europe could not be put off. Soloviëv, like Dostoevsky, recognized the great merits of Western culture, but this had adulterated that thought of Christ, which the Orient, on the contrary, had safeguarded in all its purity. That Christian ecumenism based on the *divinity-humanity* of Christ could come out of this synthesis (cf. dal Santo, 10-11). Let us not forget that what Byzantium had jealously kept and concealed to the extent possible, the Renaissance spread far and wide to everyone, recognizing the greatness of mankind. If Byzantium had forgotten to exalt mankind, however, the West was forgetting God (cf. Soloviëv, 1996, 259-261).

4.17 Western philosophy itself seemed to many Russian intellectuals embroiled in a radical crisis from which it could escape only thanks to Eastern culture. In fact, was this what some brilliant spirits such as Schopenhauer had intuited? The roots of this crisis could be traced back to Protestantism, which, finding its *raison d'être* in opposition to Catholicism, had ultimately embarked upon an abstract rationalism. Humanity had thought it could rise to the position of redeemer of nature, placing itself between this and God, but it was tending to fulfil itself independently and far from God (cf. Riconda, XI-XII and XVIII). From this point to opposing God, the way was short. Soloviëv clearly made this point in some lectures, too. Here he emphasized the final outcome of this cultural perspective, with the intent of radically changing society, revolutionaries and revolution itself would arrive at an atheistic and totalitarian view, intolerant of Christianity (cf. Riconda, XXI). Fortunately, the Russian people maintained a genuine spirituality capable of facing up to attempts of the sort. He knew all too well that the Kingdom of God was to be considered transcending history and that until the end of it, he had to conserve its mystery. The Antichrist "is none other than *a God of this world*" who has the illusion of being victorious over evil, which, in its radicalism, can never be extirpated. Victory over evil would come about only "in true resurrection". "If Christ had not arisen, if Caiaphas was right: Herod and Pilate were wise men, the world would seem to us like something absurd, like the Kingdom of evil, of deception, of death" (cf. Soloviëv, 1996, 152-153 and 249). This is further proof that evil, like sin, does not belong exclusively to personal morality, but acquires an historical dimension.

4.18 To combat evil, one must cling to another existence, different from evil itself. Here lay the dispute with Tolstoy in whose view evil is not to be understood. On the contrary, it has a real existence and cannot be considered a mere absence of good. Tolstoy seemed to be proposing the themes characteristic of that western crisis, which now seemed without any solution. The novelist insisted on a uniquely rational religiosity and an immanent mysticism from which an ethic without transcendent elements. The *Resurrection*, which Tolstoy spoke of in his novel, was reduced to an intra-worldly event (cf. Riconda, XL ff.). Liberation from evil turned out to be an illusion.

4.19 As Dostoevsky had already said, the solution to the problem of evil was to be sought elsewhere. "This vital problem must be studied lucidly and resolved only within a complete metaphysical system" (Soloviëv, 1996, LXV). That unquestionably raises problems, but certainly does not eliminate hope. Good itself, however, must be understood not merely in human and earthly terms. The consequences could be quite disastrous: absolute good could be confused with what it is not. For example, peace, any peace whatsoever, could be accepted as something good, when it could actually be bad. Peace, like good and truth seen in terms of metaphysical criteria ultimately lead to division, because the peace of Christ is not necessarily world peace. To remind us of this, Soloviëv refers to the parabola of the wine dressers. They were satisfied with their peace, convinced that the Kingdom would come to pass on earth, that is, in their vineyards (cf. Soloviëv, 1996, 115 and 129-130). They were under the illusion of having what was best, and, under this illusion, they were combating eternity.

4.20 It was clear that thoughts of this sort were leading towards paths, which the dominating philosophy in the west had abandoned. Soloviëv thoughts on compassion, modesty, and, above all piousness were in opposition to

Nietzsche's. The yearning of mankind towards something superior had been totally misrepresented. This "philosopher of the future" had written the epilogue of this "new religion" of humanity. In his attempt to teach how to attain the superman, Zarathustra became the symbol of this mission. Nietzsche's turned out to be a purely rhetorical exercise, with unforeseeable consequences. Literary fiction replaced possible truth and, to surpass a humanity aware of its vices and evils a superman was invented. Is it possible that all his followers managed to "forget the exemplary tragedy of their author"? (cf. Soloviëv, 1996, 239-243). His false truth and the sterility of his attempt led him to the insane asylum: *a terrible premonition of the century to come.*

4.21 Soloviëv, like Dostoevsky, does not offer blind optimism. He knows that evil is not easy to extirpate and that it insinuates itself into the depths of history. Russia herself, embracing the Orthodox Christianity of Byzantium, absorbed from it not only the sacred component, but also the historic sins of the Byzantine Empire (cf. Soloviëv, 1981, 87). He was, however, able to accept that yearning for salvation, which, in the orthodox religion, is not confined to the individual sphere, but is transfigured into salvation of the world. We could almost call it social salvation, which would greatly influence but also distort the events of the twentieth century. It was this very need for universalism that would lead Soloviëv to embrace Catholicism, as his life drew to its conclusion, persuaded as he was that "only Rome remains intact and indestructible in the minds of the torrent of anti-Christian civilization" (cf. Soloviëv, 1981, 89). He had entirely accepted the conviction, what had been Dostoevsky's, that *only one idea was to be considered superior* on earth: that of the immortality of the soul (cf. dal Santo, 12-13).

4.22 Dostoevsky, who read human history in the light of the Apocalypse, was convinced that the struggle against the immortality of the soul was only a chapter in the war that contemporary thought was waging against God, hence the awareness of the terrible power of evil, which, in Soloviëv, became something quite clear. Here was the charming and beguiling face of the Antichrist. He is a deceptive benefactor, without love, but filled with satanic and evil pride. From him comes *an unexpected lesson*: "evil can easily triumph if it disguises itself as good". *To attain salvation one must continually recall* the words of Christ: "My Kingdom is not of this world" (cf. dal Santo, 17-19). Whoever is not with the Antichrist must have a sole and heroic intent: "Do not allow yourself to be seduced by the visible domination of evil and do not reject invisible good for love of this one" (Soloviëv, 1981, 62). It is clear why, in my opinion albeit in a different light, Soloviëv offers an active Christianity, almost a "social Christianity" capable of giving "socialism" what there was of a purely Russian nature that was lacking. He thus believes that artists and poets must return to being priests and prophets. As Dostoevsky himself believed, art had to return to take its place alongside religion. That would not be easy to accomplish, however. For the artists it could mean ostracism since they had to defend "that ancient and eternally new truth which, given the existing order of things, the best people (morally speaking) are at the same time the worst for society" (cf. Soloviëv, 1981, 42 and 47).

4.23 All his life Dostoevsky had faith in this ecstatic vision, and thus influenced his followers. "In his convictions, he never separated the truth of good and beauty; in his artistic creation, he never exalted beauty separating it from good and from truth" (Soloviëv, 1981, 65). The theme of truth was inevitable. Dostoevsky had most clearly felt this. He "felt and understood that before that superior, divine truth, every personal truth is reduced to the ego and untruth, and that the attempt to impose this lie on others is simply a crime (…) the world must not be saved through the use of force" (Soloviëv, 1981, 49 and 65). In this, too, he was a prophet: the tragedies of the centuries to follow show this. Possession of the truth cannot be a privilege of the people nor can it be the prerogative of a single personality. Truth can only be universal. Only in this sense can Christianity be understood to be a "positive social ideal". This is true because limiting the action of God merely to the moral consciousness of human beings, "means denying His fullness and infinity, finally, it means not having faith in God" (cf. Soloviëv, 1981, 54 and 81-82). This is the understanding because one of the purposes of the believer is that of placing "*la personne du Christ au centre de l'histoire et au sommet de la perfection humaine*" (de Laubier, 12).

4.24 This choice is not painless, but confirmation of the fact that human beings cannot escape the dilemma of having to make a definitive choice between good and evil. It is impossible to think that there is a way that is neither good nor bad, the way that some call the natural one. It is only that of the animals. It is natural because it is instinctive, and so without decisions. Humans, however, are ashamed of being told that they are animals. That shows that they cannot be mere animals, but "*quelque chose d'autre et de plus élevé*" (cf. Soloviëv, 1997, VII and 48). Without this gaze towards higher realities, *aesthetics itself will turn into* a sort of cult, capable of ignoring any moral intent whatsoever. This position brings to mind the characters of D'Annunzio. The protagonist of *Il piacere* is described thus at a point of climax: "Nel tumulto delle inclinazioni contraddittorie egli aveva smarrito ogni volontà and ogni moralità. La volontà, abdicando, aveva ceduto lo scettro agli istinti; Il senso estetico aveva sostituito il senso morale" (D'Annunzio, 61). Meaning that the sense of the beautiful took the place of that of the good.

4.25 The root of this way of understanding modern life goes back a long distance. As Dostoevsky had done, Soloviëv, too, goes back to the great religious laceration of modern Europe. For him, too, Protestantism broke away from the Catholic Church over matters concerning *"le terrain de la théologie morale"*. From there, it went on to a sort of *moral determinism from which not even Kant was immune* (cf. Soloviëv, 1997, 8 and 15). Morality always implies an absolute freedom of choice, which is an interior matter above all, and does not come from the acts of practical reason, as Kant would have had it. If, finally, evil has metaphysical roots, there is all the more reason to recognize that any reference to good is a basically metaphysical matter. Thus, the actual basis of morality cannot be compassion alone, as Schopenhauer believed, but must also be sought in modesty, religious feeling and piety (cf. Soloviëv, 1997, 20-23, 73 and 96).

4.26 The thought of another multi-faceted genius of Russian and Soviet culture, who seems to move in the wake of this tendency, is equally interesting. Florensky turns the perspective upside down, going beyond purely aesthetic reflection, and implicates gnoseological and moral thoughts, which already presage the crisis of Soviet Realism. The representation in perspective used by the figurative arts, and painting in particular, is far from being the only correct one, and the only one corresponding to authentic perception. This consideration had become necessary because otherwise, any other way of perceiving art as reality could be considered a betrayal or alteration of the truth of perception. Furthermore, moving away from "the norms of the unity of perspective" had been considered a step in the direction of non-realism. For the Russian thinker, perspective unity was not the only way of relating to reality. It had been considered as such because it went hand in hand with the Kantian and Renaissance conception. "If it turned out that the conditions of perspective are violated, real experience, and also the vital importance of this conception would be confuted" (cf. Florensky, 114 and 127). In other words, rejecting a view of reality, meant calling into question all that referred to that reality.

4.27 The question of space and the three conceptions that refer to it were tied together: abstract or *geometric* space, *physical* space and *physiological* space (the latter, in turn, brings in visible, tactile, acoustic, olfactory, gustatory space, etc.). The first is only a particular case among various, extremely multiform spaces, since Euclidian geometry "is one of innumerable geometries". Where Euclidian geometry to be the sole one it would be confuted by visible space, as Michelangelo's vision of perspective shows, a subject to which we shall return shortly. At times, the world has nothing to do with the Kantian view and the visual organ ultimately represents something that is no longer submitted to the rules of geometry. The eye constantly provides artists with a corrective to keep them free of the tricks of perspective, ones that often fail (cf. Florensky, 127-129). Ocular vision is not a be all and end all. In the artist's vision there is also a psychic process, which is quite complicated and which projects the inner emotions of the artist's personality into the work.

4.28 Michelangelo is a spectacular example of what has been said. His *Last Judgment* offers a sort of "inclination". The artist did not rigorously apply the Euclidian rules. In "virtue of the perspective view", the observer does not see smaller and small figures as he or she looks further and further. The dimension of the figures actually increases in proportion to the height of the fresco. Here, Michelangelo has taken into consideration the spiritual space in which a figure is larger the further away it is and smaller when it is closer. It is this vision, which makes *Michelangelo* a figure and, at the same time, not a figure of his times, because he does not sacrifice medieval spirituality *to modernity*. His breaking of the rules of perspective is not a chance error that weakens the work of art, but, on the contrary, gives it quality. That means that the perspective view can be the result of a series of complex, artificial conventions, which have become convincing (cf. Florensky, 104-105 and 111). Half a millennium of visual training has led us to this sensibility, "but neither the view nor the hand of the child nor that of the adult, either, submit to this practice without particular training" and fall into error as, in fact, happens with educated minds (cf. Florensky, 113). In other words, perspective has become the language of a certain reality and the values that it expresses, and has turned into a vision of the world. The Kantian-Euclidian way "is one that can unify all the representations of the world, in terms of which the world is seen as a unified scheme (...) concentrating on the 'I' of the one who is observing the world". Here, the Russian thinker is explicit: "perspective is the procedure that inevitably follows from a conception of the world, in which a certain type of subjectivity is admitted". Perspective is, finally, a particular way of reading the world, interpreting and changing it (cf. Florensky, 126-127).

4.29 Then there is a dimension, without which art does not exist, but which is not easy to consider: that of time. Why do some works age and others do not? Why do some works have a meaning in one context and not in another? The answer can be simple: a work has a spirituality of its own which, under certain conditions, can weaken. Florensky indeed joins a religious work like an icon with the architectural space in which it is to be found, and not only that. A propos of space or, to further clarify, the space considered by the figurative art, it must be said that no intelligence can represent it entirely. A choice must be made as to what to represent, what to prefer. The intelligence "is lost bartering for its liberty" (Florensky, 123). It is lost because it realizes that it is not only in contact with physical reality, but that it is coming close to metaphysics. This is what the Russian thinker states in his *Reflections on Colour Symbolism*, in which he goes far beyond Goethe's considerations (cf. Florensky, 69). A propos of the considerations on space, it should be recalled that Florensky, reading Dante, had arrived at surprising conclusions. The Ptolemaic system of the world, as described in the *Commedia*, corresponded to the elliptical space of the theory of relativity, to a far greater extent than Copernican and Galilean space (cf. Misler, 31).

4.30 These metaphysics are not only inherent in the work of art, but in all that surrounds it as well. The work "does not exist except in the complete fulfilment of the conditions necessary for its existence, taking into account which ones and within which ones it was conceived" (Florensky, 61). Thus, it is impossible to take away the icons from the Monastery of St Sergei and relegate them to a museum. It also means cutting them off from the vital relationship they have to the prayer of the monks and relegating them to the superficial curiosity of those who lack spirituality. This conviction is quite clearly expressed in *the orthodox rite as a synthesis of the arts*. Artificial light cannot give new life to the icons. Outside of their cells, even though these have subdued light, they can never come to life. Indeed they are altered and they die. In a temple or sacred place, they bring to mind another reality, "whereas in a museum we do not see the icons, only their caricatures". Unfortunately, and as further proof that art has metaphysical and often spiritual dimensions, people do not realize that, "in the name of the religion of socialism", monasteries and icons, like every other form of art related to the monastic tradition, are eventually destroyed (cf. Florensky, 63 and 66). No image could have meaning any longer without that environment of prayer and faith. Here, Florensky was bringing out one of the basic convictions of Dostoevsky. The Russian people bore Christ and his teachings in their hearts and this was shown in the almost direct relationship with the sacred images, which were abundant in every place of prayer. The question thus became: "How can there be a real image of Christ without their being a doctrine surrounding the faith?" Taking the images from their sacred context and placing them in and arid, albeit sumptuous room of a museum was equivalent to ridiculing the genuine faith of the Russian people, but the Russian writer was "of the opinion that offending the popular feeling in all that it has of a sacred nature is an enormous abuse and an extreme form of cruelty" (Dostoevsky, 52 and 81).

4.31 For Florensky, true art bears authentic witness to the spiritual life. This conception brings us back to Soloviëv. For him, the artist can actually be a spiritual *medium*. This is yet another reason for leaving the religious work where it is, instead of placing it in a museum in fetischistic fashion. Florensky thereby underscores the contradictions of the revolutionary government and of what the aesthetics of social realism will be with the moral effects that will injure people and harm liberty (cf. Misler, 9 and 19). This confirms that a particular way of understanding aesthetics cannot do without a series of moral implications. These thoughts on art explain to us what was taking form then in Soviet society. The difficult phase of the class struggle was holding out the prospect of two utopias: "rational, positive one of socialist reconstruction and the palingenetic one of the spiritual refoundation of human beings". The revolutionary mysticism could be perceived which, in its radical intransigence, prognosticated the lagers. *Scientific and theological truth were shattering their ties and their scission was becoming a dramatic life experience* (cf. Misler, 25-26). Florensky himself was to finish his terrestrial experience in 1943 in un Siberian lager where he had been sent ten years prior to that.

4.32 Alexander Men' likewise took up this them in a religious perspective, which cost him his life. In his opinion, an important and not-to-be-ignored discovery was brought out in the Old Testament: "the moral condition of society is tightly linked to the destiny of that society (…) because evil generates evil" (Men', 48-49) almost in an endless vortex. This is why the Prophets fought against sin as against tyrannies. Evil could only be opposed by faith. This is why people, even today, should memorize the Symbol of faith "in case they were completely deprived of it" (Men', 13). "Review it" almost in the spirit so that it would become nourishment. Food for the spirit gives rise to other necessities, calls for other substances, which are not resolved in a logical demonstration. The Divinity knew that before mankind did. "In actual fact, the Supreme Reality has shown itself to be a mystery above all logic. There was nothing left to do but accept it in its paradoxical aspect, just as it had been revealed" (Men', 19). Otherwise, as Baudelaire had perseptively foreseen, there remains nothing left but to plunge into evil. In other words, when mankind detaches itself from the mystery of existence, "it deceives is own Nature and, satiated, begins to sink into anxiety" (Men', 23). If we depart from the assumption that enrichment is also an interior matter and that the soul, too, "can grow, but its growth is not material", only then will we understand that "the spirit understands the values of morality and makes the choice between good and evil" (Men', 30). The spirit and not reason alone make the choice. Going back to a suggestion of Berdyaev, Men' comes to say that explaining evil rationally "means justifying it", whereas evil is often "a blind impulse": "In human history, evil is usually an irrational state (…) evil is a form of madness from whose depths we will never immerge, and we will never understand what it is" (Men', 41-42). Perhaps only the poets are capable of intuiting it.

D) Thomas Mann's Soul Searching.

4.33 When the proportions of Nazi atrocities became apparent in 1944, great intellectuals like Thomas Mann, who, in any case, had been hostile to Nazism, began to ask themselves how a great culture like the German one could have produced such atrocities. What was the relationship of the German people to what had happened? "How could they have ended up in the condition in which we see them today? To what degree can the German people be considered responsible for the Nazi crimes?" (Mann, 1968C, 132). In Mann's opinion, that question implied the preclusion of any type of happiness for the immediate future and a struggle for liberation from the universal abject state in which they had fallen. All that was human in Germany, moreover, had been negated, and in the occupied countries, exponents of the clandestine opposition had been arrested then deported. The writer make explicit references to Catholic-inspired leaders arrested in Italy: Olivelli, Bianchi, Sartori, Petrini, Rovida, all of them in some way or other connected with the clandestine newspaper *Il Ribelle*. The situation seemed so disconcerting because, in Germany, "in quite a singular way, good and evil, beauty and fatality were confused" (Mann, 1968C, 134). Ideals of Renaissance and Bourgeois culture seemed shattered, as well as products of aesthetic value, such as Wagner's music, seemed somehow responsible for such disastrous results. Yet, one fact could not be denied: "a post-Bismarck German would never have been capable of uttering the words of Cardinal Manning: 'politics is part of morality" (Mann, 1968C, 137).

4.34 Returning to a consideration that many had put forth in various areas, Mann recalled that "fascism was the defence against bolshevism par excellence", but he quickly warned: "fascism, of which National Socialism is a singular variation, is not a German speciality. It is an illness of the time and is present everywhere. No country is free of it" (Mann, 1968C, 138-139). The economically dominating classes that "determine the policies" of not a few governments express an ignoble liking for fascism, because of a series of fears. This is a fundamental assumption if the accusation, which predominated at the time, to the effect that "Germany had been created especially for that regime" was to be rejected (Mann, 1968C, 161). Hence, it is necessary to re-examine the culture of one's own country, especially the art and religion that in conscience of humanity, hold the same rank as science (cf. Mann, 1968C, 340-341). This position was clearly inspired by a Hegelian approach, from which Mann never succeeded in freeing himself.

4.35 Despite the attention, indeed the unconditional faith in and fondness that Mann entertained for the anti-Hegelians such as Schopenhauer and Nietzsche, the Hegelian background would never be forgotten. His statements are permeated with panlogism. "It is a horrifying spectacle when irrationalism becomes popular. One has the sensation of a disaster, which must be a disaster that an exaggerated and unilateral esteem of reason could not cause. In its optimistic pedantry, reason can be funny and ridiculed by the deepest forces of life, but it does not cause a catastrophe. That point is reached only by the enthronement of anti-reason" (Mann, 1968C, 130). This is also the position of the Marxist Lukács and typical of a cultural view which, as Vico would say, is not even capable of supposing that an exasperation and absolutizing of reason can cause the exact opposite, that is, irrationality. It should be recalled that "Hegel's phenomenology of the spirit, too, tends of play down the presence of evil, considering it a necessary moment in the dialectic process of the self-realization of the absolute spirit. Within that process a positiveness of evil emerges" (Crespi, 24). Alongside the realization of the absolute spirit presented by Hegel, the myth of an absolutized science is emerging. This will be formulated in various ways by Comte and Marx (Crespi, 56-57).

4.36 Mann, however, seems slowly to redeem himself from this position. Philosophical dogmatism must be rejected to "entrust the salvation of human beings" to religion, understood, however, not as a particular religion, which does not interest him, "but as a 'transcending goal', a chance for the redemption of humanity", since earthly perfection cannot be attained. The evil of Nazism thus gives rise to "a meditation of the spirit" and human nature is seen "from an internal viewpoint" (cf. Bagnoli, 9 and 11). Hence, there are artists such as Dostoevsky and Schiller who are in agreement in solving the problem of mankind not politically, but only through the interior and morally: with religion, with Christian self-perfection *of individuals*. Christianity thereby becomes the measure of human morality. It is curious that these words come from an admirer of Nietzsche. "Christianity cannot be surpassed by bringing humanity below the moral level to which it had raised it, but, at the most, giving it a new impulse (...) however, humanity is religious in venerating the mystery, which is incarnated in mankind. Since humans are a mystery" (Mann, 1968B, 353-354). In other words, human beings are such only if they are capable of living in a human way, if they are free, but this freedom must come from moral substance. At this point, it must be recalled that that substances ultimately characterizes culture in the deepest sense of the word. "The origin of the world 'culture' (Kultur) is the same as that of another word, 'cult' (Kultus), distinguished by just one letter in the ending. Both mean 'cure [care trans. note]' (...) in the sense of purely human, aesthetic and moral refinement, freed from the religious sense" (Mann, 1968B, 169). This reflection of culture implies a distinction from civilization. "Culture means unity, style, form, self-possession, taste, a certain spiritual organization of the world, however adventurous, scurrile, savage, bloody, terrible it may seem (...). Civilization, on the contrary, is enlightenment, training, civilizing, scepticism, dissolution, – spirit" (Mann, in Marianelli, 15). In other words, culture can include all that is not rational such as oracles, magic, sacrifices, and so on.

4.37 It would be interesting to see, even instinctively and unconsciously what there is of Hegel, and, to some extent, even Kant in these statements, which, not by chance, lead to Nietzsche's way of conceiving the religious person. Unconsciously, because Hegel's "fatalistic way of thinking, with his faith in the higher reason of the winner, his justification of the real 'State' (put in place of 'humanity' and so on)" (Mann, 1968A, 17) is often rejected. This justification implied the divinization of the State with all that that implied. After recalling that Schopenhauer lashes out against Hegel, the German writer considers the State a simple institution fit to oppose the injustice innate in the human race (cf. Mann, 1968A, 101), is fully aware of the danger of idolatry of the

State, and keeps his distance from it, emphasizing how much there is of Machiavelli in the modern ethical State. "Politics are, in fact, participation in the life of the State, with fervour and passion; people like myself are anything but Hegelian in spirit, I do not believe that the State is to be 'venerated like a divinity on earth, I do not consider it to be 'an end in itself'; for me it is more of a technical than a spiritual matter, a machine to be taken care of and watched over by specialized personnel" (Mann, 1968A, 110-111). Those expressions about the spirit, those which made Schopenhauer speak of the "vapid impudence" of the Hegelians (cf. Mann, 1968A, 239), terrorize Mann who sees in them a sign of decadence, as well as the abdication of the great German culture. Yet, this culture does not manage, even partially, to free itself totally from Hegelianism, even in Mann, nor does it manage to sever the bonds of history, of the present, in other words, of the real and its rationality. In his opinion, too "art like religion, falls within the human sphere" (Mann, 1968A, 325) and is limited to it.

4.38 The same might be said of Kant, who, after the radical destruction caused by the first *Critique* "no longer addresses himself to the problem of the 'truth' but to that "of the validity "of certain ethical and sinister postulates". This highly different way of dealing with the practical sphere "has a clear national character; it is quite German to assign every radical element to the sphere of the spirit and adopt practical-ethical, antiradical positions about life" (Mann, 1968A, 141). It is surprising that Mann has such a clear view of the effects of Kantianism on the German spirit without seeing the dangers! His words are unequivocal: "So, this manner of separating and distinguishing spiritual and national from political life is extremely German, an entirely Kantian way of separating and distinguishing. The difference between spirit and politics is the difference between pure and practical reason" (Mann, 1968A, 201). This rigid separation of the spiritual from the political, implies no fewer problems than that of their complete merging in Hegel's perspective. Kant's position, however, fits into that legacy which, for Mann, is the genuinely German one. The outcome could be truly catastrophic: "Protestantism took the spiritual stimulus away from politics, reducing it to a matter of practice. From Kant, we inherited faith in the predominance of 'practical reason', of ethics and from him the social imperative" (Mann, 1968A, 208). When did this predominance come into conflict with the spiritual? There is nothing left to do: politics no longer recognize any spiritual stimulus. They are their own self-justification.

4.39 It is curious that Mann, too, like Kant, speaks of the philanthropy of Beccaria who almost led criminal law to nullify (!) the concept of guilt (cf. Mann, 1968A, 330). Here, Man's position seems a bit extreme so that it can be said that "the concept of human dignity is a product of custom" (Mann, 1968A, 361) albeit, as if to provide a justification, he refers to Dostoevsky's Christianity in order to safeguard the criterion of responsibility. Here lies *one of the paradoxes* of the German writer, on the one hand, paraphrasing Nietzsche, the sad observation that "now, being Christian is becoming something indecent" (Mann, 1968A, 370), on the other hand, wanting to save this Christianity based on support from a culture which has ended up denying it. How can we find a way out from that weariness of humanity of which Nietzsche always spoke? Did he not perhaps say that a person who has faith, a person of faith, is necessarily a limited person and that the Reformation itself was one that slowed the progress of the Renaissance? (cf. Mann, 1968A, 379 and 381). The unresolved puzzle of Thomas Mann, and not only him is to be found here.

4.40 As Kant, and also Schopenhauer, Nietzsche and Wagner had done, Mann criticizes politics from an intellectual and elitist pulpit. "Politics in themselves make one crude, vulgar and stupid; they teach nothing other than envy, shamelessness and greed. Only spiritual education makes us free. Institutions count for little. What counts are the ideas that one has" (Mann, 1968A, 193). This position is surely a bit questionable, but it did have a justification of its own. In the last phase of the First World War, the German writer drew a tragically prophetic picture. "Wherever literature and politics interpenetrate one another, the spirit becomes politicized, every great abstraction, Truth, Liberty, Justice, Humanity ceases to be a moral and philosophical problem (...) there must –inevitably it seems – be a spiritual type, who arises and who has all the features of a Jacobin" (Mann, 1968A, 285). Is it possible to react against a danger of that sort in the name of anti-politics? This is a further and aggravating drama in Mann. Even though he often leads us to believe the opposite, he knows all too well that "that anti-politics are themselves politics, since politics are a terrible force: one only needs *to know* that they exist, and one is already caught up in them. One's own innocence is lost forever" (Mann, 1968A, 309). Basically it is like Nietzsche's anti-philosophy, of which Mann was not by chance an admirer. He despised the term *philosophy* itself, and this was to become a dominating way of thinking of large areas of philosophical thought today.

SECOND PART

THE PROBLEM OF MORAL AND SOCIAL VALUES

Ch. V. The Rules of the Comparison

5.1 It has been rightly said, that "the road from fear to haughtiness is short" (Capograssi, 1976, 38). Usually, for a will that gives way, there is one that tends to go beyond its own limits. "Arrogance is none other than the promulgation of one's own law, one's own law of life, and the reduction of all experience to the dictates of this law" (Capograssi, 1976, 40). Hence, from what should be the time to be together with others, sociability, one moves on to unsociability; from the personal moment, which implies an I - you relationship on an equal basis, one moves on to selfish individualism which seeks supremacy of me over the others, over a *you* which *becomes you*, that is, from the relationship of an equal subject to that of an object to use freely, even to destroy at times. Is it perhaps not by chance, that in the confusion of a certain sort of contemporaneous language, person, individual, subject, etc. are used as synonyms when, indeed, their histories are profoundly different form one another.

5.2 Destruction of the other comes about when the rules of the comparison are ignored. If there is mutual respect in these rules, and the first of these must be respect for the other or, better yet, mutual respect, it means that fear and arrogance are totally absent and that *confrontation* has not turned into *conflict* in which there is one who succumbs and the other prevails. When the rules are not obeyed, the possibility of conflict is always present, among individuals as among peoples. "War comes to make clear and explicit the intimate destruction that is in fear and arrogance" (Capograssi, 1976,

41); indeed it synthesizes it because both are the result of a bad use of the will. What else is true peace if not the absence of fear and arrogance?

5.3 Thus, there are those who, like Ferrero, have called civilization "a school of courage" (Pellicani, X), we could call it the effort to seek legitimacy in commanding and obedience to avoid fear on the one hand and arrogance on the other. In other words, it is in order to reach the point of providing limits to the right-duty to command and the right-duty to obey. This means emerging from prehistory to reach civilization. As Ferrero always recalls quite well, symbolically sanctioned by the Bible itself concerning the first homicide: "I would be roaming and fleeing" (Gen, 4.12) to bear witness to the concern and fear that will be characteristic of the human experience (cf. Ferrero, 42). To overcome this state of mind, human intelligence invented *consensus iuris*. It is the only remedy that frees us from fear and arrogance. As I have maintained elsewhere, dissent is thus distinguished from sedition which, as Cicero warned, seeks the ruin of the civil community its very foundations (cf. Pezzimenti, 1995, 1.28). For this very reason we can say that will can be constructive and destructive. The force of the will, or more precisely engagement, seems the same, even if the outcomes are paradoxically different: the *constructive will* is arduous and achievement of the end is not always guaranteed for those who engage personally themselves; the *destructive will*, on the contrary, can achieve its goal in an instant, or, much faster than the other. The world will find a way out when it understands that only legitimacy can free it from its wild condition in which, upon close look, the few tout a ridiculous arrogance, but in which, the strong too, are stricken with fear even if they feign otherwise, as Saint Augustine says of the prostitutes who live as if they could be loved (*tamquam si amari possint*), in order to be safe and tranquil (cf. Ferrero, 349 and 235).

5.4 This all obliges us to analyze our desire more deeply. It is desire that makes up the bulk of will and the actions that come about as a result of it. It is also will, which leads to suffering, when not satisfied, leads to action only in order to be appeased. The secret of moral action lies, therefore, in opening up only to truly constructive and attainable desires. Once one opens up to desire, whatever this may be, the sense of duty, which justifies our action, comes into play, whatever the desire may be. We are all masters in the justification of duty. This duty becomes ever more present and categorical, the more present and categorical our desire becomes.

5.5 At this point, one of the most serious misunderstandings of ethical life occurs, and it can become catastrophic when it is felt not only by one person, but, at times, by a community or a people. Awareness of duty makes us feel responsible and we measure our responsibility by the need to do or not to do, to perform or not to perform an action, when we should, in all conscience, *carry* our *responsibility* back to the origin of the desire or, to be more precise, to our dissent from it. Destructive will has almost always been opposed by all the community experiences of every different civilization. The concern has always existed for listing a group of destructive actions that were to be punished and even prevented. *It is proof that ethical life came out of the individual sphere* and, through a controlled examination, became social *as well*. It is on that *as well* that it is advisable to dwell for a moment because it has kept ethical life from becoming *solely* social. The concept of responsibility rests on this *as well*. Here the conflict, not always kept within the realm of legality arises between the individual and the State. In this conflict, however, a danger, or rather a contradiction in terms, must be brought out: whereas responsibility is always identifiable and given concrete form in reference to the individual, it becomes nebulous, abstract, and not circumscribable in reference to the State. It seems to be an unequal conflict as, for example, has been masterfully demonstrated in the pages of Kafka.

5.6 Law, in any case, becomes the means for settling these conflicts. Law has a desire of its own, that of rendering justice and making it equal for all. This desire goes from the moment of its abstraction to that of its being made concrete which, not infrequently, comes into conflict with the intentions of desire. The fact remains that, even with all the imperfections, it is better to be governed by law than by the absence of law. This horrifies individuals, who have experienced the absence of law, all of them. Preference is given to changing the law, standing up to law, forcibly making laws, as mafias and various sorts of bands do, but the absence of rules seems impossible at this point. In fact, there is the awareness and certainty that beyond the rules, there is only barbarity. Unfortunately, what works among individuals does not always become acceptable among communities or States. Here, in the absence of certainties, only brutal conflict is left, even though *desire* is something else, but it is a desire *without tools*.

5.7 Here, the paradox of moral life is felt: those who want war, drag even those who do not want it into such conflict. Those who have no rules, or wish to ignore them, force those who have them to set them aside, at least for the time being. It is a *dangerous "for the time being"* because *the sense of limits is lost when the rules are not observed* and one returns to bestiality. If such were not the case, there would be no need for law, whose primary goal is to fix limits to a desire which, having been unleashed, feels itself to be unlimited: haughty and presumptuous. This is why the outcome of the war is the most delicate moment. The law of the strongest, which places limits only on the defeated, is the forerunner of further conflicts. Law, on the contrary, must bring peace, which is, first and foremost, placing people on an equal basis. As Virgil warned, *Parcere subiectis et debellare superbos*, and the arrogant one is almost always the one who was the victor or, in any case, wants to be. Certainly, after a conflict, there is no hope that an idyllic state of being will come to pass among hearts. It is essential to understand that discord remains more or less latent. The most difficult problem is that of overcoming it without suffocating it, in order to avoid its bursting out once again. What is needed is *concordia discors* to be achieved, as I have already said (cf. Pezzimenti, 2011A, Ch. I). The advantages of submitting to the rules thereby seeing to it that time attenuates and settles the controversies that have apparently calmed down.

5.8 Tranquillity and peace, if they are genuine, can never be the result of fear. On the contrary, like *order*, they must be the result *of continually sought after consensus* because, *like peace itself, they are continually being threatened*. Only in what human beings continually want can they fulfil themselves, because, continually desiring, they are the makers of their will, which freely expresses itself in every moment and in every act. In that *continually*, there is also the constant confrontation with limit that will encounters, a limit which has concurrence with the limit which will encounters, in determining and which, still with consent, can continually review things and propose things in another way. This usually happens when other goals are identified but, to change limits, these ends must be shared and, in future, experienced in common. Living together, that is *living with*, living together. This seems like a banal statement, but it becomes *undefendable* if the ends are not mutually agreed upon. Acting in accordance with these goals becomes the basis of civil life. It is the most serious matter a society can imagine, since it involves the *fullness* of being and the *totality* of beings. Here emerges "the consciousness of a necessity, which makes action the serious and dense matter of all the seriousness of life" (Capograssi, 1976, 57). It is wilful action, whether it relates to the end or whether it opposes it. If such were not the case we would not be free.

5.9 Aside from the paradox, moral life experiences a simple mystery: the pursuit of happiness. It is what everyone wants and thus seeks to satisfy the desire. Out of this comes a frenzy, which people believe can be calmed only if gratification is obtained. Happiness is the most nebulous and, at the same time, concrete thing that permeates human life. I do not think it is necessary to quote Saint Augustine in order to ask the question, which, however, is a crucial one, of why this *concrete* need for happiness comes about and where it comes from, but each person should ask this. At this point, I wish to point out that in this quest, too, will, whether constructive or destructive, plays a crucial role. Both justify themselves, saying that they seek a better and happier world, but one seems a parody of the other. Moral life lies in the culmination of the struggle between them. There is the Manichean temptation to see evil only on one side and therefore the *inability to perceive* that, on the contrary, evil insinuates itself everywhere. One need only have the humility to recognize this. There are those who believe that the only radical change that counts comes from this humility: "between the oppressed and the oppressor, between the slave and the master, emerges fraternity in the mutual recognition of the mutual need for pardon" (Capograssi, 1976, 187). This is certainly an idyllic position and always to be desired, but at times it is inadmissible. As some have rightly asked: "Can we confront the other one, 'accomodate the person' in our way of thinking? (...) and, at what price?" (Rovatti, 63). These questions are certainly typical at a time, such as ours which, rather than resting on certainties, sees the relationship with fellow creatures, as a continual is a constant, risky game. The assumption is fascinating, but what leads to ignorance of the fact that "the notion of 'game' (...) risks becoming more rigid every time we venture to make use of it without the awareness of always being somehow the object of the game" (Rovatti, 63). The risk is not to be underestimated, because, in borderline cases, it definitively prevents one from putting oneself on the line. A fact remains, one, which is certainly not secondary. To what degree can the risk and uncertainty of putting oneself on the line be accepted? Is there a threshold, beyond which, to risk would be absurd and counterproductive? These doubts, too, thrust us back into ethical life.

5.10 Attempting to answer these questions, Rosmini feels the inadequacy of natural Ethics. "Humans, that is, cannot make themselves fully virtuous nor, therefore, can they attain a total happiness, merely with the means and the forces that they naturally possess" (Manganelli, 19). Here, the entire classical model based on natural, rationally acceptable and pursuable premises is rejected, and so, the rejection of the Kantian model. In other words, there cannot but such a unilateral ethical view, but, if anything, there are two, mutually distinguishable perspectives "one, in terms of which ethics è are devised by human reason, the other, by divine tradition" protected from any human compromise whatsoever. The second satisfies human beings, and their satisfaction is quite different from the simple pleasure the first can bring about. "Satisfaction, as opposed to pleasure, consist of an interior and stable tranquillity and contentment of the soul, that cannot be reduced or compared to pleasure, which is a superficial and, above all, passing sensation" (Manganelli, 20). Giving in to pleasure "alone" means casting oneself in a constant and growing state of dissatisfaction, under the illusion of being able to satiate it with a constant revising of moral criteria.

5.11 To further explain this, it is useful to recall that morality, if reduced only to pleasure, becomes an exclusively practical science, as, in the final analysis, Aristotle and Kant maintained. In that Rosminian position I am attempting to describe, it is quite different. The opposition between theoretical and practical sciences is a convenient distinction and, perhaps, only the pursuit of pleasure is practical. On the contrary, "all sciences are speculative, even those that operate around actions; which can be called *praxiological*, if one likes, but not *practical*. A practical morality can indeed be given, in action, but moral science will always be speculative" (Pagani, 29, n.3). If such is the case, the task is that of investigating the assumptions on which morality is based. Independent of pleasure, these can certainly not change following one's whim. Only for this reason can morality be called a deontological science. If such is not the case, morality is reduced to simple utilitarianism (cf. Rosmini, 1998, 42) because it pursues pleasure only. Here lies the basic error of a moral action intended only to be practice and which, therefore, ignores the fact that morality gives rise to "the concept of *obligation* and *duty*. Human beings *must* operate through will" (Rosmini, 1998, 43). Once good is identified, it is clearly expressed in a law, abiding by which moral good is achieved, and opposing which, its opposite is obtained. This is the only reason that "*a moral norm of the sort makes this action obligatory*" (Rosmini, 1998, 81) as opposed to another one.

5.12 This acceptance requires liberty because "the will cannot be forced". If such were the case, moral action would be reduced to pure factualness. It is not, however. "Practical reason means operating reason, and, however, is a designation given to will itself, since, with its first *operation,* it judges beings, places judgment on their degree of goodness, and thereby makes the good or evil themselves" (Rosmini, 1998, 49). For the moment, let us set aside the sense that will "judges beings" (an aspect to which I shall return later when speaking of the value of intelligence), what must be emphasized, as we have just said, is that will indeed determines a practical morality, in action that is, but moral science, as such, will always be speculative, too. It is the evaluation of the will that determines the moral action since it "produces a new means of cognition with its act of estimation" (Rosmini, 1998, 50). This *position is quite close to the Augustinian one*, more than it might seem at first view. *It is the way to evaluate and to love the beings that give rise to moral action. If this action is misleading, it pursues evil, albeit under the illusion of doing the opposite.* Rosmini's words are entirely clear. We can say that when practical reason goes astray, this means that it does not recognize beings "for what they are, but judges them arbitrarily, and having thus judged them presents them to the capacity for affection to be loved more or less or to be hated" (Rosmini, 1998, 50). That faculty of affection, which *drives us* to love, is the synthesis of Rosmini's Augustinian perspective. The term *drives* has been used, because it orients will. "Liberty, then, comes before will, and its act actually consists in the choice between the contrary volitions" (Rosmini, 1998, 64).

5.13 When error triumphs, it means that the *amor sui*, to use Augustinian terminology once again, prevails, manifesting the selfish aspect of love. Thus, "every temptation is reduced *to flattery, which the subject produces* (that is, subjective good) *to what human beings place first in their esteem and in their actions before the object* (that is, to the objective good). Moral good is therefore always objective" (Rosmini, 1998, 53). Against this objectivity, one cannot proceed with the pursuit of one's own good. This does not mean that good things subjective good and goals cannot be pursued, but only that they cannot be in conflict with those objectives. This explains why "*subjective* good also known as eudemonological, on the contrary, is not morality in itself, and at times comes into conflict with morality, then giving rise to temptation against virtue" (Rosmini, 1998, 53). This ability to discern is the determining feature of human dignity and comes from the fact "that every intelligent human being has an intrinsic and absolute worth, insofar as he or she contains the divine component" (Rosmini, 1998, 59).

5.14 From what has been said of will, it is to be inferred that "a dubious positive law, does not oblige (…) and cannot be the intention of legislators that their law oblige if it is not known with certainty" (Rosmini, 1998, 91). Will is, then, not driven by full awareness. If we accept the fact that "acts of will are bound by laws or norms" we must suppose that these are clear. It is clarity itself that means that "the law is always imposed over will, and a commanded or prohibited act is the same as saying an act that the law commands or prohibits willing; willing is always internal, although its manifestation and its elaboration may be external" (Rosmini, 1998, 92). The fact that this "wanting is always internal" is of the greatest importance because it postulates a relationship between the conscience and what is external. In other words, the proper intention must be related to an action, which is not contrary to a just law. Who can determine the correctness of a law, however, without fear of refutation? *This is the central point of the Philosophy of Law.*

5.15 There is another problem and it is no less important: if will were driven by the "simple objects of knowing, all of its morality would end in the recognition of beings" (Rosmini,

1998, 101) and, since it is this will that gives rise to the law, we would have a body of law, as more than a few have suggested, which keeps after the events then regulates them after they have occurred several times. *Morality would thereby be only a consequence of acting and never a premise.* The objection can easily be raised that it cannot be otherwise, as various schools have shown. I believe, however, that that principle cannot be made an absolute, as Kant postulates in his famous imperative: "Act in such a way that the will with its maxim, can be universally considered the legislator governing itself". *In bodies of law that* somehow *concern the person, law cannot follow events*, but must precede them. In these cases, when law produces its formulations, the source must be visible, because this cannot be called into question by any event. Leaving aside the fact that the source may be God, out of respect for those who do not believe, we must not ignore the fact that the source "is human beings, there will be the formulations that contain the duties on behalf of human beings" (Rosmini, 1998, 104) and not even these can depend on the caprices of the moment or subjective advantage. As far as respect for those who do not believe is concerned, it should be said that if the source "were to" be God, it would be appropriate to recall that "believing in the divine existence is something basically moral (…) where the absolute being must be recognized and venerated what he has done in his own image" (Rosmini, 1998, 106 and 108) otherwise, one falls back into pure abstractism, which is that of recognizing generic humanity and not respecting it, then, in its concreteness.

5.16 In the light of what has been said, it is obvious that, without universal moral principles, only a formal morality is left, one that has been called "a rudiment of morality" (Rosmini, 1998, 110). This morality will only be measurable in its *historicist reason* and, as such, can never be allowed to err. Absoluteness, almost as if it were divinized, will be felt. At this point, an example might be useful: let us use Kant's considerations concerning duels. The German philosopher lists some events for which the death penalty is just and ultimately dwells on two in particular. "In both cases -- he maintains -- the sense of honour is the guide". Among these is "military honour", considered a duty insofar as there is no law that can "eliminate the stain from suspicion of cowardice on the forehead of a subordinate officer who does not use personal force, capable of facing the fear of death, against an offence" (Kant, 1968B, 458).

5.17 Rosmini has a totally different opinion. For him "the private duel (...) undertaken (...) upon private authority to settle some controversy is opposed to the office itself of conserving life" (Rosmini, 1998, 132). The reference to "private office" is interesting. It already implies the impossibility of doing justice since "an innocent party is exposed to the danger of dying or to mutilation no less than the guilty one" (Rosmini, 1998, 133). In other words, who can provide the assurance that satisfaction is obtained by the one who is right and not the strongest one? It is hardly necessary to recall that the law should protect the weakest, since the strongest profess to protect themselves on their own. Furthermore, "if this way of obtaining revenge takes root among people (...) how could the concept of virtue not be falsified? And would not manners turn to barbarity, society to anarchy, virtue to vice, when vengeance for one's own offences had become a duty, and criminal daring -- fortitude?" (Rosmini, 1998, 133). One of the cornerstones of political power would be lost due to weakness. As in some episodes out of the Far West, this power would be obliged to accept the fact that individuals can create their own justice where it is unable to intervene. This would be a step backwards, not forwards, in juridical civilization.

5.18 Only those who believe that there are reasons above and beyond law can understand rejecting the thirst for revenge. "History offers us [various] examples, the fact that generous, strong, decent human beings rise above the offence received, not paying any heed to it" (Rosmini, 1998, 133), practicing what the Latins called *clementia*. Only those, Cato Uticensis, for example, clearly show this. They know that "the duty of conserving for oneself earthly life is not an absolute one. It is relative, and conditioned by the moral end to which moral life is devoted" (Rosmini, 1998, 133-4). In other words, as long as there are those who are willing to sacrifice themselves for liberty, everyone will be able to say that they are capable of benefitting from it.

5.19 The person is the property. Emphasis on the "is" is not a mistake. Here, it is not denied that property may have excesses of its own, and as such reprehensible and to be combated, but it must still be recalled that "the word *property*, which Forcellini – a famous latinist – traces to *prope*, indicates the connection of a thing and a person. In a broad sense property means 'all that people have joined to themselves as part of themselves, as something of theirs' (...) Rosmini places the formal principle of all bodies of law in personal liberty; in property the principle of the determination of these" (Pagani, 141-2, n.132). If this is the origin of the right to property, the moral obligations are clear, and the same is true for the juridical ones. This explains why, where the public domain or the common good are involved, that law *can be revised* or, in any case, *limited*, but never opposed solely due to ideological prejudices. It is thus understandable why, "when Proudhon passes the judgment that: *La propriété c'est le vol*, the word rebels and protests against the idea, since *theft* assumes *property*, and so the very formulation of the system contains the confutation thereof" (Pagani, 143, n.132). The fact remains, however, that, *a balanced discussion of property, must* in any case *take into account that* "1st, the dominion can never have the same person as its object, since the person's dignity would be lost with the servitude (…) 2nd that dominion which has as its object the *person's deeds* must be moderated by respect for that person, so that his or her natural rights are not harmed, either because of the excessive burden or the nature of the service, especially that of his or her own moral perfection" (Rosmini, 1998, 144-5).

5.20 Having reached this point, *a definition of the common good* becomes necessary. A concept should be defined and circumscribed to keep it from becoming too abstract. This is all the more necessary when one speaks of good. Indeed, the common good poses even great restraints than good in general, because it involves everyone. Furthermore, if the common good is political, it certainly needs to be defined, since it cannot be a general or utopian good. No politician can promise the *land of plenty*, when he or she knows from the start that it can never be accomplished. In politics, to speak of common good means returning to the logic of the urgency of problems to be solved and the resources available. Thus, it is preferable to speak of a *possible common good* at a particular moment in history. It must also be kept in mind that a good of that nature may be subject to limitations imposed by events. One can think of a town, which presents a budget but subsequently finds itself facing a flood. Consequently it must divert some resources that had been set forth for other purposes. That *possible common good* has thus taken on a new dimension. This means that the common good must be considered with great realism, and the utopian visions that caused all that we have seen in the previous century must be rejected. That does not mean that the common good cannot draw inspiration from grand designs and noble goals, but, in politics, these must have a close relationship with the facts, if dramatic frustrations are to be avoided.

5.21 Let us return to human action, asking ourselves what comes from. Does it come about from a desire to have certain dreams come true? Do human beings always act according to their inclinations? Or else, is it that imaginary, or, more simply, convenient ends come into play, that lead one to act one way rather than in another. How many people, when confronted by the momentous choice of their life's work, really choose what they would like to do? How many others feel discouraged when carrying on the activity to which they think they are attracted? How many others yet pursue chimera, which they are not up to obtaining, and are thus deluded? Finally, how many people betray their ideal in order to enter a profession, already set up for them and which they do not feel match their talents, but which makes life easier and, not a negligible consideration, provides earnings? The problem, then, of the goal of the action is one of the most difficult problems to unravel and resolve. There is often a veil between the action and the end, which clouds the viewing of the ends and often distorts them.

5.22 There is another problem that must not be neglected. A certain way of understanding ethics is compromised when it is no longer capable of responding to the vital demands of a society. Or else, and it is not the same thing, when a society moves away from those founding standards that had previously characterized it. The fact remains, however, that, as Putnam would say, "an objectivism deprived of objects is created", a danger which ethics, like mathematics, seem not to be able to escape. Aside from the fact, however, that human beings are not numbers, if the change were only a process of adaptation to different moral principles, that explanation might be sufficient. Yet, the fact remains that it should explain to us why, in some societies, at times, that change also means a crisis of the values upon which that society had been based. In other words: *Is the crisis that of the values themselves or the result of those values having been set aside?* Like Dewey, we cannot have a blind faith in progress, but must be optimistic strategists. Vico himself taught us that crises exist, they cannot be ignored and the reasons for them must be found.

5.23 Ethics, in Putnam's perspective, make up a sort of collective noun, which refers to problems, situations, conflicts, etc., as Wittgenstein would say, a "jumble". Like all jumbles, they cannot always give way to a living mix. At times, they can lead to an amorphous and shapeless mix, devoid of any vitality. This means that every mix, and the ethical one cannot escape this logic, must keep in mind some limits in order to survive. To be sure, the fact that we accept the position of the "mix", gives ethics a multiplicity of positions, which, in their way, claim to be objective. The real problem is that, instead of bringing out the particular characteristics of each ethical perspective within the mix, one seeks to confer objectivity only on one rather than another, through philosophy. Kant had already attempted this. Basically, his need was that of formulating an ethical theory departing from a view based on "universal moral rules". Even his attempt to see applicable moral law, thanks to what he calls "natural intelligence", is to be seen in this perspective. "Judgment is a particular talent, which cannot be taught but just exercised. When judgment is the specific component of the so-called *natural intelligence* (*Mutterwitzes*), for which defect no school can compensate" (Kant, 1968A, 184). Did Aristotle not say the same of certain virtues such as courage? Certainly, how can one acquire courage if he is not a born Alexander the Great? Does that not, however, lead to resignation or fatalism before a Nature to which one cannot react, but just submit? Let us resign ourselves to having men or supermen, basically one is born a hero and does not become one!

5.24 I maintain that one of the most arduous takes of philosophy consists in finding a way to uphold truth remaining within the coordinates of fallibilism without falling back into scepticism (cf. Putnam, 16). In the light of what has been said, is it still possible to state "that all attempts to reduce ethics to a theory of being" (Putnam, 23-24) has failed miserably? ...certainly, if we have a vague and poorly defined idea of being. If however, by being, we mean, as an entire tradition dictates, the other, the person, it becomes a highly different matter. In this case, indeed, attention is not directed to "the Kantian principle as an abstract rule, but on the particular other person she is trying to help" (Putnam, 27). It is the person (the being) who is before me and whom I cannot avoid in any way.

5.25 If one does not speak of the person, the risk arises of describing the world rooted in a "vague" metaphysical plan or, of giving up, as Kant did, "the traditional plan of ontology", ultimately basing oneself on a theory which exalts the power of the mind (cf. Putnam, 24), with the consequences that history has shown us. Furthermore, there is the risk of giving life to which is assumed to precede "metaphysics, but which (as Hegel already saw) is riddled with metaphysics through and through" (Putnam, 24), here, too, with the risks that it entails. The foremost one is that of creating a terrible parody of metaphysics whose foundations, that is ends, become nebulous and hazardous.

5.26 "But there is another, perhaps looser, notion of meaning made famous by Wittgenstein, in which to ask for the meaning of a word is to ask how it is used" (Putnam, 41). The same can be said for life. Using words in a certain way rather than in another, means giving different senses and meanings not only to our language, hence, to our thought, but also to our actions, to our entire living. Accepting a plurality of meanings can thus be at the heart of pluralism. I say that it can be at the heart of pluralism because if pluralism is to continue to exist, it requires a minimum of concrete, if not verbal, and common references. It is only in this light that Putnam's conclusion becomes acceptable according to whom "conceptual relativity implies pluralism" (Putnam, 49) whereas the opposite does not apply. Without that minimum of concrete, common references the risk is that of agreement only with an abstract pluralism. For example, after a reading of certain of Stalin's considerations, however rhetorical they might be, it would be possible to suppose that one was living in a liberal State. If language does not respond to life there is no sense in speaking of use of words. Ultimately, it means speaking of pluralism, abstract pluralism, and sending dissenters to gulags or concentration camps. True pluralism is not just respect for ideas or words, many of which I can even criticize, but of the people who convey them. I can even not share and oppose certain ideas, such as the death penalty for example, but I must respect, and certainly not kill, a person who expresses this idea. This is true pluralism and also true tolerance, which we often confuse with a mere acceptance or acquiescence in all and everything, when considering it abstractly.

5.27 "If ethical statements are, as I urge, forms of reflection that are as fully governed by norms of truth and validity as any other form of cognitive activity (…)" I furthermore maintain that "the notions of truth and validity are internal to practical reasoning itself" (Putnam, 72). These are true statements, but it should be added that the various forms of cognitive activity involve different fields and, therefore, may have different premises and conclusions. In other words, speaking of scientific truths or ethical ones cannot always complement one another, indeed, those truths can come into conflict or cancel each other out. This is the real problem of the Galileo trial, which most people are not aware of, and which led the scientist to distinguish moral truths from scientific ones then considered, the latter, mere suppositions by Bellarmino. Another, obvious point must be recalled concerning this proper distinction: the object of interest of moral and scientific "truths" is not always the same. Although it is true that the interest "of ethics range from the statement of very abstract principles, such as principles of human rights, to the solution of situated and highly specific practical problems" (Putnam, 73), nonetheless, it remains true that the point of reference is still human behaviour. This aspect is not to be underestimated since it *involves a certain way of understanding the person* who is either responsible for or the victim of that act.

5.28 I say "a certain way of understanding" because the moral premises are not always as clear to everyone as Kant would wish, and, when they are, it is often only *a posteriori*, when it has, at times, become useless to have them clear. The Kantian moral position, upon close look, would imply the need for a social contract, which implies the advisability of being guided by principles, which everyone can totally share. As everyone knows, however, and a minimum of knowledge of history suffices to verify it, the human being is not always a fully intelligent person prior to his or her entry into society (cf. Putnam, 101). Here, Putnam is truly right in saying, when referring to Dewey, that the reasons behind ethical behaviour are not to be understood in a non-ethical or pre-ethical, and I would say post-ethical as well, perspective. If such were the case, every society, or more simply, every community, would be created on democratic premises, capable of accepting criticism, offering the same opportunities to everyone, etc. whereas all that is the outcome of a slow conquest which, most often, must be protected from the ever-present dangers of involution.

5.29 Some might still object that the moral premises, which Kant speaks of, are only part of some individuals who, the supporters of a technocratic view, designate the experts. Perhaps the realization is lacking that they tend to bring back a sort of masked Platonism to Kantianism. The experts are necessary is some specific areas, and, in any case to be checked periodically. They are highly dangerous in the moral sphere, as not a few of the recent theories pertaining to the ethical State have amply shown, especially when they succeed in gaining the support of a rigorous apparatus of coercion. Not only in the moral sphere, but also in all practical activities in general, the first premise should be that of dialogue and thus of persuasion using legitimate means and recognized as such by everyone.

Ch. VI. The Person

6.1 A speech on person can, at times, seem illusory. History has shown that the uniqueness of the person are not sufficient grounds for his or her rights to be defended and protected. There is no form of government that can leave us absolutely secure. Institutions must equip themselves with specific and independent bodies, as Rosmini had already understood, that can defend those rights from the despotism, which some particular forms of government can lapse into, but from which democracies are not immune, either. The fact of acquiring control bodies independent from politics, frees us once and for all from the absurdity of leaving the determination of those rights up to the State, in a position, which we could call typically Hegelian (cf. Armellini, 49 and 53). In other words, the person, in this perspective, does not have rights conferred by some superior entity, even the State: the person is an existing right. The rights of the person are, according to Rosmini, even "1st (…) prior to and independent of civil society; 2nd civil society can neither destroy nor reduce any of these rights". In this perspective, the concept of government must be the opposite of that of supremacy (cf. Armellini, 57-58). Only thus can rights be continually enhanced because they find their basis before confronting the contingencies of the worldliness of politics.

6.2 Away from this perspective, the ultimate result is that either of attributing to the subject, in himself or herself variable and contingent, the caprice of modifying the rules for their own convenience and advantage, or else the time and contingencies of subjectivity are attributed to objectivity. In other words, one falls back into utilitarianism or Kantianism: two sides of the same coin. However, this means confusing the inalienable rights of the person as such, with those that have been acquired. The latter are relative in a juridical sense, though, since their expansion and consistency depend on space and times (cf. Armellini, 66-67). To understand what has been said, it is sufficient to reflect on a fact of no minor importance. The liberal position of the first half of the nineteenth century tended to protect liberty and property as closely interconnected. Although Rosmini, too, defends property and considers it a form of expression of liberty, he maintains that those who do not have external and real property have, nonetheless, their own personal property, which constitutes the basis of their liberty (cf. Armellini, 70). For this very reason, everyone feels in himself or herself that the need for justice is something innate.

6.3 Indeed, as has been rightly said, "the production of positive law does not eliminate the need for continual and vigilant thematization of the prepositive nature of law, normally qualified by the expression *natural law*" (D'Agostino, 14). It is certainly no accident that in not a few cultures, it has always been maintained that positive law was incapable of fulfilling all the needs of justice. There was, in other words, unwritten law, according to some not *yet* written, to which one felt the need to refer in any case. This reference, which is a reference to reason, explains why much of enlightenment thought was based on the doctrine of natural law. This is why we can "maintain that personal *dignity*, or, if we wish, personal *identity* are inherent to every sing human being" (cf. D'Agostino, 22 and 32). Certain rights are "innate" to the person so that, paraphrasing Rosmini, we could say that the person is *subsisting right*.

6.4 Spaemann reminds us that according to some, we cannot speak of persons "if, from the start, they are denied admission to the community of recognition through which humans become persons". In other words, persons are something different, "they are individuals in an incomparable sense" (Spaemann, 10-11) and, because of their being "incomparable" *they can never lose their characteristic of being persons*. No one can every say of them: "Anyone who does not derive joy from teachings, does not deserve to be a human being", as a famous line in Mozart's *Magic Flute* says. The expression in itself is quite enigmatic because "a human being can merit or lose his or her quality of being human. However, to be able to do so, he or she must already be a human being" (Spaemann, 15-16). Let us take a moment to examine this last statement: A human being can merit or lose his or her fact of being a human. …merit or lose before whom or according to whom? It is clear that this consideration shows us that the concept of person is always relative to another, and, more often, to others. Humans, in other words, need recognition in order to be what they are. The word person tells us this. The *Person*, mask, or character, gave the performer who played the role, that role and differentiated it from the generic character of the personages. It made him or her live, because it wanted to live as the famous play *Six Characters in Search of an Author* by Pirandello reminds us. Once such recognition is granted, it cannot be taken away. This recognition is inalienable.

6.5 The person manifests more than that: he or she – as I said in the previous chapter – is also one who desires, who yearns for something. "Thus, desire is a necessary but not sufficient desire for satisfaction, because desire refers to one not identical to itself for satisfaction. That means that satisfaction thereof is contingent. The living being is must be assisted. He or she is basically in need" (Spaemann, 53). In need of understanding, in need of the understanding of others, in need of love. Even those who cannot explain it cannot gain satisfaction from the love of themselves: *this is the drama of selfishness*. Another love, practically a "disposable love" is needed, a gratuitous love or one of a gratuitous gesture, in which one feels the need to place confidence. This, too, is an authentic personal act. Indeed, how many of our interior actions require this trust? When we hear someone say that he or she is in pain, if we are inclined to believe the person, we must trust him or her. "Indeed, a direct perception of the pain of others does not exist" (Spaemann, 57). This applies to many other feelings, among which is anxiety. Pain, anxiety, but also hatred or, on the contrary, pleasure, joy, love: the description provided by a brain scan is not enough to make them perceptible in their most deeply hidden essence. This is further proof that a person is something more than a mere representation.

6.6 This state of incompleteness is obviously a metaphysical need. There is no exterior good that can totally placate our desire, our need of something else. This obvious state of mind is what really makes us have something in common with every other person. At this point the words of Spaemann are effective: "The personality is constituted through giving up considering the other as a simulation or a dream, hence, as something which is essentially for me, without my being for it at the same time" (Spaemann, 88). It is the realization and the something in common of this state of need, which builds solidarity among people. To be sure, it must be recognized that all this has an objectivity which is difficult to recognize as such because it does not yet manage to overcome one of the basic prejudices of modernity, a prejudice according to which *something becomes more objective the less it becomes subjective*. Yet, there is no lack of examples of what, to many, appears to be a paradox. One can think of moral responsibility, which "requires the relieving of universal responsibility" (Spaemann, 109). I would not like to play with words: there is no doubt that responsibility subsists above all where there is subjectivity – the person who becomes responsible – Yet, the person feels the sense of responsibility because that is objectively considered. Is it not this objectivity that provides the sense of guilt? I certainly know that at times it is not so. Awareness of guilt or the objectivity of it can also come from an objectivity that is not recognized: I am thinking of that which the saints consider sin and which a great majority of people believe, or can believe, to be normal. In this case the responsibility felt comes from the fact that for those who feel it, the criterion of objectivity becomes another and is made concrete deep down inside the conscience where no one can enter.

6.7 In the light of what we have said, let us examine the following statement: the "specificity lies in the fact that the person disposes of his or her life. For this very reason the person can also *lose it*" (Spaemann, 125). Some thought must be devoted to that *lose it*. A life can be lost in various ways. It is indeed the diversity of ways that differentiates people. Once again we find ourselves in the strange relationship between subjectivity and objectivity. However, *lose it* can also be an expression for someone who cannot conceive of the sense of sacrifice of another. In this case, the "lose" in the eyes of some, can mean giving or offering in the eyes of others. In the eyes of the former, these lives are called devoid of significance because, among other things, they ultimately disappear from the memories of most and, then, appear to be without consequences. This is certainly not an exhaustive way of considering life. It is like watching it on a screen during a Fluor graph or an ultrasound scan. Whoever can say how many of those so-called hidden lives have influenced the forming or achievement of other lives? Each of us has moments, episodes or encounters, for the most part unperceived, in our lives that have significantly marked their existence.

6.8 Why is the memory of certain moments lost? Why, on the contrary, does evidence of a contradiction remain for a long time? It would be easy, and for some, just as well, to answer that evil causes more excitement than good. This conviction is even easier to accept, since it gains consensus among pessimists, who say that true good does not exist whereas we are continually besieged by evil. I want, however, to lose myself in that saying of Boethius, quoted and commented on for centuries, which says *bonum ex integra causa, malum ex quocumque defectu*. To explain it in a few words, we must say that any sort of failing suffices to give rise to evil, good, on the contrary, cannot give up its integrity. Let us frankly say that it is a statement that frightens us and that we are inclined to look about ourselves with some perplexity. The normality that we experience in life seems to be that of the *malum ex quocumque defectu*. We are doubtful about those who have experiences of *bonum ex integra causa*. We consider them out of this world. We do not want to admit that one can live, allowing moral actions, or actions in general, not to be determined solely by present and immediate causes. We are upset that there are those, who want to appeal to reasons that are not those of everyday life. This is not a way of thinking of today however. Allowing ourselves to be guided by other reasons has always given rise to "scandal". In times of work, ordinary reason rightly suggests a way of saving one's own life, then those who reach the point of sacrificing it by taking the place of another is shocking. A Father Kolbe, *bonum ex integra causa*, goes beyond the reasons of everyday life to appeal to a good that does not seem solely an immediate one. This case is not so isolated. I also think of Salvo D'Acquisto, but we tend to forget it, since it tends to take us our of our selfishness.

6.9 The relationship between the person and his or her past experiences can be understood in this light. "Only when human beings cease to identify immediately with their life experiences, do they become *identical to themselves*; only when they cease to be pure living beings, do their souls attain their internal unity, the unity of my life's experiences, *of my soul*" (Spaemann, 170). It is this internal unity that creates the uniqueness and unrepeatable nature of the person. This conviction, expressed in all that tradition of thought which, from Saint Augustine on, has characterized an entire, specific current mistakenly called existentialistic. The mistake is due to a certain, individualistic current which has done all it could to confuse the individual with the person. "Persons, as opposed to individuals, are never part of a totality which covers everything, but every person is, himself or herself, an entirety which embraces all (…) Being a person is occupying a place, which does not exist without a space in which other persons possess their own" (Spaemann, 184 and 193). Thus, the place is their own, and unique. In other words, the person is in himself or herself an irreplaceable entity, whereas the individual is always replaceable because of the role he or she occupies in the simple social environment. Furthermore, establishing relationships as persons means that each one has a unique place and, for this reason, too, is in need of the respect of others, whereas as individuals they can easily be added. There are a great many examples. Recognizing others as persons means, *in primis*, ceasing to impose on them, since they possess our same rights.

Ch. VII. Responsibility

7.1 Paraphrasing Jonas, it could be said that the sense of responsibility is created in awareness of duality: "life is essentially a nature relational with something" (Jonas, 1994, 20) it would be better to say, first, with someone. Wishing to stop and dwell on something for a moment, more on something than on someone, it must be said that, in any case, the reality with which we come into contact – "earth, wind, water" – is "totally different from a paradigm of the *mera materia*" (Jonas, 1994, 25). It comes to mind, and we rarely reflect on the idea, that the concept of matter, so vaguely present, escapes us, almost as if it was a metaphysical conflict. Matter is, indeed, a too vague reference if referring to the three terms just mentioned: "earth, wind, water" (just imagine if we wanted to relate it to the bodies of animals, etc.). Let us return, however, to the question of relationality with someone. That person, as we ourselves, manifests himself or herself in temporality, which also underscores his or her transitory nature. The end of that person or those with whom one places himself or herself in relation led to "faith in a life after death (…). The cult of the dead and faith in immortality (…) are the constant confrontation of the point of view of life with death, a confrontation which can also turn against the same point of view defended and ultimately demolish it" (Jonas, 1994, 27). Perhaps the problem of faith in life after death, opens up other terms of a new, possible relation, however: that with Him, who sustains and guarantees that faith (this a subject treated by all religions, those, too, who express themselves, as in Kant, in the realm of reason alone). I do not attend to embark upon that subject. What I wish to bring out is that, even this relation, based on faith, rests on the problem of responsibility, because it rests on the awareness of a duality. It sets forth obligations and, hopefully, mutual guarantees.

7.2 The finiteness of temporality makes life so exception that, if we wish to be objective, "newness is the rule in the physical being, whereas life is the enigmatic exception" (Jonas, 1994, 28). We rarely reflect on a conclusion that is, in itself, so obvious. If we did so, we would have greater respect for life in all its meanings. Yet, such is the case. The fact that non-life is the rule in the physical being, has, over time, led to respect for non-life. *Pietas* towards the death, even of enemies, is evidence of this. The exceptionality of life, vis-à-vis the normality of death, ultimately gives rise to a series of questions about existence that are no less important than those created by its contrary. Hence, "one no longer asks how death came into the world, in one without life, but rather life" (Jonas, 1994, 29). The reasons behind the origin of life, or at least the search for them, have also led to reflections on life's ultimate aim. The theory of evolution seems to have given the coup de grâce to all that: "with its combination of chance variation and natural selection" (Jonas, 1994, 83) and it seems to have driven out the "theology of Nature" for good. The "end" now seems to have become superfluous or, at least, Jonas advises us, it has retired "totally into subjectivity". This is a very interesting consideration. Indeed, no one can think that every single subject wants to, and can, pursue his or her own end without taking account of the others, at least one other. The end always seeks a relation and, within this, objectivity, for the very reason that it expresses itself within a relation, and once again re-presents the problem of responsibility.

7.3 I would also like to dwell on "material" life, which, as I discussed in a previous work (cf. Pezzimenti, 1999), which always produces a "moment of evolution" within a system seeking a dynamic balance. That system always produces a *limit* beyond which life either degenerates or introduces a process of involution. *This limit exists in moral life, too, obviously of a totally different sort.* It is provided by the other to, whom one places oneself in relation. It is the *person* who places the limit on acting of our person. *The other is as necessary for our liberty as much as for our responsibility.* It is not a dialectical relationship, with all due respect for those who still believe this, because the various and possible manifestations of liberty are anything but necessary or made necessary, otherwise, there would be no sense in speaking of responsibility. Not only that, *doing* manifests a considerable range of possibilities in the area of liberty, but also *omitting*, with its inescapable responsibility, appears to be a choice of liberty.

7.4 Let us, however, return to what is one of the most often recurring statements from the current culture: that of the definitive crisis of a teleological vision or, more specifically, of the lack of meaning. If such were the case, however, we should stop speaking of responsibility since, for any form of behaviour to be deemed in conformity, it requires the presence of one or more purposes. These can be individual or social, but it is on the basis of them that we judge ourselves and are judged. No one can fail to know that *responsibility is measured in relation to an end* and to the consequences that it manages to bring about. This problem comes from afar. Moral action has always led to the sense of responsibility and it was this that led to judging the action itself. It was such in the classical and medieval world, but also in much of the modern world. In the latter, however, another possibility of judging moral action has gained ground: the viewpoint of success. Something of this sort is typical of a precise philosophical approach, which, albeit criticized by many, dominates human relations nowadays and *tends to cancel out that limit to action, which is represented by the person* with whom we find ourselves face to face. This sets of the drama that leads to our considering the human being with whom we are face to face no longer a subject but an object to make use of. The overall result of acting as it develops from the viewpoint of success thus changes the elements for evaluation.

7.5 I have spoken of individual or social goals that orient single or group actions, but if there is a multiplicity of goals, a scale of greater or lesser goods will be set up wittingly or unwittingly or, if one prefers, less important and necessary one. In this case there is always a *quid* in the inevitable discussions of ethics, which escapes the description of everyday matters and which implies, in our argumentations, a metaphysical approach. This is oriented by a choice of values, which we cannot avoid, even if it can be changed, as conversions demonstrate. I am not unaware, to be sure, that this metaphysical approach, called a spiritual question by many, is considered by others are sort of "epiphenomenon of matter, without its own causality" (Jonas, 1994, 229). At this point, however, I consider it important to point out that when a good to be attained is identified, a private one or one for the community, this cannot but be judged in terms of universality, even if individuals represent it in concrete as well as diverse and various forms. In this, we are somewhat like the primitives who represented images in their grottos. "the primitive hunter did not draw this or that buffalo, but *the* buffalo: every possible buffalo was evoked, anticipated, remembered" (Jonas, 1994, 288).

7.6 Let us return to the fact that every metaphysical approach is oriented by a choice of values: once this premise is accepted, it becomes difficult to argue, as some people do, that it is possible to create a science leaving aside values and that these must not be the object of scientific analysis. Basically, *rejecting them is already a choice* of values. This problem is that this choice refers to something other than science, but closely connected with it. It is often said that this choice of values can harm science, but no adequate thought is devoted to the fact that *science, too, can harm values*. This concern is indisputable in an ethical context that aims only at success. Yet, to accept this latter approach we must be certain that exasperation of the success ethic is truly capable of creating justice and reaching that goal by means of justice itself. Who, however, can perform such an act of faith?

7.7 It has been said that the limit of moral life is identified in the other, in the person whom we have concretely before us day after day in our life's spaces. In the past, this vital space had precise spatial connotations. The urban, if not, actually rural environment, in which one circulated delimited it. To be sure, it has not always been so. The crisis, especially the cultural one that passed through the ancient world when the political dimension of the *urbe* was mixing with that of the *orbe*. In a similar inter-human situation that "mix" of ethics, which seems now to have come back into fashion was established. Now, however, the context has become more dramatic. "No ethic of the past had to take into account the overall condition of human life and the far-distant future, if not the survival, of the species" (Jonas, 2003, 28). We are responsible towards those who we realize are on earth that we can see at home, that we hear laugh, cry, and fall into despair. Furthermore, we are responsible towards those who do not yet exist, because we know as never before that our actions are changing that world that we inherited from the past generations and that we should leave equally liveable on behalf of those who will come after us. The person, understood as a limit, is thus a concept which is spreading and the rights of the person, the need of which is being felt more and more universally, are extending to objects as well as to subjects, nature, in one word, which people need in order to live.

7.8 Thanks to the progress of science, some irresponsible people could even put the future of humanity in jeopardy. Jonas peremptorily summarizes this dramatic situation. "The individual right to commit suicide is subject to discussion, but not the right of humanity to commit suicide" (Jonas, 2003, 80). In his opinion human existence cannot be a gamble. One can rightly say, paraphrasing Pascal, that one can only bet on the *great beyond*, the *here and now* needs certainties and not wagers. A bet can be placed on the great beyond (a subject to which I shall return), because faith "cannot be placed on order" (Jonas, 2003, 94) hence, a bet becomes a tool in the dispute among duellers, that is, between believers and non-believers. In this world there is the obligation to think of others in the present and of those who will come in future, others, who constitutes not only an obligation but also a limit to my action. This cannot be directed by scientific knowledge alone, to blame science for reaching inhumane conclusions, but must also be guided by moral choices based on respect for the person. Let us not forget that *science is a way of explaining* and discovering, *but it leaves the responsibility for acting up to our sensitivity*. Some have maintained that science is, in itself, a-evaluative, but that does not mean that it is not up to us to confer value on our knowledge. On can think for example, of the choices, many of which cannot be put off, concerning the human habitat and its future. Which are the choices, with the values that accompany them, compatible with that and which are not?

7.9 Let us confront a problem, for a moment that is only apparently distinct from responsibility. In a statement of a certain importance, Searle maintains that our mind "is not so much an aspect of our life, but in a sense, it is our life". This statement is directed towards those who have attempted to reduce our conscience to a trifle, considering it nothing other than one aspect of our lives, when, obviously, "biologically speaking, it is just one aspect, but as far as our actual life experiences are concerned, consciousness is the very essence of our meaningful existence" (Searle, 2004, 10 and 158). From this premise it is easy to understand why Searle goes far beyond the analysis of language *strictu sensu* and no longer considers the philosophy of language exhaustive. He actually attempts to work out a "philosophy of the mind". The implication of this reflection are indeed far-reaching and lead him, for example, to refuse to "consider artificial intelligence as a second mind, more or less perfect in comparison to the first, or a surrogate of mental activity", assuming a "position in favour of the central place of mankind" and arriving at the conclusion that "a comparison can never be made between human beings and artificial intelligence" (Pititto, 115-116).

7.10 It is not just this sort of dualism that is opposed in Searle's thought, but dualism in general, in other words, that of Cartesian derivation which has deeply engaged the minds of not a few thinkers. On this subject, there are peremptory statements aimed at eliminating even the possibility of imaging that we live in several, diverse worlds, or, as it seems to some, in two: "a mental world and a physical world, a scientific world and a world of common sense. Rather, there is just one world; it is the world we all live in, and we need to account for how we exist as a part of it" (Searle, 2004, 304). Now, the task is to understand the relationship of words, strictly tied to our mental world, with the world we have before us. "Searle points out that more than an action, speaking is a social activity and, in particular, an activity of human beings, and this proceeds following certain rules" (Pititto, 117). In other words, "speaking is a rule-governed form of behavior". That explains why "speaking a language is engaging in a (highly complex) rule-governed form of behavior" (Searle, 1990, 17 and 12). This, in my opinion, means discovering, basically, *the moral value of language*. It is moral in its strictly etymological sense, that is, acquiring mentality, culture, traditions, customs, in other words, *mores maiorum*. This is what Ennio himself said. He could say that he had three souls because he spoke three languages (cf. Pezzimenti, 2011A, 1.2). Hence, "talking is performing acts according to rules" (Searle, 1990, 22).

7.11 This awareness of the moral value of language also implies a responsibility. Speaking, obviously with meaning, is always addressing oneself to someone, to a listener who can be judged as such only if made to understand what he or she is being told. The meaning inherent in our intentions must be revealed to this person. If such is the case, it can be maintained that "the semantic structure of a language may be regarded as a conventional realization of a series of sets of underlying constitutive rules" (Searle, 1990, 37), but it is certainly not enough. Can we really maintain that language completely expresses the rules of existence to the point of ignoring what can be called the tacit agreement? How can one forget pre-linguistic traditions? For example, English common law, but also legislation, refers to texts written in Latin, which, in turn, refer to traditions and "linguistic acts" certainly assimilated and no longer translated. Thus, it is not a question of having left "unresolved a series of problems such as the relationships between language and perception, between language and knowledge, as well as between language and society" (Pititto, 122), but also between language and the past, more or less remote and aware, which, in any case makes itself present even when there is not total awareness? No one can deny that all that is ultimately important in life and cannot be neglected by a philosophy of the mind, which intends to recognize the centrality of the subject. There is a tacit mutual relation of intentionality, latent perhaps, but surely not negligible. It all contributes to making human beings what they are in actual fact and helps us to answer the crucial question of Searle which, basically, is ultimately a question of considerable moral content: "Who are we, and how do we fit into the rest of the world? How does the human reality relate to the rest of reality? One special form of this question is: What does it mean to be human?" (Searle, 2004, 11).

7.12 Overcoming dualism, and not just Cartesian, means realizing that all realities, more or less tacitly accepted, are unified in our minds, whether or not we are aware of this. This is why we can in fact be responsible for each of our actions. As with language, we can say that each of our responsible actions has its intentionality, whether intrinsic or derived. Thus, it is unlikely that human intelligence can be manipulated, as can happen with even the most refined of machines, since human language is never defined as programming may be at a given moment. Indeed, "it is a typically human activity, that can never be formalized in its entirety, insofar as it is a reflection of thought, arising and developing as a product of the social reality, and reflected in that" (Pititto, 126).

7.13 Speaking, stating things in one way rather than another, has its effect in life. *Language, in fact, is not only the distinctive character of philosophy, but of existence.* This is perhaps why Wittgenstein thought that the meaning of a word or a statement always depended on how it was used, even if we must ask ourselves what we mean by use and what 'use' consists of. On this subject, I think it is useful to go back to Vico who pointed out that whoever (peoples, civilisations, individuals) lose their own language, end up losing their own habits and customs. Perhaps for the few, like he himself, the statement to the effect that "philosophers have a strong intuition that the concepts of truth and meaning are inextricably linked" (Dummett, 2006, 39) is appropriate. For him, too, as for Wittgenstein from the opening lines of the *Tractatus,* the facts are closely connected to the truth of the language that relates and transmits them. It is then obvious that the real problem becomes that of verifying or at least to have confidence in what has been told.

7.14 Concerning the problem of responsibility, there is another problem that we must not overlook. It has been said that moral action is based on three components: *motivation, choice* and *realization.* "Motivation is what gives action its impulse, that is, the reason why one acts; the choice is the act by which a motivation is accepted; the realization or result is the concrete taking shape of the action in experience" (Rigobello, 41). All three components are fundamental to an action's being truly free. Moreover, their tie with temporality removes them from that abstraction, which is the temptation that always "courts" moral action. It is this immersion in temporality, which marks the relationship between subjectivity and objectivity, but it is always temporality, which confers felicity, discomfort or uncertainty on action, depending on the cases. This is why every action "implies finding a meaning, understanding the meaning" (Rigobello, 81). That means the true liberty seeks first of all to "give a meaning". It has been noted by many, Rigobello among them (cf. 48), that choice is an act of liberty that coincides with it only for an instant. When choice is a determination already decided, choice and liberty oppose one another, because, after the choice has been made, in some cases one is no longer free.

7.15 It is clear that the choice must be ongoing like the motivation, the motivation being inspired by will: liberty is a continual wishing. Liberty is continually sustained by the choice. If such were not the case, Sartre would be right in supposing, terribly, that we could by rigged by nature: "*Ça serait terribile, se dit-il, on serait truqués par nature*" (Sartre, 1976, 219). Certainly, in order to be morally free, which is quite different from being politically or socially free we should have a "pure" conscience capable of sorting out the most noble of motivations and, as a result, the freest of choices. It is the extreme result of evidence that leads to the rejection of all that, linked to time, can harm the freedom of our inner life. Otherwise, why die for liberty, if we can no longer exercise it once we are dead? That "*liberty is seeking, what is so precious, as the person who rejects life for her knows*", it is the greatest song to true liberty, willing to cut itself completely off from temporality and all that ties us to it.

7.16 Now it is understandable why, as Bergson says, there are individuals who "as for nothing and yet obtain. They have no need to exhort; they only need to exist: their existence is an attraction. That indeed is the character of this other morality. While natural obligation is pressure or urging, in complete and perfect morality there is an attraction" (Bergson, 30). Armed with their convictions, those persons are capable of waiting, and it will certainly not be by chance that "genius is has called a long period of patience". To be sure, that patience is often of a heroic nature, a bit like that Augustinian *amor Dei*, forgetting of oneself, which almost seems a love to be disposed of. Moreover "the truth is that one must pass through heroism in order to arrive at love. Heroism, furthermore, cannot be preached, it has only to show itself, and its mere presence can set other people in motion" (Bergson, 42 and 51). It is a bit like the lines of Dante just quoted. Only as long as there are subjects prepared to incarnate them, will we be able to say that we have a truly free society. *Rationality is fundamental to morality, but it is not enough by itself.* A rationality which claims to create all moral obligations by itself leads, sooner or later, to constrictions and criteria of force that have nothing to do with morality properly understood, that based on free, personal responsibility. For this reason, I will never be a Kantian.

Ch. VIII. Pluralism, the Ethics of Conflict and the Right to the Truth

8.1 As far as pluralism is concerned, it must immediately be said that it is not just a problem of rights, although this problem remains a necessary point of departure. However obvious it may seem to say it, pluralism itself must be reformulated. It is all too often considered only formal or, worse yet, abstract. By abstract pluralism, as I have already said it point 5.23, I mean formality in ideas, many of which can also be criticized, but not the people who express them. In many of these cases, one ultimately speaks so much of pluralism and, at the same time, dissent is sent to the gulags or concentration camps. True pluralism, on the contrary, is that which allows me not to share and even to fight certain ideas, for example the death penalty, but which obliges me to respect those who convey these ideas.

8.2 Concrete pluralism forces us to reinterpret the handling of conflict itself, which can be an inexhaustible source of improvement, when it talks place in a legal context. This means arriving at the development of actual *ethics of conflict*, which, understood in these terms, can become a genuine *social value*. Developing the ethics of conflict, where no legal system can be considered complete and definitive, ensures the possibility of change, with respect for the plurality of opinions and, above all, the plurality of persons that maintain them. All of this means that no one must ever be obliged to abandon the legitimacy of the cause on behalf of which he or she is fighting, unless it cancels or jeopardizes the convictions of others. Only this way are the minorities respected and the majority is constantly led to believe that its position is not total but also *the result* of the need to be obliged to take decisions. This aspect is at the heart of politics.

8.3 It must also be said that it is the ethics of a continuous confrontation that keeps alive the possibility for that *conversion* whose importance is not only religious, but also social, and tends to cause us to be more mature and to delve more deeply into matters. Some might think that this is a ridiculous, because of being continuous and frantic, race for novelties that have little to do with the sorting out of one's own convictions. Such people should, however, remember the true meaning of conversion. "Conversion also means persevering in a moral decision taken some time earlier, persevering in a dimension that always has the character of the *beginning*, hence, what is new in relation to the natural *continuum*" (Spaemann, 228). This is a right that everyone has. In this context, each person must claim the right not to be deceived by another. This, too, is another right in the relationship among persons that cannot be eliminated – a consideration that allows us to return to what was said in points 1.43 to 1.49 and to reach a conclusion: *There is no juridical sense, properly understood, that can protect false promises*. Indeed, law can make it obligatory to keep the promises properly formulated. Forgetting a promise does not invalidate the obligation to keep it. It should not have been forgotten. A right is not extinguished if its possessor does not remember it. When we make a promise, we give up a part of ourselves, and we grant others a right to a portion of ourselves (cf. Spaemann, 239). If such were not the case, no community, or human consortium, could survive. Not only would the carrying out of the promises fail to be guaranteed, but also the liberty to make them and, with this, one of the finest aspects of liberty: *generosity*.

8.4 At this point, there is no need to repeat that the value of the person, as anyone can intuit, is a concrete value. This is why, "respect for the personality of others is the true basis of ethical life. This absolutely does not reduce morality to pure legal schematism, but shows the exacting and profound value of all political, social and economic activity". This statement shows how impossible it is to formulate a discussion with the intention of emphasizing the role of the individual in society and, obviously, vice versa. Indeed, it is, "impossible to establish an ideal form of behaviour for the individual, without establishing and ideal form of society at the same time (Geymonat, X-XI)". This also explains the extremely close connection between politics and morality, despite all the considerations against it that have been offered. One also understands why, favouring, or worse yet, carrying to the extreme the role of the individual or of society involves, in any case, injustices which "utopian" forms of socialisms as well as liberalism can fall prey to.

8.5 The incongruence in utopian socialism, that which is called "real" in other words, are obvious to everyone, but a certain liberalism, which I would call "anarchical", must look closely at its own. Liberalism promises equal liberties for all. However, "as everyone knows, limitation of the practice of activities and development of the human personality comes not from the terms indicated by that postulate, but the economic class divisions and antagonism between society and society" (Juvalta, 33). I used this quotation, somewhat extreme for some, to point out that civil society, even in the liberal perspective, requires a positive role in dictating a set of rules and in its ability to reinforce them (cf. Pezzimenti, 2004). A balance between individuals and societies must be found, naturally one, which I like to call dynamic, otherwise, there is no escaping a basic contradiction, which makes it impossible to speak of the ethics of conflict. Indeed, no one cannot fail to know, "that if it is not legitimate (…) that individuals consider themselves as ends and society as a means, it is not legitimate either that society, for the mere reason that it is a society, sets itself forth as the end, and individuals, or many or some individuals, as a means" (Juvalta, 37). Let it be understood: that it is not limiting rights of individuals to increase those of society disproportionately, but to see to it that all individuals can have certain rights, at times, that cover the few.

Ch. IX. Tolerance

9.1 Let us depart from a consideration, not at all original and which I will come back to shortly, of Barrington Moore according to whom the cases of unhappiness and suffering are different, to come to the point of maintaining that society must provide incentives for "human beings to find forms of happiness in their lives' designs *in their own way*, as long as their quest does not cause others to suffer" (Veca, 1997, 101). How can the suffering of others be assessed, however? Is it measurable, perhaps? Does it not also depend on the sensitivity and expectations of each person? Curiously enough, the utilitarians make a similar mistake. They "believe that they can have a uniform scale of measures of utility and happiness" (Veca, 1997, 103). In other words, to solve the problems of suffering, must we not ask *to what degree* are you suffering, but *why* you are suffering? The why transfers the interest of the suffering individual to the suffering person. As I have had occasion to say, the distinction is not only a question of terms. Speaking of individuals one can only speak of "deficits in the supplying of social goods" (Veca, 1997, 105), if one also wants to speak of the person, this deficit is insufficient if, first, those who find themselves in that condition, are not aware of such a deficit and of the urgency of eliminating it.

9.2 Does having a clear idea of "urgency", to attain happiness as well, not bring us back to the never resolved question of what meaning we want to give to our lives? Wittgenstein, often erroneously classified among the post moderns, on

December 8, 1914, wrote as follows in his *Secret Diaries*: "Certainly Christianity is the sole *sure* way to happiness. What happens, then, if that type of happiness is rejected?! Would it not be better sadly to drift in the hopeless struggle against the outside world? However, such a life has no meaning. (…) why not lead a meaningless life, then? Is it unworthy? (…) What must I do so that my life will not be wasted? I must always be conscious of the spirit – always be conscious of it" (Wittgenstein, 1991, 50).

9.3 Therefore, it is not always acceptable for rights not to be "other than *resources* that ensure the stability of recognition over time" (Veca, 1997, 111) if not also the result of a conscience that has acquired it, and so, of a culture which shows that it is always conscious of it. Culture is not to be understood in vague and general terms. Indeed, without wishing to perturb those who believe that *"le savoir est et sera produit pour être vendu"* (Lyotard, 14), the fact remains that knowledge and intelligence have enormous significance in the practical sphere. They go so far as to differentiate between one who knows and one who does not know, hence, among one who possesses and one who does not possess (cf. Lo Giudice, 51). Since "application of the thesis on socially avoidable suffering" (Veca, 1997, 117) is referred to, it would be appropriate to speak of well-being or uneasiness. These terms can be more easily measured or assessed, because they refer to criteria of a social nature or to *Welfare* models. Not only that, *but speaking of well-being or uneasiness* surely makes it easier to put into practice that consent by intersection that characterizes the *"public good* fundamental for a democratic society and its stability in the long term" (Veca, 1997, 167) which can be called a veritable value of civil living together. The latter is possible when society emphasizes *cooperation over time* based on the ideal of *reciprocity*. These are certainties, others may call them values, which give stability to the social body and guarantee liberty, which can bee seen as the possibility of casting doubt, as long as "something must be removed from doubt in order that one may doubt" (Veca, 1997, 168).

9.4 From this comes that "common sense of law" which is based, as Veca says, on reasonableness, what Vico called *iuris prudentia*, an area in which *consensus* operates, and this leads to mutual respect based on common foundations as well as the constant chance to improve certain rules. In other words, *iuris prudentia* does not legalize life in its totality, which would mean the end of all creativity and innovation, but lays out the rules to make it possible to harmonize stability and change, tradition and need for originality. In conclusion, *iuris prudentia* brings out a set of political values without which it is impossible to co-exist with others. *Iuris prudentia*, still, gives rise to one of the fundamental political values: tolerance. Without this *prudentia* itself, which is the basis, is nullified. *Tolerance* is, in fact, nullified when face to face with intolerance, when prudence suggests to us that an attitude, which is not reciprocated makes no sense and, indeed, cancels out the criterion *of reciprocity* on which living together, based on equal rules for all, is based. Only in this case, to paraphrase Popper, could we say that violence can be used only to demolish a violent system that does not accept tolerance.

9.5 According to some, what has been said requires a distinction: the "judgement on the political order is separate from the judgement on a good and holy life (...) Here, the usual model, which is based on the distinction between a good life and a just life must be complicated to say the least" (Veca, 1997, 203). There must be agreement on the meaning of the term separate, which cannot be seen merely in Crocian terms. There is no doubt that, in any society, the criterion of the good conditions every other value of civil life, constitutes the *a priori* logic of it which no civil context can be without.

9.6 In this light, it can be seen that tolerance can also meet the criterion of good, so that it can be said that this "must be interpreted as a value in itself in the pluralistic area of what is worthy". Thus, it is a value in itself as *all* are capable of experiencing in a certain cultural dimension. It is appropriate to emphasize that *all*, meaning that we all have a requisite in common which enables us to understand why tolerance implies common premises, despite many differences and after many difficulties. As Berlin perceptively maintained, "if we were different in every important aspect, we could not understand what is meant by trying to live a life moulded on values which are not ours" (Veca, 1997, 217). It is what we have in common that makes possible *sharing*: a true "resource in order to face challenges, threats, and risks coming from significant uncertainty" (Veca, 1997, 295), which call tolerance itself into question. If, as Hume maintained, it is true that any pleasure languishes if not savoured in company, it is equally true that even passions, in total solitude, can become a punishment. Ambition, pride, avarice, etc. what sense would they have, even selfish, if there were not others to aim them at? (cf. Hume, 363).

9.7 In a curious observation, Williams claims that death cannot necessarily be an evil, because a life without an end could even fail to have any meaning. That should mean that a finite life indeed has a meaning: what we are not capable of gradually giving it. Is it really true, however, that all finite lives are capable of giving themselves a purpose? If they are not, do they have the same dignity as those that indeed succeed in giving themselves a meaning? Moreover, if the meaning was not that recognized by the majority? The theme of suffering is ready to flood us with questions and avoiding them does not eliminate the problem. Philosophical reassurance cannot do so, either. Even Veca is forced to admit this. "Philosophy does not and cannot appease the anxiety of the being before death, of the *Dasein* of which we consist, in the language of Heidegger" (Veca, 1997, 354). It is not sufficient to say that all of this obliges us to meditate. One must be honest in meditating. From Saint Augustine to Descartes, albeit in different ways, meditation served to *overcome doubt*. Nowadays, from too many thinkers, meditate means *wrap oneself up in doubt*. At times they do not at all want to free themselves from it.

Ch. X. The Sense of Limits and Faith in Society

> "We must take care not to trust humans too much but more careful not to be too trusting"
> (Tommaseo).

10.1 We have said that each person must claim the right not to be deceived by another. Every person has this right and one, which cannot be eliminated in a relationship among persons. There is indeed no properly understood juridical meaning that can defend false promises. It all comes from a sense of limit, which constitutes one of the crucial achievements of our civilization. For this reason, it has been properly observed that "only a culture which accepts a sense of limit and the distinction among areas and claims of validity, is more likely to achieve unstable and temporary balances, among the beliefs as to how the world is made up" (Veca, 2005, 9). This sense of a limit is extended, here too, to the moral sphere and constitutes a guarantee of pluralism. Plurality of cultures is the only chance to enable effective application of human rights "moving from evil rather than from good". This means that while the idea of good can divide us, that of evil, and aversion to it can unite us more easily. Not a few have criticized this approach of Veca, which I, on the contrary, believe is worthy of careful consideration. Departing from a well-known saying of Terence, *nihil humanum a me alienum*, Veca invites us to consider the "saying" in its entirety. "The area of the *nihil humanum* is, indeed and unfortunately, more inclusive"

(Veca, 2005, 18), there is also evil in this whether it is understood as *privatio boni* or considered an anti-value, which aims at the destruction of good and goods.

10.2 In this "more inclusive" form of the human it is possible to arrive at the "common victims of humanity and executioners. To do evil out of love for evil" (Veca, 2005, 19), as, in different forms, Poe or Baudelaire maintained. Perhaps I shall shock some people, but I believe that the real drama of the human adventure and its culture lies here, as well of that which has taken place and continues to do so in the religious and Christian perspective. The pages of Saint Augustine on the fascination of evil and inability of humans to escape it should be reread more carefully and courageously. For the Fathers of the Church, sex, theft and other things aroused strong interior emotions and it was difficult if not impossible to escape them. It is true that he prayed, but he was "afraid to be cured immediately". In actual fact, "he preferred to satiate rather than extinguish" evil. Then, he asked himself why, as all of us should do. The honest reply came: since "a passion is produced by perverse will, obedience to the passion leads to habit, acquiescence in the habit gives rise to necessity" (Augustinus, 1975, VIII, 7,17 and 5,10). How can we come out of this? Paradoxically, a sense of limit was the answer here, too. Evil is produced by an almost unbeatable love: the self-love, which sweeps us along, but never satisfies us, as with love in general. However *amor sui* slides ever so slowly into pure selfishness, which it never attains, and leads us to ignore each other. Here is the reason for the turning point: to discover the other, whether God or our neighbour, as the limit to our selfishness. *It is certainly not a political solution*, with the meaning we give to this today, *but it could be a premise for it*. Here, the priority is that of a limit not to exceed in order not to settle down into evil.

10.3 It should be added: not concerning ourselves with the sense of a limit in fact leads to give legitimacy to violence, not to be confused with force. "While force can be called an *activity-against*, it possesses a *measure*, which allows it be legitimately used in accordance with justice to oppose the blindness of violence" (D'Agostino, 36). It is no accident that the force of law or legality of force is spoken of, because a law that cannot be enforced, or one devoid of the force of coercion, is nonsense.

10.4 I just said that the solution is not a political one, not because politics are inadequate in seeking the reasons for evil, or because they are incapable of doing so, but because a single solution may not suffice, speaking in human terms. Veca indirectly admits this, quoting Todorov. "Evil is not something accidently added to the history of humanity, and it could easily be eliminated: it is tied to our very identity; to eliminate it, it would be necessary to change the species" (Veca, 2005, 15). Since this is impossible, present-day philosophy offers us various chances/proposals. Let us take one of these: "We shall say that it consists in the offering *i*) of reasons which justify given beliefs or ones alternative to those (which are assumed to be such) give and *ii*) in the constitution or in production, *via* corroborated or altered beliefs, of sharing communities" (Veca, 2005, 82-83). Accepting the philosophical offers contributes to creating the collective identity. However, philosophical offers so understood lead, at least for point *i*, to serious perplexity typical not only of political philosophy, but of law itself. Indeed, the offering, as with legislative activity, seems *to come after the events* and, somehow, *justify them*. Is this the only task of political philosophy and law? However, beyond justifying given beliefs or ones alternative to those, philosophy and law should also regulate and anticipate, in order to avoid, some possible deviations. Here, though, another question arises and presents not a few difficulties: anticipating or regulating is tantamount to holding firmly onto some premises of the philosophical contribution and they cannot be bartered in any way. Bartering them could mean also losing the chance to make philosophical contributions of a certain type.

10.5 For further proof of what has been said, I depart from another of Veca's considerations: "The domain of values is where they are fragmented and that of their persistent metamorphosis, an intrinsically pluralistic space, in the drastically anti-platonic sense supported by Berlin on many occasions" (Veca, 2005, 29). However, Berlin seems to mean that this intrinsically pluralistic space exists where there is a tradition that sustains and justifies it. Suffice it to think that when Berlin seeks to redefine liberty, by reformulating classical elements taken up by Constant and Mill, he does so in the wake of Vico and Montesquieu, hence, in the wake of a tradition that certainly cannot be called an "odd geographical notion" (cf. Veca, 2005, 69-71). The differences, in history as in life, are not the result of odd notions or caprices. The same must be said of the "costs". If, "no liberty is free of charge" and if its cost is, depending on the case, different, it is because it has a different history behind it. In other words, it is often the diversity of the tradition that leads to the diversity in costs. So, let us ask ourselves: *why* has a genuine pluralism developed within a tradition, of which, fortunately, we are a part, and not in others?

10.6 Upon close look, it is a certain tradition, that of the culture of the limit, that has developed the mutual faith, which chases away fear. Can being perennially "guided by the heuristics of fear" really give rise to a better world or can it create a sort of neurosis capable, over time, of becoming chronic illnesses of our nature? As the twentieth century has amply shown there are also the ethics of hope, even in the perspective of centuries, which attempt to place themselves outside of the immediate to avoid that ethical void to which fear would carry us. We are inclined to fill this void, as long as we do not experience dramatic shocks, with whatever we find, especially when we do not have a full awareness of our tradition and our values. Only then, Berlin would say, could we discover that, in this perspective, there does not exist "so much the fact that we choose certain values, as the fact that it is characteristic of our values that they are plural and exemplify ultimate goals, independently of our choices" (Veca, 2005, 153). To be sure, we must not stop here if we wish honestly to be philosophers. We should return to wondering why, as opposed to other "geographical oddities" we have the fortune to experience this plural liberty, more generally called pluralism, which generates social confidence without which it would be impossible to live, without causing suffering. One of the causes of suffering and the evil that this leads to "is the violence committed by human beings on human beings (…); in its relational structure – dialogic – the evil by one finds its replica in the evil undergone by the other" (Ricoeur, 16). It is the dramatic evidence of history, which is attenuated only after true social trust sets in.

10.7 To be sure, speaking of social confidence, it may be difficult to come to an understanding. Despite all his efforts to cure evil starting from its deepest roots, Freud, too, maintained that it was impossible to contest Hobbes' observation *homo homini lupus*, given the wide variety of experiences in life and history. If such were the case, however, how could we maintain that human beings "construct themselves from the mutual, demanding relationships with others"? Does not their innate sociality perhaps reveal, as many have implied, that a root of good subsists in their intrinsic nature? It is perhaps here that that empathy so appropriately emphasized by Edith Stein comes out: "the original act that places us in relation to otherness, that makes us enter the realm of others' experiences, without any identification, keeping the identity with which we were constituted". This means that only in an authentic, interpersonal relationship, does one acquire his or her must truthful personal reality (cf. Pititto, 2005A, 33 and 71). If, though, one seeks to dominate in this relationship, one risks ending up not only in slavery (cf. Stein, 145-146), but lapses into a sense of bewilderment which gives rise to fear above all. It is the sense of domination that makes us visualize the other as an enemy more than as a part of otherness. So the reflections of Ferrero once again become relevant.

10.8 A free choice must be established that subverts a certain way of understanding human relationships and that controls that sense of suspicion that drives us always to see others as enemies. It is not a matter of being unprepared, but of understanding that relationships based on the logic of fear and so, "of evil, are always ones of conflict and separation, when they are not ones of violence". In this perspective "only mistakenly can humans believe that they are asserting themselves, because in actual fact, they always come out defeated" (Pititto, 2005, 72). Not a few have wanted to see, in those who want this new type of human relationship, a sort of Mr Godot who awaits a regenerated humanity. Here is where the error lies: this new humanity must not be awaited. It must *seek* and seek by constructing it. Otherwise, why have there apparently been ages better than others, if not because there have been people more determined than others to carry on this quest? Outside of this questioning there is only what, for some people, is the universal and Hobbsian pessimism that cannot be eliminated. *Seeking* implies a commitment, typical of people of faith and hope and not dominated by curiosity and suspicion. In others seek as did Abraham, not Ulysses. Lévinas was already saying this and indeed led some interpreters to speak of *nomadic truth* (cf. Petrosino- Rolland).

10.9 By way of conclusion, I wish to add for the sceptics that refusing to believe in "social confidence" is the equivalent to being belied by reality at every moment. Every day, everyone appeals to this feeling. Our actions are continually entrusted to strangers in whom we place our faith. "Social confidence" is an *inescapable premise for civil life* without which everything hurtles towards madness. I bring into this trust what has been called the value of moral directive wisdom, "as specific quality of the practical intellect" (cf. Quintas, 126 ff.). This is encountered in many rôles, fundamental in the daily lives of each of us, whose functions we continually make use of.

Ch. XI. Intelligence and its Development

11.1 That the problems concerning culture in general and, more specifically, intelligence, are truly critical and apparent to everyone, above all, in today's world is no surprise to anyone. Who can fail to know that knowledge is the source of wealth, prestige and independence, hence liberty? Most often, "Not knowing" implies not possessing (cf. point 5.56). This means that an effective improvement cannot be achieved without a rigorous analysis of the problem of intelligence and those factors, which aid or else hinder development of it.

11.2 From the body of thought developed on the subject, I prefer to return to Rosmini's, starting from the distinction between *the speculative reasoning of individuals* and the *practical reason of the masses*. These two types of rationality are distinct from one another. It is useful, however, to recall that reason expresses itself in an overall human dimension because, among other things, it is ontologically based. Two different faculties in this reason must be distinguished: that of thinking and that of abstraction. With the former, real entities are selected, the order in which they must come and their ultimate goals; with the latter, ideas, the relationships among them, are formulated and, above all, the means by which to achieve the ends. When the relationship between the two faculties breaks down the *harmonisation of the intelligence*, which always consists in *bringing the abstract back to the concrete* fails. Human reason is thereby satisfied and asserts its presence, as well, as the principle capable of organizing political society. If, on the contrary, the faculty of abstraction is lost in the irregular multiplication of needs, a great many of which can be called "artificial", intellectual forces are concentrated solely in the faculty of abstraction and they come to predominate over that of thought. Reason ends up losing its indepence, becoming reduced to the level of pure and simple sensations. A process of degeneration thereby begins, as Vico would say. The "quantity of intelligence" is reduced and so the creative capacity of a society. What counts the most is that a process of that sort almost leads to a loss of vital energy which brings about a disarticulation of the society, a slow breaking up which even reaches the point of gradually decomposing it (cf. D'Addio, 1972, 32-33).

11.3 In the light of what has been said, it is clear that the practical reason of the masses "is a sort of *social instinct* which suggests immediately usable goods to the masses and fall within the area of the common one: in this case it has a positive effect on society" (D'Addio, 2000, 74-75). The real problem is that this "instinct of the masses" is easily inclined to become corrupt since individuals are driven, as indeed happens with all instincts, selfishly to favour some private benefits at the expense of the common good. This means going back to privileging the accidental to the detriment of the substantial to the point of giving rise to those disrupting elements that lead to the crisis of the civil context and institutions. Therefore, the speculative reason of individuals must be brought to bear. It constitutes "the basis of politics on a rational level" and can bring about a rebirth of institutions and society, albeit among highly noteworthy difficulties. This is what had already happened in the ancient world: "Rosmini's conviction is that one of the historical merits of Christianity is that of having regenerated speculative reason – characteristic of individuals – after the crisis of the ancient world" (D'Addio, 2000, 75). In a certain sense, it can be said that governments who seek to avoid the dissolution of the social body have a true "mission" to perform since they protect the very essence of civil life represented by the unity of the social body. "The society which we qualify as political or that of the state is characterized by a unity of decision and command, the unity of power and the force applied over a determined territory and the continual converging of activities of a large number of individuals to achieve a common goal" (D'Addio, 2000, 79). The identification and achievement of the goal once again bears witness to the fact that politics, for Rosmini, is activity, hence dynamism ensured by an order which cannot, in any case, be static, but which converges on the goal to be achieved. When ensures movement is the *spirit,* which is certainly not to be understood as idealism had done. "Spirit, to conclude, is the intelligent and rational subject: its activity, made possible by the presence in it of the extremely general idea of being, which presides over the intellective perception of things, begins with reflection, thanks to which *it produces* new ideas and performs all the other intellectual operations which enable it to attain more profound knowledge" (D'Addio, 2000, 81). In other words, it is an activity, which we could call eminently social with reflexes and perspectives of gnoseological dimensions. This comes back to showing that *the development of society is also the development of intelligence* and vice versa.

11.4 Important conclusions come out of what has been said. Since society is created by people to for the purpose of carrying out specific goals, this is the result of the people themselves who operate in view of the aforementioned goals within a system of relations expressed in laws and institutions. Society is thus an artificial entity and cannot have its own, autonomous *raison d'être* nor can it be the foundation of the morality of those associated, as some think, as Rousseau would like (cf. Rosmini, 1972, 67 ff.). Furthermore society, as we view it, is the expression of a process of interiorization. What appears is created by the interiority of those associated. "The relationship between external and internal society must be kept in mind if we are to understand the dynamics of the society: according to Rosmini's argument, the great political and social transformations develop in the invisible society, in the souls of those associated, to manifest itself and then be carried out in the invisible society" (D'Addio, 2000, 91). Thus, politics cannot but be concerned with interior problems. Satisfaction of the citizens is a problem that must concern governments, perhaps before any other. Since the accomplishment of its end cannot be irrelevant to any society, the contentment of human souls cannot be a problem the concerns individuals and nothing else. Governments must not only refrain from placing obstacles before all those who seek to achieve their own true well-being, but they must make it possible for everyone to pursue what he or she considers useful to their own satisfaction, in a legally and morally positive way. So, it must also be said that governments encounter quite precise limits in their functioning. Since individuals make up the society, they have reserved the right autonomously to adopt the ways of achieving their ends with total independence and liberty. This means rejecting all those conceptions, in many ways utopian and unjust, that claim the omnipotence of society over individuals and minorities. This is a modern form of despotism, which, moreover, makes use of a legality considered legitimate (cf. D'Addio, 2000, 93-94).

11.5 It is obvious that in this approach Rosmini opposes all those theories, which, albeit claiming to put into effect democratic systems, as did Rousseau himself, end up, in actual fact, eliminating the most basic forms of liberty. Liberty, on the contrary is the "highest subjective good of humanity", the origin of every activity of the person. "And liberty, for Rosmini, means freedom of conscience, religious freedom, freedom of thought, freedom of opinion, of discussion and so recognition of a plurality of orientations" (D'Addio, 2000, 96). Out of this come the parties, which contribute to the ongoing debate. Parties can also be an expression of the negative side of political life, and everything must be done to reduce their number, but, in any case, they convey interests and opinions that justify political action.

11.6 How can the imminent end of a society be determined? It "is determined by the practical reason of the masses and the speculative reason of individuals, who, at times, move forward in agreement, at other times, find themselves in conflict: the end is always the result of the two opposing forces" (D'Addio, 2000, 105). It is a vital relationship, which, as Vico would say, leads to the civilizing of humanity. With their practical rationality and the conflicts that this causes in social life, the masses bring about the imminent end of the society, which changes according to the ages, which mark the various phases of development of the society itself. It is within those phases that the stimulation and opportunities are to be found, which enable human intelligence to grow and exercise its faculties. The problem is that this practical reason of the mass is inclined to lose strength and to become corrupted. This happens when it is stimulated solely by pleasant sensations because, in this case it "is the expression of a minimum amount of intelligence, practically none at all". This is the age in which the "unrestrained craving for pleasures" predominates. Everything is aimed at the immediate, the determined, and reason, following the passions almost idly, ultimately becomes sterile, thereby becoming inoperative. The force of the intellect diminishes and also the cognitive capacity. Intelligence becomes the tool to refine the quest of pleasures more and more. This result is that of losing one's own independence, and the passions of the masses are exasperated, to the point of paroxysm. Intelligence is no longer directed towards social activities and ends up withdrawing into its own selfishness (cf. D'Addio, 2000, 109). Although religion itself is the only means capable of recovering objectives thereby regenerating social life, risks being overcome if it does not cling to its genuine values and does not place them in their proper dimension, which is meta-temporal, and meta-political. Only this way, even if indirectly, can it have an effective influence in society.

11.7 In a highly opportune way, Rosmini makes a distinction between satisfaction, a pleasant state and happiness. He reminds us that "the latter is the essence of mere sensitivity, the former and the third are joined to intelligence, since a judgement by which we recognize that we are satisfied or happy is necessary. Satisfaction is a satisfying state, whereas happiness corresponds to perfect satisfaction, great enough to put an end to any possible desire" (D'Addio, 2000, 115). That the aforementioned problems have an interior nature and are in a close relationship with intelligence is proven by the fact that lack of satisfaction and unhappiness, only in intelligent beings, can lead to suicide. This does not take place in beings devoid of intelligence and so is not in the essence "of the animals or of the savage". It is on this interiority that liberty is based and this leads Rosmini to be highly critical of all those egalitarian and levelling conceptions that do not manage to understand that well-being itself, understood as the sum total of goods available to a society, is determined by the free activity of individuals, by their capacity, their expectations and their choices: "this *position* favourable to the individual is the work as part of fortune, that is, of the complex of circumstances not depending on human beings; part of the virtue and industry of individuals themselves. It can never be the work of the government" (Rosmini, 1972, 382). The government's only task is not to hinder free activities of individuals and to favour the development of their capacities.

11.8 A widespread opinion held by the theoreticians of utilitarianism was that only leaps forward would occur in societies. It was as if they had inherited an abstract Enlightenment optimism. They consider any pressure exerted on the social body useful. This idea is all the riskier since it induces governments to think that the increase in not-satisfied needs itself drives individuals and society to act in the proper direction to satisfy them. That can lead to the uncontrolled multiplication of artificial needs without any limit (cf. D'Addio, 2000, 126-127). The problem of needs produces social and political repercussions of extremely great importance because of the imbalances that can result. Here, too, there is reason for regret: even during the so-called period of decolonisation, people did not draw on the surprising reflection of Rosmini to suggest a possible solution to the many problems arising from development processes often chaotic but certainly confused. Returning to some analyses of Tocqueville, Rosmini believes that "having suggested to Indians the needs of a society far further evolved had the opposite effect of what had been foreseen by the theoreticians of creating incentives for and acceleration of economic development: the measures did not give rise to new working or intellectual energies, but caused the existing ones to disintegrate (...) The industrial economy with its system of needs cannot be put forth as a model to communities and *nations* set up on a tribal and village basis with a subsistence economy" (D'Addio, 2000, 129).

11.9 In addition to risks of disintegration of the social fabric, a policy based solely on utilitarian criteria is dangerous for single individuals as well because people are inclined to confuse feelings of pleasure with happiness, which, in this case, cannot help but cause the need for abstraction to increase. The outcome can only be that of "going from one passion to another as soon as its effect has worn off: happiness is a fleeting illusion, but we must believe in it however short a time it lasts, in order to renew the expectation, the illusion that once again sparks hope in our hearts" (D'Addio, 2000, 137). That dangerous sophism then comes out, one that claims happiness not only to be fleeting, but impossible to attain unless in the incessant succession of diverse suggestions which transform life into continuous agitation, if they are to be obtained (cf. Rosmini, 1972, 450-454). From that come two different feelings of individuals, both unsatisfying. *On the one hand* one lives with the vague hope of achieving complete satisfaction using means which, given their inconclusive nature, show themselves to be absurd; *on the other,* growing indignation arises, which often turns into anger, as one sees the vapidity of our efforts and the deception that they lead to. In other words, improvement of material life does not, by itself, improve the quality of life and generalized dissatisfaction accompanies discontent, irritation and resentment against everything and everyone. It is useful to recall that "free competition is no expression of the criterion of justice, on the contrary, it is justice which gives it legitimacy and governs it" (D'Addio, 2000, 140). Only thus can the problems concerning satisfaction be placed in their proper dimension.

Ch. XII. Citizenship, Brotherhood, and their Corollaries:
liberty, dignity, equality, justice, solidarity

12.1 There are not a few and I, too consider myself one of them, who consider democracy an "uncompleted" project. This conception is easy to verity if one observes close-up the progressive expansion of a value such as that of citizenship, with all the corollaries associated with it. Over time, there has been an attempt to minimize "suffering and cruelty". On the contrary, one has sought to maximize "the respect for and protection of rights, the creation of equitable life opportunities for women and men". This requires "keeping up *loyalty* to a group of values or ends in themselves, liberty, dignity, equality, justice, solidarity" (cf. Veca, 2008, 12-13). Perhaps the term corollary is not the proper one. The fact remains, however, that values such as *liberty*, *dignity*, *equality*, *justice*, *solidarity* not only come within the others examined thus far, such as that of the person, which is implied in all of them, but also mark the concrete development of citizenship to the point that they cannot do without this.

12.2 I would add the value of *association*, closely connected with citizenship. As Tocqueville recalls, "after the freedom to act on one's own, the most natural idea of human beings is that of combining their efforts with their peers and act in common. The right of association thus seems to me almost as inalienable as individual liberty" (quoted from Veca, 2008, 33). Above and beyond being a right, that of association, it is a true value, at the heart of all civil life, as we are reminded by a long series of reflections the arrive at the unsociable sociability of Kant and depart, as I pointed out in another work of the ancient *concordia discors* of the Latin peoples (cf. Pezzimenti, 2011A, 2.25). It should be forgotten, either, that the value of association makes possible the realization of another value: that of pluralism. I used the term realization because there is the risk of carrying on abstract discussions of certain values such as pluralism. In order to overcome this dangerous abstraction, and in addition to what has already been said (cf. point 5.23 and Ch. 8), I must underscore what Veca said, and that is: the concreteness of pluralism is not only measured by what comes of it, but by the fact of its being considered a *precondition* for civil life (cf. Veca, 2008, 40). To accomplish it, the sense of a *limit* must be strongly developed for everyone, and for the institutions as well (cf. Ch. 10).

12.3 In addition to a sense of a limit, the institutions must maintain a degree of neutrality with respect to some interests to enable each one to carve out its own destiny. All of that seems to give rise to "a first version of citizenship", which I would call of an exclusively liberal character (cf. Veca, 25 and 34). This position, while not cancelled, has been adequately corrected, as Veca also sees by the socialist perspective. I believe, however, that such a view is somewhat limiting because it not only ignores the contribution of modern and contemporary Christian thought, but also democratic thought, even if not always socialist. In this perspective I feel I can acknowledge that citizenship is a complex, which has received a contribution from a diversity of ideal points of view. Basically, the same can be said for liberty (cf. Berlin). All of this has helped give rise to "a right or group of rights to non-interference. The premises are based on the idea that the existence of preferences, desires, purposes and individual interests – whatever they may be – is a question of value". Hence the need to protect these "preference spaces" from violations and interference (cf. Veca, 65, see also Dahrendorf).

12.4 That of "non-interference" is certainly not easy to carry out because it implies a continual revision of what we can call a demarcation line between action by the authority, even if acknowledge, and that of individuals. It is in this perspective that some people (cf. Veca, 101) have wanted to rediscover the political and civil feeling of fraternity, understood, however, to be "as the solidarity of citizenship". Fraternity, which has quite definite Christian roots, however, (cf. Baggio, 2007B, 36 ff.), is something quite different and can indeed be called a fundamental and independent political category (cf. Baggio, 2005A, 45 ff.). Only if this important distinction is made, is it possible to understand why certain values are the result of a complex to which various ideal points of view have contributed. Fraternity, for example, has strong Christian roots, which prevent if from being confused with other values, however respectable they may be (cf. Baggio, 2007A, 9). Seen in its particular nature, fraternity constitutes a fundamental element because "it guarantees the survival and quality of a political society, which operates through its diversities" (cf. Baggio, 2007A, 15 in footnote). It follows that fraternity is forgotten in every situation, where the path of terror rather than that of living as a community is taken. This is what happened in France.

12.5 Fraternity and citizenship seem to be two entities capable of sustaining one another because, if the *latter* in fact implies equality, the *former likewise* tends to enhance diversities, which guarantee actual mutual respect. Real equality of treatment is essential for effective citizenship. "*Equality* does not imply having *same expectations*, but that all be recognized as being in possession of fundamental and inalienable expectations. Many of those expectations may, *prima facie,* seem *identical*, but, upon closer inspection they actually seem analogous" (D'Agostino, 33, where the right to good health and a variety of therapies stand out).

12.6 At the heart of what we have said, there is a question: "Who ensures this citizenship?" (Donati, 176). To answer the question, one must identify what type of government is most suited to the various criteria of citizenship. In other words, the classic problem of authority and, above all, what its requirements are arises. "In other words, when a citizen requests rights, her or she must know what obligations are involved" (Donati, 183). Citizenship, legally constituted of course, must be circumscribed in terms of this relationship with authority. "Considered as a whole, citizenship, in fact, loses its character of belonging, its consisting of a structured ensemble of titles" (Donati, 193-194). This takes the concept of citizenship away from those recurrent and dangerous abstractions, which quite often constitution its negation.

12.7 This conclusion brings us back to a reconsideration of Robert Nozick's approach. "Central to the model of the basic of ethics is the concept of value, which manifests itself as a *push* and a *pull*. On the one hand, moral behaviour expresses myself (*push*) and, on the other, depends on the value of the other with whom I compare myself (*pull*)" (Maffettone, 394). In other words, it is a question of viewing ethics in general and citizenship in particular to find the compatibility of my patterns of behaviour with that of the other person or persons. This mutual duty can, according to the perceptive perception of Maffettone, give rise to more than one danger. If uncritical acceptance is involved, there is the risk of "the difficulties associated with ethical relativism", quite a central theme nowadays, when "the subject of multiculturalism" is dealt with. Such a discussion must not allow us to forget the dangers behind certain generalizations. That explains why it is not "at all clear what is understood by moral relativism" (cf. Maffettone, 402). It must also be observed that, to "understand the relevant moral differences, we are in need of a sort of ethical metalanguage which operates, as Davidson says, as a *system of common coordinates*". Otherwise how could we set up international courts – an example, for example, could be the case of genocide in Bosnia and not only that – to judge what has happened in situations different from those being judged? However anyone wishes to answer this, the claim is a criticism of ethical relativism (cf. Maffettone, 404-405) and, in my opinion, confirmation that rights, so-called inalienable ones, exist, which no political and juridical context can cancel with impunity.

12.8 These inalienable rights enable us to keep another danger at bay. Much is said nowadays, in a multi-cultural society, of the need to move from the right to equality to the right to diversity. On the contrary, it can be said that it is "the right to equality that postulates recognition of the identity of each person". So, any integration must be "careful to guarantee the right for one to guarantee the that of maintaining his or her own identity" (cf. Dalla Torre, 10-11). This right to diversity must, however, encounter some limits, obviously set by the juridical order. These limits come from "determined values implicit in the juridical order" itself (cf. Dalla Torre, 11). If such were not the case, the right to diversity could be a factor of disintegration rather than a source of enrichment for individuals and the community. This is a further proof that such inalienable rights constitute a guarantee not only for individuals, but also for civil society itself.

12.9 Some people tend to define these inalienable rights using the term absolute. I certainly do not wish to venture into a matter, which is not solely of a terminological nature. What I wish to consider is one of MacIntyre's convictions, expressed in the *Postscript to the Second Edition* of his justifiably famous *After Virtue: A Study in Moral Theory*. According to the American philosopher, we cannot speak of absolute values in an historicist perspective, because, as Hegel teaches, these are tied to their era and, therefore, cannot be called absolute, but only relative, like the truth that creates them. What I would like to point out is that Hegel and his many-sided school do not exhaust the subject of historicism. There are, in the Italian tradition above all, views of history that have nothing to do with the dialectical conceptions. From this point of view, certain values convey content which becomes increasingly rich so that they become essential for a true civil life.

Ch. XIII. Security and Authority

13.1 The problem of security, closely connected to that of order, has always been felt even though the solutions proposed have been quite different from one another. They range from the order in legality, which found expression in the Latin world, and which was inherited by the Anglo-Saxon world, to the order expressed by the Leviathan and guaranteed by force. Considering then the contemporaneous world, we observe that the problem of security arose for the French revolutionaries in the midst of those uprising that would give rise to the *terror*. Art. 8 of the 1793 Constitution takes care to emphasize the "protection offered by the society to each of its members for the conservation his or her person, rights and property". This conviction has been reformulated by some neoliberals who, speaking of a social market economy referred to "decentralized coordination of economic activities in a framework of general rules". This gave rise to the designation of "ordoliberals" (cf. Felice, 25). This explains why security and order are often seen as almost synonymous and they cannot exist without peace. "Peace, in turn, is the necessary premise for the recognition and effective protection of the rights of man in the individual states and in the international system" (Bobbio, VII). It is clear the security, understood in those terms, requires rules capable of giving expression to serious objectivity, that can be improved in space and time but, in any case, objectivity that guarantees universal, acceptable and accepted points of reference. Too many sectors of post-modern thought call these references into question nowadays. Those "philosophers" ultimately refer to thinkers who have sought to ban objectivity even from philosophical discussions. Such is the case of "Nietzsche (who has been courted for some time by a new left without any sense of direction)" (Bobbio, 103).

13.2 This objectivity is the basis of the most elementary criteria for security. It has been appropriately written that "no reasonable expectation of our acting or our not acting in our relationships with human beings would not be possible, if other laws, *positive laws* (political, social, of custom), did not guarantee us the effects of this acting and abstaining from doing so. This is that certain *order* without which human life is not *feasible*, as physical life would not be feasible if a natural *order were not guaranteed*. Every provision presupposes an order and every order presupposes a law" (Juvalta, 387-388). The law ends up being "a means or condition for an end, which varies between general benefit and individual benefit; to say this in ancient terms, a condition for a time of virtue and happiness" (Juvalta, 392). This balance is fundamental to respect for the dignity of the person, which is the real purpose of security and is based on the certainty of law. Law, says Guicciardini, must never leave – "anything at the judge's discretion – that is in free will – of the judge, so that it never makes him a master free to give and take away" (cf. Pezzimenti, 2011B, 1.16). It is understandable why law presupposes and aims at "an *order* outside of which no reasonable, and moral act as well is possible" (Juvalta, 388).

13.3 Again to paraphrase Guicciardini we could say that lawmakers, on the social level, must above all feel the need to ensure order and security. This possibility becomes concrete especially when two needs, always present in society, are made to converge: that of wanting to change everything and do so immediately and that of not wanting to change anything at all cost. The *former*, left on its own with its revolutionary and utopian excesses, would drag civil life into perennial instability, thereby marking the end of any certainty. The *latter*, with its absurd defence of the past and its unquestioned privileges, would anchor civil society to reactionary models incapable of understanding the changing world. In the former, social equilibrium would become impossible, in the second it would be tied to sclerotic, senseless models that would cut off any reference to the new exigencies of justice. Bringing about change within the rules is what gives everyone the security and tranquillity required so that the rules will not be broken. This is why "political law has a double content and meaning: it is *law-from the legal order* and is *law-order*. Thus, law-order like law from the legal order have as their postulate the state and sovereign will which is the incarnation of authority, and exercises the power thereof (…) the state and the power on the basis of empirical rationalism essentially have the duty of recognizing, sanctioning and enforcing the rights of the person; to prevent and repress any violence against the life, liberty, property of each one and of all" (Juvalta, 398). It is, in other words, authority as the guarantee of liberty and security.

13.4 Security understood in the proper sense brings us back to analyzing the problem of authority, which is denied only in anarchical views, and these, thus far, have never been well received in history. Perhaps no one has summarized this dilemma better than Tocqueville, who came to maintain that there is no room for history in anarchy and the will to supplant legitimate governments only leads to despotism. In this view, authority arises with society itself. "The authority we have discussed thus far, is absolutely the first juridical achievement of human beings, and it proceeded by far the possession of any other right; and because it was created together with human beings, it can be said to be in itself *native* and *inherent*" (Vico, 110). Created together with human beings, *native* to them and *inherent*, are terms of great importance if the meaning of the problem is to be understood. All this means that authority, for Vico, arises even before society itself. Even in solitary life, using their intelligence, human beings exercise a sort of authority over themselves in order to regulate their lives. "The first juridical authority possessed by human beings in solitude may be called *monastic*, or *solitary*". Vico hastens to say that it is a form of authority that a human exercises when in "uninhabited" places, "threatened in his or her person, and unable to have recourse to the law" (Vico 110). There is no need to recall that juridical civilization begins at this point, with the distinction of the juridical meaning of "major peoples" as opposed to "minor peoples". A first reflection on the meaning of justice comes out of this.

13.5 It is obvious, therefore, that the crisis of authority is also the crisis of legality and the meaning of justice related to it. This all means the loss of security, authority and legality is deeply rooted *unless* a new form of authority is established, which broadens or transfers the criterion of legality and creates new forms of security. In these cases a growth "crisis" can take place without dangerous voids in legality arising. This has happened in not a few modern societies, which increased intervention policies in anticipation of possible post-war crises, not only the *Welfare state*, but also new criteria for security. *The Beveridge* Plan, devised in the United Kingdom and passed on to various western countries, is evidence of this.

13.6 The close relationship among authority, security and justice brings us to question ourselves as to the true meaning of the last term. Human beings of every era have questioned themselves about justice, but the present debate can be synthesized by pointing out two different positions. Is justice strictly connected with its time or, in the terms of Rosmini, does it depend on a meta-empirical concept? Accepting the *first* perspective, as much of present-day thought does, means saying the only valid principle is that of the "empirical I and its present things" (Capograssi, 1977, 219); in the light of the *second*, which must also not lose contact with the reality of the present, it is maintained that some rights exist which must be kept away from the momentary authority of lawmakers, even when empirical facts change. Otherwise, how could inalienable rights be spoken of? In other words, if this balance between empirical facts and meta-empirical premises is lost, justice, authority and, above all, security could become solely mere and easily disputable opinions.

Ch. XIV. Work

14.1 Great respect for the person, or as some say, the personality, is certainly not something measurable in merely theoretical terms, but in actual practice. One of the most common ways for individuals to express their personalities is work, which can certainly be universally considered a value.

14.2 No one can doubt that work is a social value. To be sure, this value must constantly be improved. Emerging Christianity made a crucial improvement, bringing it to free people, taking it away from the mere dimension of the hard labour of slaves. That message did not immediately make its way into the social situation. Resistance was overcome in the course of time, and not everywhere, so that the term work, itself, (*labour*), so long replaced by others, such as craftsmanship or art was recovered in the modern world with all its emotional content of fatigue and exploitation rather than creativity. The latter, on the contrary, seemed to be the sole possibility for the personality of the individual to assert him- or herself. Together with property, this theme has be the object of a great deal of discussion, especially in difficult periods of transition, such as during and after the French Revolution. It would perhaps be useful to return to the considerations of Fichte for whom "the right to property does not indicate a static relationship with things", as the aristocratic class would have liked it to be, "but an essentially dynamic relationship" based on the liberty and dignity of human beings. The close connection between property and work, is such that the latter, too, "is part of the activity with which the individual fully realizes his or her personality" (cf. D'Addio, 1992, 119), manages, in other words, to become a property owner.

14.3 At this point, problems of an ethical nature begin to arise for Fichte. He clearly says so: "No person on earth has the right to allow his or her strengths to go unused, and to live off the strength of others" (Fichte, 324). If the world in which we live is the result of our activity, property cannot help being the result of our liberty, and so, of our work (cf. D'Addio, 1992, 120-121). It follows that work becomes the means for guaranteeing an effective participation in the life of the society and a chance to become a property owner. It follows that anyone who does not have a job cannot claim effectively to be free. This needs arises from the inequality existing among various human beings who give life to a society precisely in order to give life to a tie capable of reducing the overly marked differences that can influence a different way of experiencing liberty. *Work* thus begins *the condition, which can ensure a position of equality* among human beings insofar as they are rational and free.

14.4 Concepts such as alienation, given expression by Hegel and further refined by Marx, are now within reach of everyone. *Respect for the activity* follows the no less important and certainly more actual *alienation from the product*: it is not the person who chooses the job, but the job, which chooses the person in the sense that he or she adapts to performing any sort of activity. Human beings thus feel as if they are turned "from an end into a means, from a person to a tool in an impersonal process that subjugates them without any regard for their needs and exigencies" (Abbagnano, 213). As can be read in the *Economic and Philosophical Manuscript of 1844*, they turn into "human commodities". Alienation thereby arises *in their Wesen*, because the process of production ultimately "alienates them (...) from themselves". Not only that, in production "relationships with other human beings [also exist]; and these relationships, in the form they take because of the effect of private property, tend to fall apart thereby cutting human beings off from Nature and other humans, alienating them from their relationships with them" (Abbagnano, 213). Marx was to say: "a human being becomes objective for him- or herself or rather an alienated and inhuman object". A further form of alienation is thereby created, *from one's neighbour*, seen as an antagonist and a rival, when, on the contrary, he or she should be an ally in transforming the society.

14.5 To be sure, the forms of alienation referred to above, at least in the most advanced societies, have been greatly mitigated, even more could be said about the latter, especially from a Christian perspective, which exists in reference to some "vocational" criteria. Furthermore, it is not only for these reasons brought about by alienation that work has known moments of inhumane and demeaning conditions which have led to dramatic splits in the world of workers. One can speak of conflict among ways of understanding work, and, more generally, existence, more than alienation. The splendid pages of Antonio Baggio, on the logic of the workers' movement confirm this (cf. Baggio, 2005A, 172 ff.). Paradoxically, from the French Revolution on, that idea of fraternity, which might have changed human relationships as a whole, has weakened. Although repeatedly proclaimed, fraternity has remained practically a dead letter. This is perhaps because, in view of the anti-religious deviation of the revolution, "it was impossible to manipulate the idea of fraternity beyond a certain point" (Baggio, 2005B, 11). The weakening of fraternity implies a different view of liberty and equality and, in extreme cases, their irreducible conflict. It is not absurd, then, to say that there can be various ways of understanding the famous revolutionary triptych. Furthermore, it should be recalled and has been shown, that it was "the Christians who introduced the principle of the triptych into European culture" (Baggio, 2005B, 12). That explains why fraternity has come to be considered in a reductive light, even among those who have not been unaware of the principle of brotherhood.

Conclusion

14.6 There has always been great debate among those who believe in values to seek a possible means to find roots for these values. There are two main positions, which have opposed each other on this matter. According to the *first* "only through an expansion of the theme of transcendence and careful development of the relationship between conscience and liberty can the theme of values be rooted in an ontological sense that does not immediately construct it outside of human decision and choice" (Thaulero, XXXII). The *second* considers values the result of a precise historical and cultural approach, claiming the strong influence of tradition. As far as I am concerned I see no conflict between the two positions, which can and indeed should complement one another. In this case, with all due caution, we could accept the following statement of Hartmann: "In a certain sense it can be said that philosophical ethics discover values. However, this is rarely a truly first discovery. At most, it is only the retroactive appropriation of what was originally present and effective in the moral conscience" (Hartmann, 1949, Ch. 6°, § a). This position enables us to overcome a problem posed, above all, by relativists: that of the subjectivity of values. "Relativity to the subject" can also not mean "relativity of values" (cf. Hartmann, 1949, Ch. 15°, § b), but it means the subjective way of living and interpreting the values which, often, become separated from the values themselves. Also with Hartmann I believe in the difficult of bringing about a "hierarchical order of values" (Hartmann, 1949, Ch. 64°, § a), even though social values all depend on the value of the person however one wants to organise them. They are in relation to the person, in fact, and depend on the person. To speak of the person and of subjective interpretation, if not an actual detachment from values themselves, means to attach the value of responsibility, as I think it is, to the person.

THIRD PART

DEVELOPMENT OF THE SUBJECTS

Ch. XV. Boudon and the Problem of Values: In order not to reduce Tocqueville to banality

15.1 "The fact that values are experienced as something established does not indicate that the subject clearly perceives the reason behind them: in most cases, he or she will intuit it as a matter of feeling" (Boudon, 12). The statement can be accepted as long is the meaning of "clearly" is explained, because if the meaning is intended to be that the subject is incapable of giving others, rather than "giving to himself or herself" a *complete and exhaustive* rational explanation, we can agree. That cannot, however, mean that the subject is feeling about in the darkness, otherwise, his or her values would give not meaning to their action and to life, as well. I say this since Boudon, on the subject of the Münchhausen trilemma, tells us that from the first of the three solutions one can obtain a fideistic conception of knowledge, in the sense that each one can say to himself or herself: I know that the principles on which my theory is based cannot be demonstrated, but they seem solid to me. From this, as Boudon also reminds us, sceptical conceptions also arise, which ultimately maintain that nothing can be certain for the very reason that they consider the principles upon which theories are based not demonstrable. This, however, is a position quite close to that of faith. It is certainly not by chance that faith is always besieged by doubts, as, in fact, is scepticism, and since it cannot prove its validity to others, is forced to admit the inadequacy of reason. At this point, however, I believe that a question arises automatically: is a faith not besieged by doubts still a faith?

15.2 Given these premises, and since "our knowledge cannot be presented, even ideally, in the form of an immense hypothetical and deductive theory coming from a few first principles: it takes on the form of a complete and patchy network of hypothetical and deductive theories" (Boudon, 29). I wish to recall that if science reached this conclusion in the twentieth century, metaphysics underwent this affliction in the eighteenth century. I shall make a brief digression, by way of summarizing what I maintain, to take up some considerations offered by my friend Michele Malatesta. Why does Kant refuse to consider metaphysics a science: simply because he cannot apply the synthetic method to this *a priori* or for some other reason? Kant feels a sort of revulsion towards metaphysics, because their object cannot be explainable, hence definable, like those of other sciences and, in his *Prolegomena to any Future Metaphysics*, he says so explicitly: "*how* are metaphysics possible and *how* does reason go about arriving at them (...) Not a single book can be indicated, more or less as a *Euclid* appears, and then say, as Kant does: This is metaphysics; here you find the highly excellent purpose of this science, – the awareness of a supreme being and a future world, – demonstrated through the principles of pure reason (...) in every era, one set of metaphysics has contradicted the other, either the statements themselves, or proofs of these, and each has nullified the direct claim of the other to a lasting consensus". The statement is important because saying that one set of metaphysics has contradicted the other is tantamount to saying that the truth, or presumed truth, is contradicted by other truths. Basically, even though Kant, in the pages just quoted, set forth the task of holding back scepticism, he only ended up increasing it, since it is now the sciences that are in this position. The progress of scientific thought has clearly demonstrated that more than one geometry exists (it might be said more than one Euclid), and more than one set of mathematics. So, is it shocking that more than one way of approaching metaphysics exists? Or is it not necessary to say that they came, before the other disciplines, to the present-day way of understanding and known, scientifically and inexhaustibly?

15.3 In the light of what has been said, it is understandable why the thesis of those who maintain that the legitimacy of values cannot be supported is absurd, because scientific theories can be freed from doubt thanks to a rigorous system of control, whereas "the theories of norms and values" do not have scientifically objective tools capable of validating or invalidating them. That can all be erroneous ultimately if one departs from the assumption that values, too, can be confuted or proven (some would say falsified) only, however, if it is accepted that they be judged through the "length" of historical times and, perhaps in certain cases, accepting the dramatic nature of certain verifications (we can think of the German conscience which acquires the awareness of the real aims of the racist and Nazi ideology). It is history, which, in this case at least, confirms or denies the validity of certain principles.

15.4 However, a *serious risk* lies behind this solution: that of justifying Machiavelli, "whoever wins in whatever way never feels shame", or Hegel with his tragic "Cunning of Reason", an updated version of the Florentine secretary's cynicism. This position has perhaps led to what Weber called "The Polytheism of Values" and the consequent "war of the gods", a metaphor which, as Boudon always reminds us, would indicate that values can be marked by conflict. If such were the case, we should honestly admit that not all conflicts supported by values are identical and not always do the values, which prevail *nowadays* (there is always a need to ponder over this adverb of time) are, in actual fact, those most commendable.

If we ignore this conclusion, we end up accepting that of Nietzsche, according to which belief in a morality, like the theory of resentment, is assumed when it satisfies certain impulses or physical needs in a subject. The disinherited tend to judge society as something bad. Believing in the theories that promise them a better condition in future gives them psychological satisfaction. This position must respond to two provocations, which Nietzsche intentionally did not look at: the cross, in the broad sense of the word, and conversion. Conversion, however, if it is indeed that, constitutes giving up pursuing the path upon which one had embarked and whose perspectives one thought he or she knew, to embrace a solution, once considered absurd or, at the least, unknown.

15.5 Is it possible, however, to perform a real conversion in any cultural context, which, might, for some, be called *the acquisition of a new process of rational selection of ideas?* Furthermore is that process "typical of democratic societies or does it extend over society as a whole? (…) Weber indicated, rightly I believe, that 'rationality' is a universal anthropological given" (Boudon, 77-78). This position may be acceptable, but not fully to be shared, since, Converting is not easy and permissible everywhere. What I want to bring out, however, is another aspect which puts Weber's position in the wake of Kant's as a logical consequence. I indeed believe that those who convert consider both the cultural and prescriptive Kantian-type theories fallacious.

15.6 Kant takes for universal, in morality, what is not universal as the facts show. Paraphrasing Boudon, it can be maintained that "if one holds to this interpretation, one inevitably ends up with an irrational theory of axiologistical beliefs" (Boudon, 155-156). Kant's claim, that of being able to consider elements that have moral connotations universal, was typical of others, suffice it to think of Marx and Nietzsche, in their way of dealing with religious beliefs. For Marx, these "should be analyzed in terms of being at the service of class interests (...); for Nietzsche, these are dictated to individuals by psychological interests that arise from their social status" (Boudon, 164). I referred to Marx and Nietzsche who, to be sure, cannot be called Kantian for various reasons, to emphasize that they, too, do not succeed in freeing themselves from the need to base morality on principles that are, in some way, considered unquestionable, almost *a priori*. The result is that they, too, and others, have ultimately placed scientific, religious, philosophical, etc., premises on the same level. I agree with Boudon when he says that Weber escaped that temptation, but the reason behind his motivation leaves me with some perplexity. "Religious beliefs are based on 'revealed' truths, Weber tells us, belief in which implies an act of faith. It cannot be ignored that religious explanations of the world are not to be submitted to the principle of realism that governs scientific activity" (Boudon, 174). Even the latter, however, is based on postulates, which, as I have just said, constitute actual acts of faith, as the reflection on scientific paradigms has amply demonstrated to us. It is all very well that Weber says that the first, religious beliefs (or theories), do not develop and do not prevail unless "they are accompanied by convincing arguments". The conclusion is at least somewhat debatable. What do we mean by convincing arguments? If they were really so, religions would not require faith. Then, saying that religion without theology cannot be put forth, does not prevent one from *maintaining the opposite as well*. There are, *in fact*, those who maintain that theology takes over when initial faith weakens and the first doubts begin to insinuate themselves.

15.7 I would like to return to the problem of "revealed" truths to deal with a subject not theological in nature, but more simply anthropological and cultural. Boudon rightly reminds us that Tocqueville practically saw in the inevitable progress of equality proof that "the hand of Providence is working on its behalf" (Boudon, 188). Tocqueville's statement is to be taken more seriously than has been done. *Let us ask ourselves* indeed *why* only certain cultures affected by certain traditions, and not others, are capable of coping with certain stimulations towards equality, liberty and, in general, human rights. Irreversibility, like progress towards certain values, must lead us to open our eyes to understand multiculturalism properly, upon whose "altar" we cannot continue to "burn incense" uncritically. No one can deny "that very few among the 'multiculturalists' would accept the idea that, for example, sexual mutilation or the inferior status of the woman are good things, that magic is as valid as science or certain sectors of production are set up on a slavery basis" (Boudon, 190). In other words, let us ask ourselves why that concept of *person*, which, I believe *is one of the basic pillars of ethics*, belongs to some cultures and not to others? Perhaps it is in this perspective, that Dostoevsky's conviction, "if God does not exist, everything is permissible", takes on its true meaning, otherwise it would end up being a maxim like so many others.

15.8 "One can thus speak of axiological truths just as one speaks of scientific truth and call one or the other conclusions drawn from solid reasons (...) how can it be assumed that axiological certainties are rationally founded, when they vary rationally in space and in time?" (Boudon, 221-224). This correct observation merits two considerations: the *first*, concerning the fact that scientific truths have more universal value because they have prevailed due to their utility. The decimal system is one example. It is based on the use of two hands and ten fingers, considered more convenient than the quinary one, likewise efficacious, but considered more limiting only after some cultures came into contact with the other. The same could be said of numerical systems: the Latin world used Roman numerals until they came to consider Arabic ones superior. The latter, in turn, preferred then to utilize the Indian one, which it still uses. Moreover, what can be said of systems of measure? It could be hypothesized that the same will happen for values (we can hope that sexual mutilation or the inferior status of women will be avoided in future) even if resistance is greater, because more interests are involved. The *second*, concerning the fact that "revealed" truths, for believers, imply the intervention of the supernatural in space and time. Furthermore, it is undeniable, as Kierkegaard would say, that this intervention only modifies that space and that time (more precisely speaking, the individual ones) that come to be contaminated by the infinite as it penetrates the finite. The rest continues to be extraneous, ignoring those values brought by the infinite. Perhaps it will accept them later. No one can say, but the fact that they continue to infiltrate and permeate history is equally undeniable.

15.9 From what has been said it is certain possible to retain "that, however strange this proposition may sound in the relativist context characteristic of modern societies there is indeed moral progress" (Boudon, 230). Certainly this does not mean, as Boudon hastens to confirm, that human beings have become better or that they will no longer commit the worst of atrocities, it only means that, practically speaking, the concept of human dignity is certainly making progress. True, and because there are those who do not consider multiculturalism equivocally or surrender to it, but this conviction does not allow us to flee from pressing questions on the moral level: how can we act to see to it that what is worthy, in general, on a more and more universal level is fully valid on the particular and concrete level, as well? How can we keep declarations of principles from remaining dead letters?

15.10 Boudon's studies suggest further reflections. I believe that what Boudon calls "ideological inertia" is not exclusive to certain products of the social sciences (cf. Boudon, 236, n. 1), but is also practiced in metaphysics. It cannot be forgotten that this discipline continues to be present and viable, and submits to continual renewal (cf. Pezzimenti, 1992). Is this not perhaps why it has been deemed justifiable to move from what was considered a "harsh positivism" to another considered "mild positivism"? Here I do not wish to bring in the discussion of what are considered "non observable terms" in the sciences, hypotheses that some consider "psychological" which continue to be valid, even when they cannot be observed (cf. Boudon, 384), I wish only to recall that, *quite often, daily life is based on the correctness of this hypothesis*.

15.11 There is another point in Boudon's thinking that deserves being taken into consideration, and which I feel I can share, albeit with some reservations. Tocqueville was among the first to sense that a transformation from aristocratic to democratic societies was taking place, and he did not criticize this at all, *he turns banality into a positive value*. Our author quotes these forceful words of Tocqueville to the effect that modern societies elude individuals when they suggest that each person can be self-sufficient, so that they can put forth their own personal convictions above everything. "Humans are related to one another not be ideas any more, but just interests, and it might be said that human opinions create nothing but a sort of intellectual dust which flies about in every direction without any possibility of being collected or of settling (...) The inclination to believe in the mass is increasing, and it is always common everyday opinion that guides the world" (Tocqueville[2], 432 and

---

[2] A. DE TOCQUEVILLE, *De la démocratie en Amérique*, in *Tocqueville, De la démocratie en Amérique, Souvenirs, L'Ancien Régime et la Révolution*, Paris, Laffont, "Bouquins", 1986.

434 in Boudon, 300). The various opinions become the basis for various values and, in this state of affairs, "relativism is the natural philosophy of modernity: more precisely, it tends to be the only admissible philosophy" (Boudon, 302). It can be taken for granted, however, that Tocqueville does not place himself on the side of relativism. He clearly says: "I am not more inclined to bow my head under the yoke for the mere fact that the yoke is presented to me by a million arms" (Tocqueville, 435 in Boudon, 304). For him, relativism is, for the most part, "imposed on the social subject rather than this subject's being persuaded". Boudon (cf. 302) puts the two verbs "impose" and "persuade" between inverted commas, but the meaning does not change. Indeed, "Tocqueville sees relativism not as an undeniable truth, but as a point of view which tends to prevail under certain historical and social conditions; The fact that these conditions are long-lasting is not enough to make a truth of relativism" (Boudon, 304), *otherwise, we would be obliged to acknowledge the law of the market as far as values are concerned.* This means that any "point of view", if cleverly put forth, can be made to prevail. This position seems supported by that "universal benevolence" according to which "there is no need to oppose the truth put forward by a guru: one is free not to subscribe to it, but one should try to stop those who have been seduced by it" (Boudon, 310). At this point we must not allow ourselves to be misled by a superficial idea of tolerance, but we must keep in mind that one should not favour "the development of irrational beliefs" using the excuse that it will be the market that eliminates them. The past century amply showed that the price to pay, in these *idola fori*, could be unbearable. *Not everything can be bargained over* or priced. In this, I am fully in agreement with Boudon and with his considerations concerning Rorty since the idea "that facts do not exist, only interpretations, no truth, nor objectivity, is not only false but can become dangerous" (Boudon, 320).

15.12 The greatest danger coming from bargaining over values is not, however, that of giving rise to relativism or, worse yet, scepticism, but that of falling back to the level of conformism. There is a consideration of Boudon that would merit further examination: "the media popularisers can benefit by advertising ideas that seem more or less in tune with the times, since their conformism has strategic value; this is why they have been flattering the gurus of relativism for a long time" (Boudon, 332-333). We have reached this goal, Boudon reminds us, because some thinkers, the so-called "masters of suspicion" have come to consider values as illusions. Apart from Boudon's criticism of these people, I think it would be useful here to return to the subtle difference between the two fundamental faculties of reason, that of *thought* and that of *abstraction*, developed by Rosmini and that I examine in the value of intelligence. It is hardly necessary to recall that this explains the outcome of what we encounter is that of making the human beings, who devote their attention more and more to the capacity for *abstraction*, more and more unsatisfied, their attention more and more, losing sight of the situations before them and which they view in more and more artificial ways. Boudon reaches a similar conclusion, departing from a different position: "the gurus of relativism", having to discredit everything and everyone, contribute "with their reactions of doubt and discontent to creating that climate of *disaffection* which characterizes democratic societies nowadays (…) since it is not consensus that forms the basis of justice, but, inversely, justice that forms the long-lasting basis of consensus" (Boudon, 347 and 397). It must be further said that once a minimum of justice has been attained, it must not be claimed that this was attained by chance, but always in conformity with guidelines, *however general they might be*, which have accompanied our action. That of the *person*, with his or her values, seems to me one of these, and we must never, for any reason, be willing to give it up.

Ch. XVI. The Relationship between Command and Obedience and the Thought of Father Theodossios

16.1 The relationship between command and obedience is certainly one of the most frequently debated questions in political thought, but not only that. Suffice it to think that its ramifications have involved the social, economic, moral and last but not least, religious dimensions. I think that everyone can agree, in any case, that the relationship between command and obedience is the greatest pillar of support to a social structure. Indeed, when this structure is lacking, the model of society with its way of life and understanding of human relations is ultimately called into question. I wish briefly to trace Father Theodossios' religious thought on the matter. His argumentation may seem apparently far from social subject, but I believe that it useful in coming to understand the reasons for the crisis in the relationship between command and obedience on a civil level as well. The critics of obedience, and there are not a few of them, maintain that the latter humiliates liberty and reduces human beings to a state of total subjection. They are referring to the hierarchical conception of civil life, which is a manifestation of a military mentality: The obeying subject must submit to any command of his or her superior. Obviously, an extreme condition is involved which, most often, is not relevant to the essence of the problem.

16.2 According to our author "it may happen that on one occasion I obey out of fear; I must repent for that"

(Theodossios, 64). Hence, the tie with authority cannot and must not at all be fear. The latter, as Montesquieu would say, can only be created by tyrants. Why, then, should one obey? This question cannot be avoided. However, one must obey in life, obey people or laws, whether against my will, alien to certain commands, or a will with which I sympathize. Suffice it to think that to obey "is in itself a change of realm: one leaves one realm to go into another. One leaves one leader, to enter the service of another one". It seems, as our author further points out, an "uprooting one one's own will (…) our will is submitted to another person" (Theodossios, 60 and 61). Upon close examination, however, this subjection is a free act, totally free, freely renewed every time, otherwise, it has no value, either on a mystical and religious level, but also on a social one. In other words, obedience, in this perspective, requires liberty and has meaning only thanks to liberty. The problem is to see what the motivation, free motivation, is that drives the will to obey.

16.3 Religiously speaking, the answer should be simple, because "when we obey, we are free and all of our lives are free". We have not, however, reached the basis of obedience, which, once it is identified, could also turn out to be valid in other areas as well, albeit adequately re-examined. "If this fundamental point is not observed, obedience has no meaning" (Theodossios, 62). For the Greek Father, the answer, on a religious level, is simple: "if I spend my life obeying out of obligation, out of fear, my love falls apart", so, what unites command and obedience in a relationship that cannot be dissolved is love. This is the meaning of the maximally free act, which is the act of love, so that "our act of obedience has greater value than the thing commanded in itself" (Theodossios, 63), whether this is more or less perfect. Just as in "civil" life, but, naturally, more than that, true obedience needs free spirits and ones, which, above all, know how to love. If this love is lacking, obedience risks not having any more meaning and, in any case, is reduced to pure formalism.

16.4 Religious obedience is a "more absolute manifestation that that for which everyone is called upon" (Theodossios, 64), even in simple, daily life. Cicero recalled: "*Legum servi sumus ut liberi esse possimus*", once again to bring out the very close links among liberty, command and obedience on the social level, as well. That means that when one no longer obeys there is not only a crisis in the relationship between command and obedience, but the innermost reasons that upheld it, for which one makes sacrifices, obeys and loves. It follows that a social crisis is also a crisis in the bonds of the society itself, a crisis of that confidence on which that society is based. There can be many causes. The fact remains, however that the intimate reasons supporting a civil relationship have come to be lacking, have lost their *raison d'être*, shattered the bond of solidarity and love which kept society together.

16.5 Revolutions are not only an act of disobedience of the preconstituted order, they "love" a new type of order, a new relationship between command and obedience. The condition cannot be escaped. I repeat: "in itself it is a change of realm: one leaves one realm to enter another. One leaves one leader, to enter into the service of another leader". Anarchical solutions have no place in this perspective. For love one obeys, and in a certain way, for love one betrays. Paraphrasing Sorokin, we could say that there is also *a social aspect of love* which requires is logic of obedience in order to be maintained.

16.6 One of the conditions that uphold civil living, in addition to social confidence is, upon close examination, altruism. What is altruism, however, if not a manifestation, albeit a limited one, of humility on a social level? Is it not, perhaps, a small step aside on someone's part, the giving of a new dimension to "my" space to enable the other to find it (otherwise, what altruism are we talking about)? Following the usual logic, is it not becoming poorer? For this reason "poverty and obedience, imply humility in any case" (Theodossios, 65). This humility is present, in its most highly diverse forms, in every situation and in all human relationships.

16.7 It was such in Old-Testament tradition. In the Judaic tradition, what concerned the household often had social implications and vice versa. Suffice it to think of those relationships based on propriety (cf. D'Agostino, 14), a premise indispensable for justice. The simplest example comes to us from Tobias who, in his "obstinacy" to fight on behalf of good, experiences the solitude that follows the bitter conviction that there are few who fight on behalf of good. Tobias, which means good, himself bears witness to this solitude: "I went alone ..." (Tb, 1,6). Solitude obviously turns into lack of comprehension, even in those who should sustain it and who, on the contrary, criticize it. Once, having been injured, his wife scolded him: "Where are your alms and your good works? Now, everything can be clearly seen, the condition you are in!" (Tb, 2,14). To be sure, Tobias turns this situation into an interior epic, but his bitter observations, "I am the one who has to hear false reprimands" (Tb, 3,6), do not free us from asking some questions. Why is does the just one find himself in solitude? Why is there his lack of comprehension? Why listen to his lamentations, however just they may be? In short, why is he no longer obeyed and supported by those close to him? Is it not because he is no longer loved? "Why obey if there is not this love?" (Theodossios, 85). The other side of obedience is summed up in this brief statement. The other side of obedience is love. It is the other side that explains why one should obey, at least in these cases. It is a free act to the greatest possible degree. It is so, because to love, to want to love, is the highest expression of liberty.

16.8 Often, solitude and lack of comprehension are the price that must be paid for liberty, so that "to conquer and overcome that suffering from solitude, sovereign love and willingness to die are necessary" (Theodossios, 84). This is so not only in a figurative sense, but at times, in the real sense of the term, like Dante's Cato: "Liberty goes in search, of one, who is so dear, as it knows who rejects life for her" (Dante, Purg. 71-72). Interior solitude and obedience! Madness? Perhaps, but would there be true liberty without the evidence, always possible, of these martyrs, for the most part misunderstood and derided? It is basically the paradox of the Cross, which knows how to join together, in a language, which is certainly not light and easy, obedience and liberty.

16.9 Saints and Martyrs: Who else can understand this language! Obedience and liberty are transformed, they practically transfigured, into the ability to command. "This is why the saints have always loved to obey and have commanded, when they have been obliged to do so (...) because those who oey out of love of God and with interior tenderness in the soul, are free of any false sense of responsibility" (Theodossios, 133). It is a bit as the adage says: "Only those who have learned to obey with all their intelligence, also know how to command". This is the highest meaning of the relationship between command and obedience.

Ch. XVII. Brief Itinerary for an Historical Analysis

17.1 Greek ethics have as their purpose the pursuit of happiness. This can be carried on in the *polis*, the only dimension worthy of a free person. The afterlife perspective, suffice it to consider the great poetic works from Homer on, is not to be understood from the Judaic and Christian points of view, which are aimed at the fulfilment of the human being. Here, too, one can think of Dante's Paradise. In Plato, where not a few Pythagorean premises are present, the problem of happiness is seen in relation to that of perfection of nature. Nature is distinguished by true harmony, and both the individual soul, as well as the *polis*, seen as a magnified human being, relate to it. (cf. Plato, 434e-435a). Mistrusting all the limitations, Plato lays out his design of the *polis* coming to trace out ideas of perfectism, which will have a great, often pernicious, influence on the future ethical and political schemes. Nature has, for him, definitively set forth the virtues of individuals as well as of the community, reducing the pedagogical role to simply validating Nature's directives. Thus, the ethical engagement can be said to be resolved in staticity: it is impossible to depart from what has hitherto been "marked" (cf. Vegetti, 150). Aristotle, too, falls back into an elitist view of ethics, despite his claiming the independence of practical knowledge. Some moral characteristics cannot be taught to (or learned by) everyone if nature has not already provided them with the necessary virtues (cf. the courage of Manzoni's Don Abbondio). Certain virtues, such as courage, temperance, etc., referred to as ethical virtues, are considered to be natural "gifts". It is no accident that one of the meanings of the word *ethos* is character and here, too, we have a return to Platonism. The reward for these virtues is happiness. For this reason, it can be said that Aristotle's ethics are not deontological, in the Kantian manner, but teleological (cf. Vegetti, 173). Here, too, there is a return to Plato's pedagogical view since a guide is needed to direct one towards what nature has already preordained. It follows that freedom of action itself and of choice can be placed in contrast with the predetermination of character.

17.2 In the Latin world, morality is closely related to tradition. The *mores maiorum* were shaped over time. They are a cultural fact in the etymological sense of the verb *colere* from which comes agriculture, *agri culturae studere*: to farm. What is planted also grows slowly, just like the habits that are acquired by putting oneself in the perspective of tradition. Here lies the close tie between morality and law. This is the fruit not of legislators, but fruit which has ripened as events have taken place, as will be the case for British law. Laws are not set forth *a priori* and definitively, but are the result of history and are acquired when matured by experience. For this reason, simple natural gifts or inclinations are not sufficient, and no one can hold public office if that person has not first completed the *cursus honorum* (cf. Pezzimenti, 2011A, 1.43). Tradition involves not only the individual, but also the entire community. As Seneca recalls (cf. epist. 94), the vices of the peoples manifest themselves in those of individuals and, for this reason, too, one can speak of *publicus error*. For those who live in a certain context, morality and law become a *habitus*, which guarantees and allows certain forms of behaviour. This "habit" constitutes a form of juridical personality, which eventually completes the physical one of nature.

17.3 This concept of the person is taken up and redefined in Christian morality, which basically presents itself in a totally different way from preceding ethical conceptions as well as those that would follow. This perspective is characterized by its being a sort of acceptance of the person of Christ who, for the true Christian, becomes the root and basis of any sort of behaviour. Christian indeed means another Christ, a position, which Saint Paul so well elucidated, that he comes to say "I live, but no longer as myself, Christ lives in me" (Gal, 2.20). In Him, and only in Him can we overcome evil "always and forever rejected and conquered in God" (Coda, 273). It is no longer reason or nature, as for the Greeks, nor is it tradition, as for the Romans, which give meaning to our moral actions. It has meaning only "starting from the revelation of Jesus Christ, indeed, in our being in Christ" (Coda, 312). This imitation, above and beyond all the reflections that can be made on grace, on merit and guilt, remains the fulcrum of all of Christian morality. Without this imitation, Christianity is reduced to a mere cultural expression or sociological dimension, since, the acceptance of Christ, tends to remove every type of cultural or social conditioning, if one looks closely at the situation. This indeed means: to convert.

17.4 Machiavelli has always been thought of as having been responsible for the split between politics and morality. The Florentine secretary is alleged to have been the standard bearer of immoral, or at least amoral thought. A closer look suggests that Machiavelli can be considered the theoretician of the morality of success. The end justifies the means, a motto that he never wrote but which sums up his thought quite well, expresses a logic of life that has, since then, and above and beyond hypocritical denials, the norm in a certain understanding of social life. There are a great many disciples and they have constantly increased in number thanks to the contribution given to this perspective by the philosophy of Hobbes. Using more or less toned down formulae, this has become the dominating position of society and life, which departs, in any case, from a pessimistic view of human nature. This position, purified by typical Renaissance individualism, was to become characteristic of the conflicts among nations, peoples, classes, etc. The dramatic vicissitudes of contemporary history bear witness to this.

17.5 The value of tradition, as the basis of morality expressed in culture and law, will be emphasized in most of British tradition. As Rawls, among others, brought out in his famous text *Lectures on the History of Moral Philosophy*, Hume relates his conception of justice to the regulating of property and the agreements governing it: its stability, its possession, its transfer through consent and the keeping of promises (cf. Pezzimenti, 2011B, 3.38 ff. and the entire chapter concerning the role of tradition). These points have been stated throughout many centuries of history and constitute the cultural, social and juridical basis of a people. Latin and British institutions have a clear characteristic in common. Neither left free play to selfish conceptions because they sought to anchor tradition in more stable premises, that is, natural ones, as Locke or Berkeley did. Hume himself, who spoke of *sympathy*, sees in it a natural tendency and one, which is totally disinterested. The fact remains that Latin and British institutions are two juridical entities that grew a little at a time and, for these reasons, must be considered the most flexible ones in history. Their rich tradition is, to be sure, characterized by documents that have made this history of law, but also a *ius non scriptum* was traced out that is evidence of the moral strength of their traditions, that is, the *mores maiorum*. It is tradition itself, in the opinion expressed in a memorable study by Bryce, that keeps the *ius non scriptum* from being easily altered or distorted on behalf of momentary interests. *Ius non scriptum* indeed provides the premise capable of bringing about changes, even far-reaching ones, in continuity, for the very reason that it manages to keep unaltered those moral premises on which it is based. A close look reveals that it was one of these polemic motives that inspired those who did not perceive any continuity between the English and French Revolutions. The latter, with its pretension of rebuilding everything *ab imis*, aimed at placing itself radically outside of tradition.

17.6 Kant sought to react to what could be called a morality oriented towards "sentimentalism", also expressed by personalities such as Rousseau and other proto-romantics. In his opinion, a morality that depends on a palpable reality cannot be accepted, because nature cannot be the basis of morality. That basis is liberty. The obligatory nature of the categorical imperative comes from a pure form of reason. It is, however, a reason for supporting himself and for saving morality. On one hand, he must admit his inability to demonstrate the postulates for morality itself, but on the other, he must admit that he cannot do without it if he does not wish to resort to coercion as an end in itself. This is one of the many contradictions of Kantian ethics, as the first chapter of this book has attempted to show. The question of postulates seems also to be oriented towards a morality, understood in a religious sense, but a religiosity which does not allow, to put it in the terms of Jacobi, that step towards transcendence which constitutes the meaning itself of religion and enables humans to perceive God. Religion is thus reduced to pure rationality, as is morality itself. This is all shown by the fact that Kant eventually writes *Religion within the Limits of Reason Alone* in 1793, a work almost unthinkable without the moral premises of practical reason.

17.7 Another orientation develops with Hegelian ethicity, and it makes extreme use of Fichte's ethical idealism. The problem of ethics ultimately dissolves into the historical and social dimension, where Hegel himself establishes the moment of ethicity. The dialectic perspective, with Marx then turns into dialectical materialism. It can be said that ethical relativism begins with Hegel and Marx. Truth, moral truth, too, is relative to history and its evolution. Morality itself, as with all ideologies, is a reflection of reality, economic especially. It is, in other words, a superstructure. This bit of positivism, present in Marx, is turned into social utilitarianism in the positivists. Not even the Italian idealism of Croce and Gentile will be immune from this relativism (I intentionally do not specify Italian historicism because this, in some of its expressions from Guicciardini to Vico, cannot exist in relation to the dialectic view). Historicist moralities will end up being deleterious to morality itself because, with the requisite of dialectical necessity, they will ultimate call into question the pillar of morality, which is liberty.

17.8 Existentialism tried to react to the drama of these convictions. As with Kierkegaard, it condemned every dialectic and historicist logic. The philosophers of this trend in thought, starting with their "posthumous" father, contributed, however, with their extreme subjectivism, to increasing ethical relativism. The subjectivist – it would be better to say individualistic – experience enhanced certain tendencies present in European culture at the time of the Reformation. A close look shows that in some of his *Dialogues*, Giordano Bruno, who does not indulge in sympathizing with many aspects of the Reformers had already presented this redemption of individuals by the will of the gods. People, in any case, failed in their attempts to find a balance between the objectivity claimed by the claims of the dialectics and subjectivity of the existentialists. Proof of this is the existential experience of Nietzsche whose dramatic end many try to not to see. It seems to me that much of postmodern ethics (it is difficult for me to call them that) is the natural offspring of this individualistic position, as is that of various philosophical currents in periods of crisis.

Works cited

AA. VV.,
2005, *Dopo Beveridge. Riflessioni sul Welfare. Con una ristampa de Il Piano Beveridge*, a cura di L. Troiani, Agrilavoro Edizioni, Roma.

ABBAGNANO N.,
1974, *Storia della filosofia*, vol. III, *Filosofia del Romanticismo. Filosofia tra il secolo XIX e il XX*, UTET, Torino.

ARMELLINI P.,
2008, *Rosmini politico e la storiografia del Novecento*, Aracne Editrice, Roma.

AUGUSTINI (SANCTI),
1975, *Confessionum libri tredecim*, in *Opera Omnia*, vol. I, Città Nuova Editrice, Roma.
1969, *Epistolae (1-123)*, in *Opera Omnia*, vol. XXI, Città Nuova Editrice, Roma.
2001A, *De Mendacio*, in *Opera Omnia*, vol. VII/2, Città Nuova Editrice, Roma.
2001B, *Contra Mendacium*, in *Opera Omnia*, vol. VII/2, Città Nuova Editrice, Roma.

AYER A.,
1936, *Language, True and Logic*, London.

BAGGIO A.,
2005A, *Lavoro e dottrina sociale cristiana dalle origini al Novecento*, Città Nuova Editrice, Roma.
2005B, *Etica ed economia. Verso un paradigma di fraternità*, Città Nuova Editrice, Roma.
2007A, *La riscoperta della fraternità nell'epoca del Terzo '89*, in BAGGIO A. ed., *Il principio dimenticato, la fraternità*

nella riflessione politologica contemporanea, Città Nuova Editrice, Roma.

2007B, *L'idea di "fraternità" tra due rivoluzioni: Parigi 1789 – Haiti 1791. Piste di ricerca per una comprensione della fraternità come categoria politica*, in Baggio A. ed., *Il principio dimenticato, la fraternità nella riflessione politologica contemporanea*, Città Nuova Editrice, Roma.

Bagnoli R.,
2001, *Introduzione* a T. Mann, *Pace mondiale e altri scritti*, a cura di R. Bagnoli, A. Guida Editore, Napoli.

Baudelaire C.,
1975A, *Les Fleurs du mal*, in *Oeuvres Complètes*, vol. I, Éd. Gallimard, Paris.
1975B, *Journaux intimes*, in *Oeuvres Complètes*, vol. I, Éd. Gallimard, Paris.

Bergson H.,
1976, *Les deux soueces de la morale et de la religion*, puf, Paris.

Berlin I.,
1969, *Four Essays on Liberty*, Oxford University Press, Oxford.

Bobbio N.,
1990, *L'età dei diritti*, Einaudi Editore, Torino.

Boudon R.,
1999, *Les sens des valeurs*, P. U. F., Paris.

Brandt R.,
2000, *Presentazione* a Falcioni D., *Natura e libertà in Kant. Un'interpretazione del progetto Per la pace perpetua (1795)*, G. Giappichelli Editore, Torino.

Bryce J.,
1901, *Flexible and Rigid Constitutions*, in *Studies in History and Jurisprudence*, vol. I, pp. 145-252, Clarendon Press, Oxford.

CAPOGRASSI G.,
1976, *Introduzione alla vita etica*, Edizioni Studium, Roma.
1977, *Riflessioni sull'autorità e la sua crisi*, Giuffrè Editore, Milano.

CICERONE M. T.,
1976, *De legibus*, in aedibus Livianis, Patavii, MCMLXVIII.

CODA P.,
2003, *Il logos e il nulla. Trinità religioni mistica*, Città Nuova Editrice, Roma.

CORAGO J.,
2001, *Dar vita a una vita*, Jaca Book, Milano.

CRESPI F.,
2006, *Il male e la ricerca del bene*, Meltemi, Roma.

D'ADDIO M.,
1972, *Introduzione* a A. ROSMINI-SERBATI, *Filosofia della politica*, Marzorati Editore, Milano.
1992, *Storia delle dottrine politiche*, vol. II, Ecig, Genova.
2000, *Libertà e appagamento. Politica e dinamica sociale in Rosmini*, Studium, Roma.

D'AGOSTINO F.,
2006, *Giustizia. Elementi per una teoria*, Edizioni San Paolo, Cinisello Balsamo (MI).

DAHRENDORF R.,
1979, *Lebenschancen. Anläufe zur sozialen und politischen Theorie*, Suhrkamp Verlag, Frankfurt am Main.

DALLA TORRE G.,
2000, *La multiculturalità come dato di fatto e come programma etico-politico*, in AA. VV., *La cittadinanza. Problemi e dinamiche in una società pluralista*, a cura di G. Dalla Torre e F. D'Agostino, G. Giappichelli Editore, Torino.

DAL SANTO L. V.,
1981, *Prefazione* a SOLOV'ËV V., *Tri reči v pamjat'Dostoevskogo*, tr. it., *Dostoevskij*, Coperativa editoriale "La casa di Matriona", Milano.

D'ANNUNZIO G.,
1985, *Il piacere*, Mondatori, Milano.

DE LAUBIER P.,
1997, *Introduction* a SOLOV'ËV V., *La justification du bien. Essai de philosophie morale*, Editions Slatkine, Genève.

DERRIDA J.,
2005, *Histoire du mensonge. Prolégomènes*, Éd. de L'Herne, Paris.

DESCARTES R.,
1972, *Oeuvres philosophiques*, vol. I, Éd. Garnier, Paris.

DONATI P.,
1999, *La cittadinanza*, in PELLICANI L. (a cura di), *Dimensioni della modernità*, Edizioni SEAM, Milano.

DOSTOEVSKIJ F.,
1981, *Diario di uno scrittore*, Sansoni Editore, Firenze.

DUMMETT M.,
2004, *Truth and the Past*, Columbia University Press, New York.
1994, *Origins of analytical philosophy*, Harvard University Press, Cambridge (MA).

FABBRO C.,
1995, *Introduzione* a S. KIERKEGAARD, *Opere*, vol. I, a cura di C. Fabbro, Piemme, Casale Monferrato.

FALCIONI D.,
2000, *Natura e libertà in Kant. Un'interpretazione del progetto Per la pace perpetua (1795)*, G: Giappichelli Editore, Torino.
2001, *Aporien des Strafrechts bei Kant. Eine Alternative zum Jus Talionis*, in *Kant und die Berliner Aufklärung*, Akten des

IX. Internationalen Kant-Kongress, Band IV: Sektionen XI-XIV, Walter de Gruyter – Berlin – New York.

FELICE F.,
2008, *Economia sociale di mercato*, Rubbettino Editore, Soveria Mannelli.

FERRERO G.,
1981, *Potere. I Geni invisibili della Città*, Sugarco Edizioni, Milano.

FICHTE J. G.,
1964, *Beitrag zur Berichtigung der Urtheile des Publikums über die französische Revolution*, in *Werke*, Band I/1, 1791-1794, F. Frommann Verlag, Stuttgart-Bad Cannstatt.

FLORENSKIJ P.,
1984, *La prospettiva rovesciata e altri scritti*, casa del libro editrice, Roma.

FONNESU L.,
2006, *Storia dell'etica contemporanea. Da Kant alla filosofia analitica*, Carocci Editore.

GEYMONAT L.,
1945, *Avvertenza* a JUVALTA E., *I limiti del razionalismo etico*, Einaudi Editore, Torino.

HABERMAS J.,
1992, *Faktiztät und Geltung. Beiträge zur Diskurstheorie des Rechts und des demokratischen Rechsstaats*, Suhrkamp Verlag, Frankfurt am Main.

HARTMANN N.,
1949[3], *Ethik*, Walter De Gruyter, Berlin.

HEGEL G. W. F.,
1986, *Grundlinien der Philosophie des Rechts*, in *Werke*: Band VII, Suhrkamp Verlag, Frankfurt am Main.
The quotations refer to the paragraph.

HEIDEGGER M.,
1927, *Sein und Zeit*, Tübingen.

HUME D.,
1981, *A Treatise of Human Nature*, At The Clarendon Press, Oxford.

JONAS H.,
1994, *Das Prinzip Leben. Ansätze zu einer philosophischen Biologie*, Insel Verlag, Frankfurt am Main.
2003, *Das Prinzip Verantwortung*, Insel Verlag, Frankfurt am Main.

JUVALTA E.,
1945, *I limiti del razionalismo etico*, Einaudi Editore, Torino.

KANT I.,
1968A, *Kritik der reinen Vernunft 1*, in *Werke*: Band III/Band IV, Suhrkamp Verlag, Frankfurt am Main.
1968B, *Die Methaphysik der Sitten*, in *Werke*: Band VIII, Suhrkamp Verlag, Frankfurt am Main.
1968C, *Über ein vermeintes Recht, aus Menschenliebe zu lügen*, in *Werke*: Band VIII, Suhrkamp Verlag, Frankfurt am Main.
1968D, *Kritik der Urteilskraft*, in *Werke*: Band X, Suhrkamp Verlag, Frankfurt am Main.
1968E, *Zum ewigen Frieden. Ein philosophischer Entwurt*, in *Werke*: Band XI, Suhrkamp Verlag, Frankfurt am Main.
1968F, *Idee zu einer allegemeinen Geschichte in weltbürgerlicher Absicht*, in *Werke*: Band XI, Suhrkamp Verlag, Frankfurt am Main.
1968G, *Über den Gemeinspruch: Das mag in der Theorie richtig sein, taugt aber nicht für die Praxis*, in *Werke*: Band XI, Suhrkamp Verlag, Frankfurt am Main.
1968H, *Der Streit der Fakultäten*, in *Werke*: Band XI, Suhrkamp Verlag, Frankfurt am Main.
1968I, *Rezensionen zu J. H. Schulz: Versuch einer Anleitung zur Sittenlehre für alle Menschen*, in *Werke*: Band XII, Suhrkamp Verlag, Frankfurt am Main.
1974, *Von der Vahrhaftigkeit*, in *Kant's Gesammelte Schriften*, Band XXVII, t. 1, Berlin.

Kelsen H.,
1994, *Reine Rechtslehre. Einleitung in die rechtswissenschaftliche Problematik*, Scientia Verlag Aalen, Amsterdam.
1922/23, *Gott und Staat*, in *Logos*, vol. 11, 1922/23, pp. 261-284.

Kierkegaard S.,
1962, *Enten-Eller* af Victor Eremita, *Samlede Vaerker*, Bind II, Gyldendal.
1963A, *Frygt og Baeven* af Johannes de Silentio, *Samlede Vaerker*, Bind V, Gyldendal.
1963B, *Begrebet Angest* af Vigilius Haufniensis, *Samlede Vaerker*, Bind VI, Gyldendal.
1963C, *Sygdommen til Döden* af Anti-Climacus, *Samlede Vaerker*, Bind XV, Gyldendal.

Lo Gatto E.,
1981, *Introduzione* a Dostoevskij F., *Diario di uno scrittore*, Sansoni Editore, Firenze.

Lo Giudice S.,
2005, *Profili della contemporaneità. Temi e problemi di etica sociale*, Pellegrini Editore, Cosenza.

Lyotard J.-F.,
1979, *La condition postmoderne*, Les Éditions de Minuit, Paris.

MacIntyre A.,
1984, *After Virtue. A Study in MoralTheory*, University of NotreDame Press, Indiana.

Maffettone S.,
1999, *Etica alla fine del secondo millennio*, in Pellicani L. (a cura di), *Dimensioni della modernità*, Edizioni SEAM, Milano.

Mann T.,
1968A, *Betrachtungen eines Unpolitischen*, in *Politische Schriften und Reden*, Erster Band, in Thomas Mann, *Werke*, Fischer Bücherei, Frankfurt am Main.

1968B, *Politische Schriften und Reden*, Zweiter Band, in Thomas Mann, *Werke*, Fischer Bücherei, Frankfurt am Main.

1968C, *Politische Schriften und Reden*, Dritter Band, in Thomas Mann, *Werke*, Fischer Bücherei, Frankfurt am Main.

MANGANELLI M.,
1998, *Introduzione* a A. ROSMINI, *Compendio di etica e breve storia di essa*, Città Nuova Editrice, Roma.

MARIANELLI M.,
1997, *Introduzione* a T. Mann, *Considerazioni di un impolitico*, Adelphi Edizioni, Milano.

MARITAIN J.,
1990, *Neuf leçons sur les notions premières de la philosophie morale*, in JACQUES ET RAÏSSA MARITAIN, *Oeuvres Complètes*, 1947-1951, vol. IX, Éd. Universitaires Fribourg, Suisse, Éd. Saint-Paul, Paris.

MEN' A.,
2007, *Io credo. Il Simbolo della fede*, NMR, Roma.

MISLER N.,
1984, *Il rovesciamento della prospettiva*, *Premessa* a FLORENSKIJ P., *La prospettiva rovesciata e altri scritti*, casa del libro editrice, Roma.

NIETZSCHE F.,
1980A, *Jenseits von Gut und Böse*, in *Sämtliche Werke*: Band 5, Deutscher Taschenbuch Verlag GmbH & Co. KG, München Walter de Gruyter, Berlin/New York.

1980B, *Zur Genealogie der Moral*, in *Sämtliche Werke*: Band 5, Deutscher Taschenbuch Verlag GmbH & Co. KG, München Walter de Gruyter, Berlin/New York.

PAGANI G. B.,
1998, *Note* a A. ROSMINI, *Compendio di etica e breve storia di essa*, Città Nuova Editrice, Roma.

PAGANINI E.,
2006, *Introduzione all'edizione italiana*, di M. Dummett, *Verità e passato*, Raffaello Cortina, Milano.

PELLICANI L.,
1981, *La Rivoluzione e i Geni invisibili della Città*, Saggio introduttivo a G. FERRERO, *Potere. I Geni invisibili della Città*, Sugarco Edizioni, Milano.

PERISSINOTTO L.,
2005, *Prefazione* a Putnam H., *Ethics without Ontology*, tr. it., *Etica senza ontologia*, Paravia Bruno Mondadori Editori, Milano.

PETRARCA F.,
1996, *Canzoniere*, A. Mondatori Editore, Milano.

PETROSINO S. – ROLLAND J.,
1984, *La vérité nomade. Introdution à Emmanuel Lévinas*, La Découverte, Paris.

PETRUCCIANI S.,
1997, *Sul rapporto fra morale e diritto in Fatti e norme di Habermas*, in *Fenomenologia e Società*, anno XX, n. 2, 1997.

PEZZIMENTI R.,
1992, *Homo Metaphysicus*, Ler, Napoli-Roma.
1999, *Dynamic Order. The Problem of Method in Evolvine Nature. With letters from N. Rescher, L. Pauling, J. Eccles and K. R. Popper*, Gracewing, Leominster.
2004, Politics and Economics. An Essay on the Genesis of Economic Development, Leominster: Gracewing.
2008, *Política y religión. Legado cultural de la secularización*, *Prólogo* de Jean-Yves Calvez. Ciudad Nueva, Buenos Aires, 2008.
2011A, *The Open Society and its Friends, with letters from Isaiah Berlin and Karl R. Popper*, Leominster: Gracewing.
2011B, *The Open Society along the Arduous Path of Modernity, with letters from Isaiah Berlin and Hilary Putnam*, Leominster: Gracewing.

PITITTO R.,
2005A, *Ad Auschwitz Dio c'era. I credenti e la sfida del male*, Edizioni Studium, Roma.
2005B, *Dalla teoria degli atti linguistici alla filosofia della mente. John Roger Searle critico di Russel*, in Metalogicon, anno XVIII, n. II, 2005.

PLATONIS,
1957, *Res Publica*, rec. J. Burnet, tomus IV, Oxonii.

POLANYI M.,
1958, *Personal Knowledge. Towards a Post-Critical Philosophy*, Routledge & Kegan Paul, London.

POSSENTI V.,
1996, *Introduzione* a J. Maritain, *Neuf leçons sur les notions premières de la philosophie morale*, tr. it., Editrice Massimo, Milano.
1998, *Terza navigazione. Nichilismo e metafisica*, Armando Editore, Roma.
1999, *Filosofia e rivelazione, un contributo al dibattito su fede e ragione*, Città Nuova Editrice, Roma.
2004, *Essere e libertà*, Rubbettino Editore, Soveria Mannelli.

PUTNAM H.,
2004, *Ethics without Ontology*, Harvard University Press, Cambridge (MA).

QUINTAS A. M.,
1979, *Analisi del bene comune*, seconda ed., Bulzoni Editore, Roma.

QUINZIO S.,
1995, *Kierkegaard, il cristiano moderno*, in S. KIERKEGAARD, *Opere*, vol. I, a cura di C. Fabbro, Piemme, Casale Monferrato.

RAWLS J.,
2000, *Lectures on the History of Moral Philosophy*, Harvard College.

RICOEUR P.,
1986, *Le mal. Un défi à la philosophie et à la théologie*, Labor et Fides, Genève.

RICONDA G.,
1996, *Introduzione* a SOLOV'ËV V., *Tri rasgovòra*, tr. it., *I tre dialoghi e il racconto dell'anticristo*, II Ed., Casa Editrice Marietti, Genova.

RIGOBELLO A.,
1983, *Certezza morale ed esperienza religiosa*, Libreria Editrice Vaticana, Città del Vaticano.

RORTY R.,
1989, *Contingency, irony and solidarity*, Cambridge University Press, Cambridge.

ROSMINI A.,
1972, *Filosofia della politica*, Marzorati Editore, Milano.
1998, *Compendio di etica e breve storia di essa*, Città Nuova Editrice, Roma.

ROVATTI P. A.,
2004, *Adesso ci vuole più pensiero. Ma non metafisico*, in Reset, n. 86, Nov. – Dic., 2004.

SARTRE J. P.,
1964, *Les mots*, Éd. Gallimard, Paris.
1976, *L'âge de raison*, Éd. Gallimard, Paris.
1977, *L'être et le néant*, Éd. Gallimard, Paris.

SCHOPENHAUER A.,
1986A, *Die Welt als Wille und Vorstellung*, in *Sämtliche Werke*: Band I, Suhrkamp Verlag, Frankfurt am Main.
1986B, *Die Welt als Wille und Vorstellung*, in *Sämtliche Werke*: Band II, Suhrkamp Verlag, Frankfurt am Main.
1986C, *Preisschrift über die Grundlage der Moral*, in *Sämtliche Werke*: *Kleinere Schriften*, Band III, Suhrkamp Verlag, Frankfurt am Main.

SEARLE J. R.,
1990, *Speech acts. An Essay in the Philosophy of Language*, Cambridge University Press, Cambridge.
2004, *Mind. A Brief Introduction*, Oxford University Press.

SENECAE L. A. (SENECA),
Ad Lucilium Epistulae morales, rec. L.D. Reynolds, 2 volumes, Oxonii, 1965.

SOLARI G.,
1971. *Introduzione* a I. Kant, *Scritti politici e di filosofia della storia e del diritto*, UTET, Torino.

SOLOV'ËV V.,
1981, *Tri reči v pamjat' Dostoevskogo*, tr. it., *Dostoevskij*, Coperativa editoriale "La casa di Matriona", Milano.
1996, *Tri rasgovòra*, tr. it., *I tre dialoghi e il racconto dell'anticristo*, II Ed., Casa Editrice Marietti, Genova.
1997, *La justification du bien. Essai de philosophie morale*, Editions Slatkine, Genève.

SOROKIN P. A.,
1954, The *Ways and Power of Love. Types, Factors, and Techniques of Moral Transformation*, Beacon Press, Boston.

SPAEMANN R.,
1996, *Personen. Versuke über den Underschied zwischen "etwas" und "jemand"*, Klett-Cotta, Stuttgart.

STEIN E.,
1962, *Die ontische Struktur der Person und ihre erkenntnistheoretische Problematik*, in Edith Stein Werke, vol. VI, *Welt und Person*, L. Gelber und P. R. Leuven, Archivum Carmelitanum, Edith Stein, Gelen (NL).

TAGLIAPIETRA A.,
1996, *Introduzione* a I. Kant, B. Constant, *La verità e la menzogna. Dialogo sulla fondazione morale della politica*, Bruno Mondatori, Milano.

THAULERO V. F.,
1969, *Nota introduttiva* a N. HARTMANN, *Ethik. Phäenomenologie der Sitten*, W. De Gruyter, Berlin, 1949³, tr. it., *Etica. Fenomenologia dei costumi*, Guida Editori, Napoli.

TAYLOR C.,
1999, *A Catholic Modernity? Charles Taylor's Marianist Award Lecture with Responses by W. M. Shea, R. L. Haughton, G. Marsden, J. B. Elshtain*, Oxford University Press, Oxford.

THEODOSSIOS MARIA DELLA CROCE,
2008, *Sui passi dell'Agnello. Insegnamenti sulla vita consacrata*, Città Nuova Editrice, Roma.

TODOROV T.,
2000, *Mémoire du mal. Tentation du bien. Enquête sur le siècle*, Robert Laffont, Paris.

VASOLI C.,
2005, *Introduzione* a SCHOPENHAUER A., *Il fondamento della morale*, Laterza, Bari-Roma.

VATTIMO G.,
1989, *Introduzione* a A. SCHOPENHAUER, *Il mondo come volontà e rappresentazione*, Mondatori, Milano.
1996, *Credere di credere*, Garzanti, Milano.

VECA S.,
1997, *Dell'incertezza. Tre meditazioni filosofiche*, Feltrinelli Editore, Milano.
2005, *La priorità del male e l'offerta filosofica*, Feltrinelli Editore, Milano.
2008, *Cittadinanza. Riflessioni filosofiche sull'idea di emancipazione*, Feltrinelli Editore, Milano, prima ed. 1990.

VEGETTI M.,
1989, *L'etica degli antichi*, Laterza, Bari-Roma.

Vico G. B.,
1974, *De universi iuris uno principio et fine uno. Liber unus – De uno universi iuris principio et fine uno*, e *Liber alter – De con stantia iurisprudentis*, in *Opere giuridiche*, Sansoni, Firenze.

Wittgenstein L.,
1985, *Tractatus Logico-Philosophicus*, with an *Introduction* by B. Russel, Routledge & Kegan Paul LDT, London.
1991, *Geheime Tagebücher 1914-1916*, Turia & Kant, Wien - Berlin.

Index of Names

ABBAGNANO N., 216-217, 245
ABRAHAM, 77, 79, 193
ARMELLINI P., 157-158, 245
AUGUSTINI (SANCTI) OR AUGUSTINE, 14, 44-48, 50. 85, 90, 138, 142, 163, 185, 188, 245
AYER A., 49, 245

BAGGIO A., 205, 217-218, 245- 246
BAGNOLI R., 130, 246
BAUDELAIRE C., 5. 107-110, 127, 188, 246
BECCARIA C., 11, 28, 133
BERDJAEV N., ?
BERGSON H., 83, 175-176, 246
BERLIN I., 15, 184, 190-191, 204, 246, 253
BEVERIDGE, 212, 245
BISMARCK S.O., 129
BOBBIO N., 209-210, 246
BOUDON R., 223-232, 246
BRANDT R., 33-34, 246
BRUNO G., 64, 244
BRYCE J., 242, 246

CAPOGRASSI G., 137, 142, 213, 247
CICERONE M. T., 247
CRESPI F., 14-15, 83, 130, 247
CODA P., 241, 247
CONSTANT B., 30, 190, 256

CORAGO J., 247
CROCE B., 61, 244

D'ADDIO M., 16, 196-202, 216, 247
D'AGOSTINO F., 158, 189, 206, 236, 247
DAHRENDORF R., 205, 247
DAL SANTO L. V., 116, 119-120, 248
DALLA TORRE G., 207, 247
D'ANNUNZIO G., 121-122, 248
DE LAUBIER P., 121, 248
DERRIDA J., 44-45, 248
DESCARTES R., 12, 14, 57, 77, 185, 248
DONATI P., 206, 248
DOSTOEVSKIJ F., 248, 251, 256
DUMMETT M., 174, 248, 253

ECCLES J., 253

FABBRO C., 76, 79, 248, 254
FALCIONI D., 33-35, 38-40, 43, 95, 246, 248
FELICE F., 209, 249
FERRERO G., 138, 190, 249, 252
FICHTE J. G., 215-216, 243, 249
FLORENSKIJ P., 249, 252
FONNESU L., 19-21, 50-51, 74-76, 249

GENTILE G., 244
GEYMONAT L., 179, 249
GUICCIARDINI F., 210, 244
HABERMAS J., 103-104, 249, 253
HAMLET, 69
HARTMANN N., 218-219, 249, 257
HEGEL G.W.F., 16, 19-21, 23, 26, 32, 38-40, 42-43, 53-55, 58-59, 65-66, 72, 77-79, 82-83, 86-87, 101, 130-131, 133, 153, 208, 216, 225, 243-244, 249
HEIDEGGER M., 104-106, 185, 250
HOBBES T., 18, 66, 68, 191, 241
HOMER, 239
HUME D., 184, 242, 250

JACOBI F. H., 243
JONAS H., 165-166, 168-170, 250
JUVALTA E., 179-180, 210-211, 249-250

KAFKA F., 140
KANT I., 11-19, 21-44, 46-51, 57-59, 61, 68-73, 76, 79, 82, 90, 95-96, 101, 122, 131-134, 144, 147-148, 152-153, 155-156, 165, 204, 224, 226, 243, 248-250, 256, 258
KELSEN H., 95-103, 251
KIERKEGAARD S., 51, 74-81, 229, 244, 248, 251, 254
KUHN T. S., 58

LÉVINAS E, 193, 253
LO GATTO E., 110-111, 251
LO GIUDICE S., 182, 251
LUKÁCS G., 130
LYOTARD J.-F., 182, 251

MACHIAVELLI N., 18, 24, 55, 66, 68-69, 132, 225, 241
MACINTYRE A., 208, 251
MAFFETTONE S., 206-207, 251
MALATESTA M., 224
MANGANELLI M., 143, 252
MANN T., 11, 128-134, 246, 251-252
MANNING (CARD.), 129
MARIANELLI M., 131, 252
MARITAIN J., 48, 50, 252, 254
MARX K., 21, 32, 38, 87, 130, 216-217, 227, 243-244
MEN' A., 127-128, 252
MICHELANGELO BUONARROTI, 123-124
MISLER N., 125-127, 252
MONTESQUIEU CH. L., 16-17, 190, 234

NIETZSCHE F., 44, 53, 55, 61, 73, 82-94, 107-108, 119, 129-131, 133-134, 210, 226-227, 244, 252

PAGANI G. B., 144, 149, 252
PAGANINI E., 253
PAUL (SAINT), 44, 241
PAULING L., 253
PELLICANI L., 138, 248, 251, 253
PERISSINOTTO L., 253
PETRARCA F., 253
PETROSINO S., 193, 253
PETRUCCIANI S., 103-104, 253
PEZZIMENTI R., 28, 36, 72, 95, 100, 138, 141, 167, 172, 180, 204, 210, 230, 240, 242, 253
PITITTO R., 171-173, 192, 254

PLATONIS, 254
POE E. A., 188
POLANYI M., 254
POPPER K. R., 183, 253
POSSENTI V., 254
PUTNAM H., 15, 151-155, 253-254

QUINTAS A. M., 193, 254
QUINZIO S., 75, 254

RAWLS J., 242, 254
RESCHER N., 253
RICOEUR P., 191, 255
RICONDA G., 117-118, 255
RIGOBELLO A., 12-14, 174-175, 255
ROLLAND J., 193, 253
RORTY R., 84, 231, 255
ROSMINI A., 82, 143-150, 157-159, 195-202, 213, 232, 244, 247, 252, 255
ROUSSEAU J. J., 16, 22-23, 37, 39, 85, 198, 243
ROVATTI P. A., 142-143, 255
RUSSEL B., 254, 258

SARTRE J. P., 13, 25, 175, 255
SCHILLER F., 11, 67, 130
SCHOPENHAUER A., 53-74, 77-78, 81-82, 117, 122, 129, 131-132, 134, 255, 257
SCHULZ J. H., 250
SEARLE J. R., 171-173, 254, 256

SENECA L. A., 64, 240, 256
SOLARI G., 18, 21-23, 256
SOLOV'ËV V., 248, 255-256
SOROKIN P. A., 235, 256
SPAEMANN R., 15, 84, 159-161, 163, 178, 256
STEIN E., 192, 256

TACITUS C., 91
TAGLIAPIETRA A., 30, 41-42, 256
THAULERO V. F., 218, 257
TAYLOR C., 257
THEODOSSIOS MARIA DELLA CROCE, 61, 244, 257
TOBIAS, 236
TOCQUEVILLE A. DE, 201, 203, 211, 223, 228, 230-231
TODOROV T., 48, 189, 257
TROIANI L., 245

ULYSSES, 193

VASOLI C., 68-69, 73, 257
VATTIMO G., 53-55, 84, 257
VECA S., 181-185, 187-191, 203-205, 257
VEGETTI M., 239-240, 257
VICO G. B., 130, 152, 174, 183, 190, 196, 199, 212, 244, 258

WEBER M., 225-227
WITTGENSTEIN L., 54, 152-153, 174, 181-182, 258

www.ingramcontent.com/pod-product-compliance
Lightning Source LLC
Chambersburg PA
CBHW020945230426
43666CB00005B/169